Testing for Athlete Citizenship

Critical Issues in Sport and Society

Michael Messner and Douglas Hartmann, Series Editors

Critical Issues in Sport and Society features scholarly books that help expand our understanding of the new and myriad ways in which sport is intertwined with social life in the contemporary world. Using the tools of various scholarly disciplines, including sociology, anthropology, history, media studies and others, books in this series investigate the growing impact of sport and sports-related activities on various aspects of social life as well as key developments and changes in the sporting world and emerging sporting practices. Series authors produce groundbreaking research that brings empirical and applied work together with cultural critique and historical perspectives written in an engaging, accessible format.

Jules Boykoff, *Activism and the Olympics: Dissent at the Games in Vancouver and London*

Kathryn E. Henne, *Testing for Athlete Citizenship: Regulating Doping and Sex in Sport*

Jeffrey Montez de Oca, *Discipline and Indulgence: College Football, Media, and the American Way of Life during the Cold War*

Jennifer Guiliano, *Indian Spectacle: College Mascots and the Anxiety of Modern America*

Testing for Athlete Citizenship

Regulating Doping and Sex in Sport

KATHRYN E. HENNE

Rutgers University Press

New Brunswick, New Jersey, and London

Library of Congress Cataloging-in-Publication Data

Henne, Kathryn E., 1982–
    Testing for athlete citizenship : regulating doping and sex in sport / Kathryn Henne.
        pages cm.—(Critical Issues in Sport and Society)
    Includes bibliographical references and index.
    ISBN 978-0-8135-6591-0 (hardcover : alk. paper)—ISBN (invalid)
    978-0-8135-6590-3 (pbk. : alk. paper)—ISBN 978-0-8135-6592-7 (e-book)
    1.Doping in sports. 2. Athletes—Drug use. 3. Athletes—Sexual behavior. I. Title.

    RC1230.H46 2015
    362.29'088796—dc23

                                                                2014027495

A British Cataloging-in-Publication record for this book is available from the British Library.

Visit our website: http://rutgerspress.rutgers.edu

Manufactured in the United States of America

To Andrew G. Nelson, who did not live to see this book in press but always told me that writing was in the family, and to Elizabeth L. Nelson, for first opening my eyes to places and worlds beyond my own.

Contents

Preface

The research for this book formally began in 2007, but its origins can be traced to a conversion about drug testing in sport that took place in 2003. I was talking with a mentor of mine who had retired from a very successful career as a high-level athlete. This was before I began contemplating a venture into competitive sport. Of her many accomplishments she had represented the United States in international competitions and been inducted into her university's hall-of-fame for sport. Her reflections on the lifestyle of competitive athletes and her concerns about the intrusiveness of anti-doping measures directly informed the questions motivating this book: how does anti-doping regulation contribute to attitudes toward athletes and their abilities, as well as the expectations to which we hold them? Moreover, what do these insights tell us about broader social beliefs about the human body, be it an athlete's body or our own, and its capacities?

The particular conversation I reference here made me think more deeply—and more critically—about anti-doping regulation in sport. My mentor considered drug testing one of the most humiliating moments of her athletic career, referring to it as "one of the most degrading things you can imagine for a female athlete, especially when you are so young and have no idea what's going on. There you are *bare*—I mean standing there on display—with someone watching over you, just watching you pee in a cup. Can you imagine being exposed like that?"[1] Admittedly, I had not thought much about it at the time. When I asked her to clarify whether only women, not men, had observed her, she responded,

> Yes, only women. But, it really doesn't matter when you are in that vulnerable of a position. It still feels like a violation, but you have to do it, or you're basically telling them that you are doing something wrong. Even afterwards you still feel

like they think you are guilty of *something*, even though you didn't do anything. When I was on the national team, I wouldn't even eat a piece of bacon, because the coach told us not to. There's no way I would've taken drugs! It was ridiculous. I mean talk about a *violation of basic rights*. How can they get away with that? It's just not right to do that, especially to young kids just entering college.

The way she stressed "*a violation of basic rights*" stayed with me. The humiliation she had felt seemed to underpin the words.

Those words prompted me to later ask how drug testing and other forms of bodily surveillance in sport have been justified, both ideologically and legally. My mentor's story was that of a student who was among the first generation of collegiate athletes in the United States to undergo regular drug testing endorsed by the National Collegiate Athletic Association in the 1980s. Olympic drug testing preceded that development by nearly twenty years. Today, random drug testing and the systematic monitoring of high-level athletes are common practice. In addition to having blood and urine samples tested, an increasing number of athletes are subject to the Whereabouts Program, which requires elite athletes to notify authorities where they are one hour per day of the year so that they can be subject to random testing during those windows, and the Biological Passport, which is an electronic record of blood profiles documenting abnormalities that may serve as indicators of banned substance use (or lack thereof). Forms of surveillance pervade workplaces and other spaces of everyday life; however, athletes are subject to unique and compulsory requirements. Under current anti-doping rules, an athlete's refusal or resistance results in disqualification. How then has sport developed into a space where overt forms of bodily surveillance are fundamental aspects of elite competition? In short, why are athletes treated differently?

This book explores the development and deployment of anti-doping rules in sport, considering the cultural conditions that have enabled them to be expanded in scope and jurisdiction. Its aim is not to substantiate or prove whether these testing apparatuses undermine individual rights per se, but to explore how this regulation reveals a broader issue of legality: that elite athletes occupy a unique position as citizen subjects. Studying how anti-doping regulation has taken shape since the mid-twentieth century, I argue, demonstrates how elite athletes have become a visible transnational group of citizens that is akin to a distinct caste. Athletes not only represent nations, but their bodies are also held accountable to a host of regulatory, normative, and ideological expectations that other subjects are not. Further, the regulation to which they are held accountable is global in scope, not limited to the nation-state.

To explain what these regulatory practices entail, how they come to bear on athlete subjects, and the nature of their authoritarian claims, this book genealogically explores the emergence of anti-doping regulation and the actors—both human and nonhuman—that have shaped and implemented these rules. In so doing, this analysis examines two, interrelated concerns: the first is how earlier ideas about what athletes should be became refashioned and adapted to fit the contemporary conditions of elite sport participation, and the second queries what these regulatory developments can tell us about the changing nature of citizenship in a globalized world. Athlete citizenship, though a distinct formation of citizenship, reveals broader tensions around how ideology and surveillance converge in the differentiation and policing of subjects.

This project—or any book project—is the result of collaboration on many levels. I must thank the incredible support I received from people at the University of California, Irvine; the California State University, Long Beach; and the Australian National University. To my advisers throughout graduate school, Justin Richland, Susan Bibler Coutin, and Kerrie Kauer, I cannot think of a better group of mentors, and I feel privileged that I was able to work with you at formative times during the genesis of book. I am also indebted to Elliott Currie, Tom Boellstorff, and Alison Wrynn for their critical feedback, attention to detail, and words of wisdom, which made this a much more focused piece. Sora Han, Connie McGuire, Natalie Newton, Emily Troshynski, Susan Greenhalgh, Rita Shah, Lydia Bederka, Natasha Pushkarna, Benjamin Authers, Kyla Tienhaara, Roannie Ng Shiu, Valerie Braithwaite, John Braithwaite, John Tubera, and Tan Leng Goh provided generous feedback and many insightful conversations over coffee, which informed the ideas featured in the pages that follow. This book also benefited from the thoughtful comments of Gina Dent and the members of the 2010 residential workshop hosted by the University of California Transnationalizing Justice Multicampus Research Group; from Laura Kang and the Department of Women's Studies at the University of California, Irvine; and from the School of Social and Political Sciences at the University of Melbourne, which provided me with venues to present and reflect on my work during the genesis of the book.

One of the unexpected surprises that came out of this project was the incredible support that I received while doing this research and while writing this book. Farah Palmer, Nan Seuffert, Graeme Steel, Paul David, Pierre-Hugo Laurin, Regula Cardinaux, Nuria Puig, Ama Tofaeno, Joan Alleluia Filemoni-Tofaeno, Alisha Misiaita, and Albert de la Tierra as well as many participants who I cannot name here assisted me through various stages of this project. Roland Burke and Vanessa McDermott provided incredibly supportive and analytical comments on aspects of this book. The reviewers of this manuscript as well as the editors were immensely helpful in revising the text and argument. Special thanks go to the team at Rutgers University Press, especially Peter Mickulas for making it into a proper book and shepherding it through the publication process, and to the editors of Critical Issues in Sport and

Society series, Doug Hartmann and Michael Messner for providing a home for this book.

The financial support I received for this book was also critically important. Without it, this research would not have been made possible. In particular, external funding from the National Science Foundation (SES-0851536) and International Olympic Committee as well as funding from the School of Social Ecology and the Department of Criminology, Law and Society at the University of California, Irvine supported data collection and analysis. A UC-Irvine Chancellor's Club Fellowship for Excellence and a research development grant from the Australian National University Research School of Asia and the Pacific supported the writing.

I am also grateful for permission to reprint portions of previously published articles. Parts of chapter 3 and the conclusion first appeared in Kathryn Henne, "WADA, the Promises of Law and the Landscapes of Antidoping Regulation," *PoLAR: Political and Legal Anthropology Review* 33, no. 2 (2010): 306–325. Selections of chapter 2 first appeared as Kathryn Henne, "The Emergence of Moral Technopreneurialism in Sport: Techniques in Anti-Doping Regulation, 1966–1976," *International Journal of the History of Sport* 31, no 1. (2014): 884–901. Portions of chapter 4 were previously published as "The 'Science' of Fair Play in Sport: Gender and the Politics of Testing," *Signs: A Journal of Women in Culture and Society* 39, no. 3 (2014): 787–812.

In addition, my family made this book possible. To my mothers and my brothers, you are my intellectual stimulus, always inspiring. To my mother Lesley, you will never know how much your love and assistance benefited this book, and to my mother-in-law Marlene, thank you for keeping me going during the home stretch of writing. Dave and George, your critical discussions in the basement got me through some difficult aspects of my arguments, and to Katie Camarda and Meredith Edelman, thank you for being with me through thick and thin and for providing frank editorial feedback when I needed it early on. Last, but certainly not least, to my partner in crime, Kent: life made more sense when you entered it, and here's to many more years spent together trying to figure it out. You more than anyone has had to endure some heavy demands and sleepless nights because of this book. I cannot thank you enough.

Abbreviations

ACC	Australian Crime Commission	NBA	National Basketball Association
AFL	Australian Football League		
AIS	androgen insensitivity syndrome	NFL	National Football League
		NOC	National Olympic Committee
ASADA	Australian Sports Anti-Doping Authority		
		NRL	National Rugby League
BALCO	Bay Area Laboratory Co-operative	NZOC	New Zealand Olympic Committee
CAS	Court of Arbitration for Sport	PCR	polymerase chain reaction
CoE	Council of Europe	PPFN	Pure Playing Field Nation
DFSNZ	Drug Free Sport New Zealand	SPARC	Sport and Recreation New Zealand
IAAF	International Association of Athletics Federations		
		UNESCO	United Nations Educational, Scientific and Cultural Organization
IOC	International Olympic Committee		
IWF	International Weightlifting Federation	USADA	United States Anti-Doping Agency
MLB	Major League Baseball	WADA	World Anti-Doping Agency

Testing for Athlete Citizenship

1

Introduction

---●

It is November 15, 2007, and I am in the Palacio Municipal de Congresos in Madrid, Spain, observing the Third World Conference on Doping in Sport. One of over 1,500 participants in attendance, I am listening to Richard Pound, then-president of the World Anti-Doping Agency (WADA), deliver his opening remarks. In a characteristically impassioned speech about the need to preserve the integrity of sport, Pound appeals to stakeholders' concerns about doping in sport: "We do have—and I emphasize this, we do have—the hope of prevailing over doping, but only if we persevere and continue to look to the future and to hope for that future. So what better endeavor for society to embark upon? What better occupation for each of us to be part of? What better contribution can we make to history and to the generations that will follow?"[1] As it is early in my research for this book, I do not expect the harsh tone and fervor of his words; however, I would soon learn that many people working in anti-doping spaces take their mission seriously. Sport, for many of them, is not simply entertainment or recreation. Rather, as another conference presenter would explain, it is "a source of inspiration for all," but only, as many others would caution, if doping can be eliminated.[2]

As framed at the conference, this cause against doping in sport, often referred to as "cleaning up sport," is a moral crusade; that is, anti-doping advocates promote it as part of a broader normative agenda concerned with the ethics of sport.[3] In particular, the World Conference on Doping in Sport highlighted this mission as an effort to legally condemn doping, a pursuit that aims to institutionalize a particular moral stance.[4] Those lobbying for anti-doping regulation uphold sport as a socially significant space. Sport, they argue, communicates values across the globe, prompting the need for regulation to ensure it sends the "right" messages.

Opponents of doping are not alone in the value they place upon sport. Sport is often referred to as "an important cultural phenomenon in all countries of the world."[5] Some scholars even characterize it as "the most important thing in the world."[6] The fact that an estimated audience of 4.7 billion spectators, over 70 percent of the world's population, watched the 2008 Summer Olympic Games on television supports the claims of its significance.[7] Athletes play an important part in the mediated performances of sport, making them powerful symbols consumed by spectators. Fans can read about athletes in newspapers and magazines, listen to play-by-play calls on the radio, and follow analyses of individuals, anticipating match-ups between them. With the rise of social media and the Internet, sport consumers can now interactively add and "trade" athletes in fantasy leagues, follow them on Twitter and gossip websites, and join fan pages and clubs dedicated to them. Sport is thus much more than something that people watch; it is something in which fans invest their time, hearts, and money. Further, the bodies participating in elite sport are important corporeal actors who themselves enable and command significant levels of investment.

The premise of this book begins with the contention that sport, as a social field, articulates messages not simply about ethics, but broader beliefs about embodiment, physical ability, and human difference. Here I examine sport as a form of social control, one in which many of us actively participate. Jin-Kyung Park describes sport as "a central cultural technology of governing the social body."[8] Although not often thought of as a form of regulation, sport disciplines bodies by encouraging forms of organized labor that are often thought of as merely play or recreation. There are thus vested interests in the regulation of athletes' bodies, as they communicate values attributed to sport. Sport's regulatory power in part stems from the fact that many of us do not realize it as such. Anti-doping advocates, however, are attuned to sport's influence, as evidenced by their moral crusade to ensure that sport aligns with a particular set of values. Accordingly, the outgrowth of their campaign against doping is a host of regulatory mechanisms aimed at athletes' bodies, which are the subject of this book.

In this book, I explore sport as a complex transnational field by specifically attending to the protection of "fair play" through the regulation of performance enhancement. Specifically, I trace the rise of anti-doping regulation, which began as a limited number of biomedical testing practices in the twentieth century and grew into a more elaborate regulatory regime during the twenty-first century. The current regime is a global network supported by scientific testing, an array of biomedical surveillance devices, corporatized sport actors, national governments, and international law. The synergies between these actors, I argue, yield a unique transnational caste of citizen subjects—that is, elite (or aspiring elite) athletes—who are increasingly subject to expectations of bodily purity that are policed by routine bodily scrutiny, a number of surveillance mechanisms, and binding regulatory codes. This book illustrates how the moral crusade against doping in sport has taken shape amid particular historical contingencies that have become embedded in the characteristics of anti-doping regulation. In the pages that follow, I document how such legacies shape the technologies deployed, as well as the problematic inequalities that they imbue, which crystallize along racial, gendered, national, and transnational lines. The insights of this book attest to broader concerns related biomedical surveillance, risk, and legality. But, to understand the interplay of these issues in relation to sport, let us first consider the ideologies that underpin the regulation of athletes and the mechanisms used to do so.

Athletes as a Transnational Caste of Citizen Subjects

Many scholars contend that elite athletes are powerful signifiers that circulate and take on meanings through discourses of sport. According to anthropologist Susan Birrell, sport's significance hinges upon "the status of the athlete as exemplary," a role that is "incumbent with power to mediate between the individuals who comprise the audience and the moral order of the community."[9] Athletes, writes Park, "help maintain the body of the population to be healthy, efficient, and productive."[10] Elite athletes are rewarded for their physical excellence, and their performances contribute to transnational discourses about human capabilities and achievement. The celebration of their accomplishments promotes not only the valuing of their bodies but also adjoining ideologies attributed to and communicated through them, such as values of hard work and discipline.

As a group, elite athletes are uniquely positioned because of their exceptional physical abilities. As they are often representatives of their respective nations in the Olympics, world championship events, and other international competitions, it is perhaps not surprising that assumptions about their physical integrity are often connected to beliefs about moral fortitude and strength. These beliefs have historical roots. The founding father of the modern Olympics, Pierre de Coubertin, felt strongly that Olympic competitors were to be "imbued with a sense of the moral grandeur of the Games" and "a spirit of almost religious reverence."[11] Accordingly, the Olympic Games were to play an important role in promoting Olympism, a philosophy that promoted a balanced sense of individual development and necessitated a strong body, will, and mind. Sport was to be "a cult, an impassioned soaring which is capable of going from play to heroism."[12] It was to inspire moral integrity like "a religion with church, dogmas, and ritual."[13] Coubertin actually referred to such sport as *religio athletae*[14] and considered the Games to be a venue to celebrate a particular caste of men.[15] Olympic principles, he wrote, would foster a "race of sportsmen," a *race sportive*, evoking what Otto Schantz describes as an "old signification of race in its sense of distinguished class or noble lineage . . . [an] 'aristocracy of muscle,' another expression of Coubertin often used to distinguish 'true' sportsmen from ordinary people."[16]

Coubertin's understanding of athletes as citizens embraced a notion of amateurism that forbade the participation of athletes paid to participate in sport. It also explicitly excluded women and embraced imperialist ideas of class while promoting moral and bodily integrity through sport and physical activity. Sport, however, has changed significantly since Coubertin founded the Olympics in 1896. Increasingly professionalized, it now showcases many more competitors from across the globe, including groups, such as women and non-Western peoples, that were previously banned from Olympic competition.[17] Although both modern sport and anti-doping regulation seemingly disavow colonial ways of thinking, this book highlights how those earlier exclusionary values nonetheless underscore the regulations to which elite athletes are held accountable today. As global sport has changed so too have the mechanisms, both formal and informal, used to scrutinize and evaluate who is deserving of elite athlete status.

Of particular interest to this analysis is how anti-doping regulation pursues its goal of ensuring that athletes' performances are their own and not artificially manufactured or unfairly enhanced by ergogenic aids. Doping in sport is a recognizable, even regularly occurring, news headline and a topic of growing scholarly interest.[18] In recent years, high-profile American athletes, including Tour de France winning cyclists Lance Armstrong and Floyd Landis, baseball's Barry Bonds and Roger Clemens, and Olympic sprinter Marion Jones, have been punished for doping—and there are many more globally. These particular athletes have two things in common: they all achieved groundbreaking success in sport yet were condemned for how they went about doing so. Authorities determined that they had cheated. They had doped. In taking artificial enhancements, they were seen to be undermining the spirit of competition. These athletes are not simply condemned for taking a banned substance, they are condemned for failing to meet public expectations of them as elite subjects and cultural icons.

Despite the visibility of athletes accused of doping, the regulatory techniques and normative claims that inform popular understandings of doping as an offense rarely receive critical attention in public discourse. Although doping is often understood as performance-enhancing drug use, it encompasses a much broader spectrum of substances and methods, including illicit drugs that likely have no significant performance-enhancing effects. In addition, even though anti-doping regulation forbids the use of artificial substances, there are other rules in place that actually compel some female athletes to take hormonal treatments. This is to reduce their naturally occurring levels of testosterone, an androgen that is the principal male sex hormone, in order to participate in women's events. The stated justification is to protect "fair play" among women in those sports; however, as this book explores in later chapters, this rhetoric is laden with gendered beliefs that result in particular groups of women being subject to heightened levels of bodily scrutiny and surveillance.

In light of these contradictions, this book explores the following questions: How has doping emerged as a transgression in sport? What insights into the meanings of sport can we glean through the study of anti-doping regulation? And, how does the anti-doping regime reflect broader trends in regulation and surveillance? To answer these questions, I trace how doping has become a globally conspicuous issue by focusing on the cultural conditions that have informed the development and deployment of rules targeting the protection of fair play. More specifically, this analysis examines how scientific testing and technocratic practices have become the primary tools used to police fair play in sport, while attending to contradictions that underpin current regulatory tactics.

Fair play is often upheld as an important value in sport, but is a relatively ambiguous concept.[19] Articulated through different platforms with distinct aims and objectives, it is not clear what constitutes fair play or what social good it delivers.[20] The United Nations Educational, Scientific and Cultural Organization (UNESCO) posits fair play as a broad, positive value that is "much more than playing with the rules" and includes "respect for others and always playing within the right spirit."[21] WADA asserts that doping is antithetical to fair play but provides no clear definition of the term; rather, it presumes that the notion of a "level playing field"—that is, one that allows for athletes to fairly compete—relies on doping-free sport.[22] This idea of what constitutes fair competition has its roots in the foundations of modern sport, which took shape in elite schools in England and in a context where values of amateurism—a position that advocated the virtues of sport as being for love and leisure—had been employed as pedagogical tools to educate for young men.[23] The origins of fair play are thus decidedly masculine and of a particular class, emerging when the enjoyment of sport was limited to a "homogenous elite (i.e., moneyed, educated, aristocratic, leisured males)."[24] As Allan Guttmann explains, "Sportsmen for amateurism attempted to justify their snobbery with the claim that the 'lower orders' were incapable of acts of fair play and good sportsmanship."[25]

Fair play, especially as taken up by the nineteenth-century Muscular Christianity movement that promoted religious piety through physical activity, has a decidedly colonial past, as its incorporation through sport was considered a method of strengthening empire and "civilizing" colonialized peoples.[26]

Accordingly, scholars have argued that campaigns for fair play (as doping-free) in sport negate the influence of gendered, national, or socio-economic inequalities that shape the fields on which athletes play and the resources to which they have access.[27] The assertion that anti-doping regulation protects a level playing field is a misrepresentation because athletes do not begin on a level playing field. Against the backdrop of globalized inequality, athletes have access to very different resources, which are also shaped by divergent cultural beliefs about gender and physical ability more generally. Throughout this book, I critically consider how the global anti-doping regime has come to encompass a range of policies, ideas, institutions, and actors, all of which shape this regulatory field and maintain power relations that have gendered, racialized, classed, and nationalistic dimensions, even though its formal platform is to promote fair play.

In attending to these dimensions, I argue that the anti-doping regime reveals a unique cross section of citizenship, which I refer to as "athlete citizenship."[28] Citizenship, as a concept, is something we often think of in terms of rights and privileges and who is—versus who is not—entitled to those benefits. I use athlete citizenship to distinguish how high-level sport competitors constitute a transnational caste of subjects whose bodies are subject to distinct regulatory technologies. Such technologies serve to determine who is and who is not allowed to become or remain an elite athlete. No longer limited by amateurism, sport is more democratic in the sense that more bodies are able to participate; however, gatekeepers, such as anti-doping regulations, still exist and enforce boundaries in profoundly undemocratic ways. As I describe later in this chapter, athlete citizenship retains unique contours, but like other formulations of citizenship, it involves a complex demarcation of belonging and exclusion, which is underpinned by politics and tacit assumptions that inform which bodies are judged to be deserving of citizenship. Preserving an ideal of athlete citizenship, I argue, is a driving force in the regulation of fair play in sport and lies at the heart of the anti-doping regime. Regulation's aims are not simply about preventing the unfair use of performance-enhancing substances in sport, but also about protecting ideals around a presumed purity that athletes are to embody.

Regulation's valuing of purity exemplifies what Mary Douglas describes as a disdain of "dirt."[29] Athletes suspected of doping are, in fact, often referred to as "dirty." For Douglas, dirt "is essentially disorder" that "exists in the eye of the beholder"; those who aim to reorder or "clean" it are actually "re-ordering our environment, making it conform to an idea."[30] More importantly, her insights remind us that what objects are deemed to be dirt—in this case, particular bodies—is telling because it provides evidence of the symbolic orders that are to be preserved. Particularly during times of instability, Douglas explains, "any object or idea likely to confuse or contradict our cherished classifications" is likely to be condemned as dirt.[31] In the context of sport, doping emerged as threat in the mid-twentieth century, a time when there were major changes to Olympic sport. Professionalization begun to challenge its values and practices, and it was accompanied by the influx of many more bodies competitively pursuing—and excelling at—elite sport, including women and non-Western peoples from places no longer under colonial rule. This book describes how gendered and racialized anxieties reveal themselves through the bodies labeled as contaminated, even unnatural, by regulations initially developed by the International Olympic Committee (IOC). In doing so, it explains that although athlete citizenship has changed, it still maintains the tropes of earlier classist beliefs about sport and the bodies capable of participating in it.

As a complex history informs the development of formal regulation aimed at protecting ideals of fair play in international sport, much of this book examines how past events inform present practices and also documents how scientific tools have been deployed to scrutinize athletes' bodies in order to protect ideological beliefs. As such efforts often yield contradictory and paradoxical outcomes, this analysis paints a complicated picture of power, one that presents anti-doping regulation not as an oppressive regime (although many athletes who I interviewed did characterize it as such), but as one that constitutively contributes to inequality. In other words, even though regulation aims to protect fair play, it intersects with other forms of social control to reinforce, and at times exacerbate, social stratification. In order to grasp how the practices of this regime succumb to the postcolonial dilemmas described in this book, a better understanding what anti-doping regulation actually entails is a necessary first step.

The Emergence of Bodily Regulation to Protect Fair Play

Under international anti-doping rules, doping entails behaviors that include and surpass the use of performance-enhancing methods considered to be unethical or to undermine fair play. A substance or method can be prohibited in sport if it satisfies two of the following conditions: (1) it is performance enhancing, (2) it is a risk to the health of the athlete, or (3) it violates "the spirit of sport."[32] Further, even if the substance used is not performance enhancing, the rules state that it can violate the "spirit of sport" if the athlete is using it with the intent to enhance his or her performance "regardless of whether the expectation of performance enhancement is realistic."[33] Because of this clause, a broad array of substances can constitute doping without evidence of performance-enhancing qualities.

Critics often characterize anti-doping guidelines as a mistargeted attempt at leveling the playing field, not simply because fair play is an ambiguous concept, but because various forms of global inequality undermine the possibility of a level playing field being achieved. If one considers the uneven distribution of resources and technologies across regions and nations, doping is not the only factor affecting the ways that athletes pursue performance enhancement.[34] This observation thus prompts an additional question to pursue: If what constitutes doping as an offense and what constitutes fair play as a virtue appear vague, why, then, has anti-doping regulation become so prominent in sport?

History provides some insight. The Olympic Games formally upheld amateurism as a requirement until the 1970s.[35] In accordance with amateurism, athletes were not to receive payments for participating in sport, which aimed to preserve upper- and middle-class values (mostly by discouraging working-class participation). Historian John Gleaves has elaborated upon such requirements and their differential, and sometimes lax, enforcement, pointing out that amateurism was more of an ideal than a clearly defined practice.[36] In idealized articulations, though, athletes were to compete only "in 'the spirit of chivalry' and 'fair play,'" as so-called "brothers-in-arms," which Coubertin described as being "united by a bond that is stronger than that of mere camaraderie."[37]

In contrast, sport has become widely professionalized and a field made up of an array of globalized industries and corporate interests, changing the spectacles and expectations of athletes and their performances. According to David Andrews and George Ritzer, "Today, virtually all aspects of the global sport institutions (governing bodies, leagues, teams, events, and individual athletes) are now un-self-consciously driven and defined by the inter-related processes of: corporatization (the management and marketing of sporting entities according to profit motives); spectacularization (the primacy of producing of entertainment-driven [mediated] experiences); and, commodification (the generation of multiple sport-related revenue streams)."[38] Despite these changes, the Olympic Games and other international sport events still articulate claims about bodily purity. The perceived threat of doping directly implicates athletes' bodies, presuming that they are biologically pure until contaminated by drugs or methods deemed to be contaminants. Drug testing, perhaps the best-known technology used to combat doping, operates under the belief that it can detect such impurities. The detection of contaminants has, in turn, become accepted as evidence of athletes' ethical shortcomings or, at the very least, weaknesses in their moral fortitude. Although not the same as the amateur ideals posited by Coubertin, the assumption that a natural body is a marker of a virtuous body remains ideologically intact.

While ideals of bodily purity are longstanding, the technological tactics used to police athletes' bodies have emerged alongside the aforementioned economic changes to sport. In doing so, they reflect neoliberal dimensions. Given the range of ideas and theories about neoliberalism, particularly its embrace of seemingly unregulated free-market capitalism, this book does not embrace them all. Many such works concentrate on economic changes and political shifts limited to the state pulling away from providing social welfare for its citizens.[39] In contrast, this research illustrates the rise of an individualized regulatory focus on the body, a focus that many scholars argue is characteristic of risk society—that is, a society marked by a heightened awareness of risk, which can actually yield a perpetual preoccupation that seeks and manufactures more risk in the effort to control it.[40] My particular emphasis on risk in this book reflects what Deborah Lupton describes in relation to the regulation of bodies. Such risks, Lupton writes, emerge with the heightened surveillance of human bodies across contexts, including medicine, which instill a powerful medico-scientific gaze that requires the body to be open to routine scrutiny.[41] Lupton explains that these practices reinscribe neoliberal values of individualism, self-responsibility (or responsibilization), and self-awareness as citizen subjects internalize risk and surveillance. Thus, even healthy individuals become aware that their bodies may be prone to risk, disease, or contamination if they are not cautious and responsible. Anti-doping technologies amplify risk as it becomes displaced onto individuals, while also imparting a general distrust of athletes and their bodies.[42]

Anti-doping regulation polices citizens through a host of regulatory actors and techniques. The IOC initially spearheaded drug testing in international sport; WADA now leads this global effort.[43] Since its establishment in 1999, WADA has implemented a multifaceted approach against doping in accordance with the World Anti-Doping Code (commonly referred to as "the Code"), a charter drawn up for the purpose of harmonizing anti-doping efforts across geographic areas and sports. WADA annually updates an official list of banned substances, promotes scientific and medical research to enhance anti-doping detection methods, hosts a global web-based database to assist the implementation of programming, and facilitates the actions of regional and national anti-doping organizations. It also manages education, outreach efforts, and out-of-competition testing. WADA's methods thus incorporate enforcement and surveillance strategies beyond the collection and analysis of athletes' urine or blood samples. In fact, the Biological Passport system, which documents the biological profiles of athletes in an effort to detect abnormalities that may stem from doping, resulted in six athletes receiving anti-doping rule violations just days before the start of the London Olympic Games in 2012.[44]

WADA's formal mission is "to lead a collaborative worldwide campaign for doping-free sport," which it frames as transnational community-building project of like-minded stakeholders who value fair play, not as the coordination of mass surveillance.[45] Formal rhetoric reinforces anti-doping regulation as necessary to preserve the integrity of sport, but often overlooks the intrusive nature of surveillance tactics—and their cultural implications. For instance, during the 2007 World Conference on Doping in Sport, then-IOC president Jacques Rogge claimed, "Let us never lose sight of why we are here:

to give athletes at all levels the fair chance they deserve, to create an environment that allows champions to shine as role models for children, parents, and fans alike, to preserve the integrity—and the very future—of sport."[46] Like other anti-doping advocates, Rogge emphasized that regulation is not simply about ensuring that athletes comply with the rules, but also about promoting a broader ethical agenda that draws upon athletes' symbolic status.[47] His statement, however, presumes that the rules can be enforced equitably, disregarding the fact that they apply to a broad and diverse population of athletes, many of whom have access to different resources as well as varying personal beliefs and practices that affect how they pursue performance enhancement. Moreover, Rogge's words ascribe a neoliberal focus on the individual in ways that draw attention away from the broader structural dynamics at work. In particular, it overlooks the financial benefits and global prestige of sport that incentivize doping, much of which is encouraged and enabled by the Olympic Movement.[48] Further, the regulatory outcomes reinscribe risks primarily onto athletes, not governing bodies or other authorities charged with athlete welfare.

Because anti-doping rules are important considerations in understanding how doping is condemned, this book draws heavily from socio-legal studies. Law and society research demonstrates that the passage and enforcement of law and regulation often do not result in outcomes that match the original intent.[49] Although rules may prescribe standardized procedures and outcomes, divergences often surface when rules are put into action, often yielding contradictions. When legal rules interact with normative orders, the resulting convergences, according to Sally Falk Moore, uphold "general principles of application and interpretation that can themselves be interpreted in a variety of ways," which leaves us with only *partial* order and *partial* control of social life by rules."[50] In other words, law on the books is only a piece—and not necessarily an accurate reflection—of law in action. Rule making and rule breaking are not the means or ends of law, but rather, constitutive moments within the complex social milieu that make up regulatory regimes. A longstanding body of research demonstrates that the study of disjunctions and intersections, or the "breaks," in these networks can offer important insights into the social worlds undergirding regulation.[51] This book addresses how legality operates at transnational, national, local, and even intimate levels, particularly as the anti-doping regime indoctrinates a kind of risk society among athletes. Not only do international and national laws bind various individual and organizational actors to the terms of the regime, but technocratic rules, testing practices, and surveillance strategies also come to hold athletes accountable. Combined, these regulatory technologies communicate and reinscribe WADA's jurisdiction over athletes while also informing how these surveilled citizen subjects come to relate to the rules and their own bodies.

The transnational nature of anti-doping regulation's jurisdiction is an important feature of the regime. Transnational features of legal orders, according to Terence Halliday and Gregory Shaffer, entail recursive and multi-directional movements across international, national, and local levels.[52] Although WADA is intended to be a global authority, the extent to which it can exercise that power depends largely upon local agents and contexts. As Philip McMichael explains, "Global relations are inconceivable without local 'faces,' just as the 'local' has no meaning without context. The very definition of 'global' and 'local' are not only mutually conditioning, they continually change."[53] This global-local interplay has important implications for the anti-doping regime and this analysis. For instance, even though the World Anti-Doping Code requires standardized practices, sanctions levied for anti-doping violations can vary in nature and severity depending upon jurisdiction and actors involved. Many accomplished athletes caught doping have been scorned publically, resulting in their records being black-marked or "asterisked." Some have had medals and endorsements revoked. Others have received suspensions of various lengths, including expulsions, from sport. A select few have faced criminal sanctions. Perhaps more importantly, despite the very few offenders caught, there emerges a proliferation of athletes rendered suspect through the expansion of regulatory techniques.

To illustrate how these risk-laden dynamics emerge and play out contextually, each chapter of this book explores the differential treatment of athletes, even in some cases those who are under the jurisdiction of the same national anti-doping system. These divergences, I argue, evidence how bodies cast as doped (or suspected as such) reveal powerful claims around human ability, many of which have a basis in naturalized, not natural, forms of difference. Important to this book are the effects of the normative claims upon which surveillance and punishments rely. Anti-doping rules and sanctions uphold a tacit assumption that athletes are to be hard working, disciplined, and honest, never cutting corners; doping to achieve an advantage is unacceptable. This presumption often goes unquestioned. Beneath this rhetoric, however, lies a contradiction: elite athletes are never natural. They are *made*, relying on practice and specific kinds of training, nutrition, and technological innovations for physical conditioning and recovery. Combined, these actions enable athletes to achieve bodily changes in pursuit of a competitive goal.

Sport, according to historian Paul Dimeo, is "a technological process" of "taking of a physical body and making it into something new in pursuit of athletic achievement." Doping, he argues, is "only one more technological enhancement" to consider.[54] History supports this claim, as athletes and scientists have worked together in formal and informal capacities for over a century.[55] In the 1960s, anti-doping regulation was in part a response to concerns around the proliferation of so-called "unnatural" competitors; that is, those athletes perceived to rely too strongly on artificial enhancement.[56] Almost ironically, science (in the form of testing for doping agents) emerged as the regulatory response to these technological anxieties. And thus pharmaceutical knowledge has come to play an important role in both the enhancement of athletic performance and the regulation of performance enhancement.

The regulatory reliance upon technocratic and medical surveillance is arguably part of the rise of "biomedicalization," which Adele Clarke and colleagues describe as the "increasingly complex, multi-sited, multi-directional processes of medicalization, both extended and reconstituted through new forms of highly technoscientific biomedicine."[57] The anti-doping regime exemplifies key features of biomedicalization, namely its decentralized and stratified characteristics, the internationalization of risk and surveillance (by both regulation and subjects), the embrace of technoscience, and changing perceptions of and knowledge about the human body.[58] Combined, these practices influence how subjects relate to and understand their bodies, their health, and the rules governing them. Although biomedicalization has spread more generally, its manifestation in sport is unique in the sense that athletes are subject to a host of biomedical tools and techniques, which are justified as necessary to prevent and catch doping, that everyday citizens are not. Even though biomedicalization affects many populations, sport offers a site where it is particularly robust.

Differences between athlete citizens and other citizen subjects become more profound when we consider the extent to which doping is condemned in sport versus other spheres of social life. For example, working professionals in many fields, as well as university students in the United States and beyond, often use over-the-counter stimulants and prescribed pyschostimulant drugs—at times illegally without prescriptions—in order to work for long hours. Others take beta blockers or similar medications to calm anxiety in high-stress situations. Even the use of sexual-enhancement drugs like Viagra is arguably a form of doping.[59] These forms of everyday doping are not a recent trend. Over a quarter century ago, sociologist Harry Edwards argued, "Americans continue to buy and use an ever-expanding volume and variety of such drugs in search of remedies for afflictions both real and imagined. Indeed, we have so 'medicalized' the personal and social vicissitudes of life in our society that people who truly use no drugs could well be considered an extremely deviant minority."[60] Edwards's point is perhaps even more relevant today, as the competition of daily life drives many people to dope. In short, the growth in self-medication coincides with the rise of neoliberalism and biomedicalization, both of which enable cultures of doping by instilling values of individual competition, self-enhancement, and risk management.

More recent research highlights that these developments have discursive power beyond the mere act of taking drugs. For example, pharmaceutical companies, argues Joe Dumit, *define* health and how citizens understand their well-being and bodily risks.⁶¹ Similarly, corporate investments have enabled sport to expand globally, extending the reach of sport's messages in relation to human bodies and performance enhancement. As I describe in the next two chapters, the expansion of sport has brought with it a growth in anti-doping regulation. The vested financial interests in sport not only incentivize athletes' doping in order to succeed, but they also make the stakes of being caught that much more costly. Although doping is accepted in many spheres of social life, being accused or found to be doping in sport can tarnish an athlete's image and can even end careers. In short, elite athletes, by virtue of being superior physical specimens, are held to higher ethical standards than others in relation to performance enhancement and thus navigate levels of suspicion and risk that other citizen subjects do not experience—at least not in the same ways.

In light of the many media stories around doping in sport, it is easy to get caught up in doping scandals and scenes of denial, remorse, betrayal, reformation, and redemption that they depict. As publicly disseminated performances of and about sport, these tales have become accepted narratives that we often anticipate in competitive sport, as evidenced by shamed Tour de France–winner Lance Armstrong's 2013 interview with Oprah Winfrey where he, after being sanctioned by authorities, finally admitted to doping after years of denial. Such performances reinforce anti-doping discourses and the values that they communicate. I therefore ask readers to step away from these melodramatic accounts and temporarily suspend their beliefs and, if possible, their feelings toward the so-called cheaters depicted in these narratives as profiting from misleading the public. Instead of focusing on recent high-profile cases, I examine how anti-doping regulation has taken shape and changed, querying how biomedicalization and legality inform the terms of athlete citizenship. This book thus offers a contrast to the popular images of and narratives about drug cheats, which are a relatively small proportion of the athletes subject to surveillance. Such rhetoric often offers only straightforward tales of law and order. They typically convey a message that authorities must pursue and catch bad guys (or at least those so seduced by riches promised by sport and the desire to win that they cheat) in order to preserve fair play in sport. The social worlds of athletes and regulation, however, are more complicated.

My aim here is to examine the cultural conditions around regulatory claims, how those claims affect rules aimed at protecting fair play, and how regulation, in turn, affects athletes as citizen subjects. In doing so, I pay particular attention to the rhetorical and scientific devices that condemn those who are deemed unsuitable for athlete citizenship and render athletes more generally as suspect. As the book describes, this group of athletes, or outlaws, are not always those caught deliberately cheating. Rather, they are a group of suspect athletes whose diversity highlights the subjective contours of what—and who—regulation deems unacceptable for elite competition. In essence,

I argue that these stigmatized bodies reveal that regulation, even though employing objective forms of science, posits fictions about bodily purity. That is, in many cases, it is not actually cheating that warrants an offense, but other kinds of social concerns deemed to be contaminants or unnatural. The cases of suspect bodies attest that the impetus for regulating athlete citizens is much broader than concerns of taking drugs or using unfair or unhealthy substances to achieve in sport.

This book examines the various techniques used to sustain the anti-doping regime, including not only the scientific and legalistic instruments deployed through regulation, but also the persons and images labeled deviant. I pay particular attention to how gendered, economic, and postcolonial ideologies inform the frames through which they are produced to illustrate that anti-doping regulation is not simply about condemning people who cheat; it is bound to other historically ingrained and ideological beliefs about the human body. These include aesthetic judgments about whether a body appears to be enhanced naturally or unnaturally, postcolonial ideologies about whether or not some bodies are inherently pure or contaminated, as well as about beliefs that science can detect and explain the presence of these impurities. In sum, this book unearths how naturalized beliefs about the human body constitute the understandings of athlete citizens and how the partnership between science and regulation acts as an ideological gatekeeper.

Athlete Citizenship in a Globalized World

In this book, I use the term "athlete citizenship" to capture the regulation of a diverse transnational population of athletes who are subject to biomedical-ized forms of surveillance. This is a distinct departure from studies of citizen-ship that focus on how national law delineates subjects or how nation-states differentially treat their subjects. While law and regulation define athletes as a unique group, they are not marked uniformly by specific racial, socio-economic, or gender classifications (although I argue these are important considerations). Their corporeal abilities and achievements delineate them as a class distinct from other citizen subjects, and even though their bodies are held accountable to an ideal of fair play through tangible and legalized prac-tices, other nationalized, gendered, racialized, and classed inputs mediate and constrain their membership in this caste. This form of citizenship thus requires considering the tangible impacts of regulation alongside discursive barriers, including both their national and transnational dimensions.

Even beyond sport, various actors and regimes come to bear on citizens as well as those rendered noncitizens. Citizenship is no longer—and perhaps never was—solely dependent upon one's national affiliation or ethnic belong-ing; nor is it merely a matter of jurisdictional claims. Considering citizenship requires accounting for practices of governance, mechanisms of belonging and exclusion, and the ways inequality can mediate or exacerbate differences between subjects. Of contemporary formations of citizenship, Aihwa Ong writes, "Diverse actors invoke not territorialized notions of citizenship, but new claims—postnational, flexible, technological, cyber-based, and biological—as grounds for resources, entitlements and protection. . . . In addition to the nation-state, entities such as corporations and NGOs have become practitioners of humanity, defining and representing varied categories of human beings according to degrees of economic, biopolitical, and moral worthiness."[62] In light of globalized dynamics, attributes of citizenship take on myriad configurations beyond territorial jurisdictions, including, but not limited to, imagined, global, sexual, biological, and even genetic dimensions.

There are a host of theories and empirical analyses concerned with explaining citizenship in ways not bound to the nation-state.[63] A common tenet among these theories is that citizenship entails a form of "boundary work," which delineates insiders, those who enjoy a particular status and benefits, and outsiders, those who are denied such benefits. With regard to athlete citizenship, these dynamics crystallize around the bodies cast as tainted compared to athletes who retain a clean record. In keeping with Mary Douglas's observation, the judgment of cleanliness is not evidence of purity, but of normativity. The biomedicalized techniques employed to verify these judgments may appear as objective measures, but they also are stratified. This stratified biomedicalization, argue Clarke and colleagues, "both exacerbates *and* reshapes the consequences" of existing inequalities.[64] Moreover, as Nan Seuffert argues, "Colonialism haunts globalization, and is exceeded by it."[65] Thus, this analysis endeavors to show that anti-doping regulation contributes to and is enabled by globalized, corporatized, biomedicalized, and risk-oriented conditions, and it also highlights their postcolonial underpinnings.

Athlete citizenship reflects various inequalities, as sport-specific regulation operates within and alongside other domains—or what Louis Althusser referred to as "apparatuses"[66]—of social control, which fall within and beyond the boundaries of sport and the nation-state.[67] Apparatuses, be they private or public, forceful or mundane, express ideologies in a way that secures individuals as subjects under a regime. Ideology and practice are inseparable. The apparatus (*dispositif*) is a "thing," explains Michel Foucault, intermeshed with other regulatory techniques of the nation-state.[68] Accordingly, governance has various trajectories, "a plurality of specific aims," which include "a whole series of specific finalities, then, which become the objective of government."[69] Recent ethnographic work has detailed how trajectories of governance—what Foucault refers to as governmentality—inform citizen-state relations.[70] Similarly, this book explores governmentality in relation to anti-doping regulation, but in doing so, it looks beyond the nation-state to ask how various legalistic and scientific mechanisms affect individual subjects and groups in sport, addressing how they interact with—and sometimes surpass—state interests and formal legal boundaries.[71]

Although the Olympics, international sport competitions, and regulation have all changed significantly, regulation communicates many elements of Coubertin's appreciation for the body across the globe. In fact, with the growth of the Olympics and other international sport competitions as mediated spectacles watched by millions, bodies are increasingly visible and readily accessible to the public. Visually consuming and scrutinizing athlete bodies are aspects of everyday life for many people. Lawrence Wenner argues that the drama of sport narratives satiates desires for excitement stifled by the corporatized social arrangements that influence everyday life. Sports, he writes, are "commodified spectacles" enhanced by media productions and compelling story lines that indulge the populace with a kind of "compulsory fulfillment."[72] As such, scholars have examined spectator sport in the context of globalized dynamics, including citizenship, beyond nationalistic spaces.[73] Among them is sociologist Mette Andersson, who explains that contemporary international sport highlights a transnational "extension of contradictions of modernity" in that it "simultaneously values the homogenization (global village) and the differentiation processes of global modernity."[74]

International sport thus poses distinct challenges for understandings of citizenship. On the one hand, its spectacles evoke imaginaries that bring together national communities of diverse citizens to consume human spectacles and achievements, using a shared timeline.[75] On the other hand, sport is not always a clear space where citizenship and belonging are tied to collective imaginings and uniform calendars, as Benedict Anderson famously described in relation to national communities.[76] Instead, sport is a transnational field of contested meanings in which the bodies of athletes, namely their achievements, failures, and transgressions, are the focal points of sporting narratives. In this analysis, athletes' bodies and the various ways that they come to be regulated and understood emerge as central to understanding how athlete citizenship takes shape and interacts with other social norms and legalities.

This book queries sport in order to examine how anti-doping regulation mediates divergent beliefs and practices while pursuing a normative agenda against doping in sport. This builds upon critiques of Anderson's focus in *Imagined Communities*. Don Mitchell, for example, insists, "the question is not what common imagination exists," but what are "the practices and exercises of power through which these bonds are produced and reproduced."[77] I describe how these conduits work constitutively to maintain the anti-doping regime, unveiling the interpersonal elements that can go overlooked when we emphasize the outcomes of performance enhancement over the factors that contribute to and enable them. Relying upon insights provided to me by athletes subject to anti-doping rules and protocols as well as regulators who develop and implement them, this examination looks at both imagined and tangible dimensions of athlete citizenship. The imagined elements include the perceptions and expectations of what athletes are and should be. The observable forms include the practices of policing and gatekeeping that attempt to shore up the boundaries of a global sport community concerned with fair play, itself an imagined construct.

The Biopolitics of Athlete Citizenship

This study of citizenship in relation to sport is expressly concerned with biopolitical dimensions of regulation; that is, the "numerous and diverse techniques for achieving the subjugations of bodies and the control of populations."[78] In doing so, it focuses on three aspects of embodiment: the discourses around and symbolism of particular bodies (particularly those rendered deviant), the tools and techniques aimed to policing athlete bodies, and the power dynamics of surveillance that implicate athletes' embodied subjectivities. As chapters 2 and 3 describe in detail, anti-doping regulation relies upon and reiterates suspicions that many athletes are doping, even those who do not look deviant. While the athletes punished for transgressing the rules aid in sustaining anti-doping regulation because they provide evidence of the need for the anti-doping regime,[79] we can also observe that spectators often expect certain (often professional) athletes to be deviant and immoral.[80] Further, in the absence of evidence of doping, some, but not all, athletes become suspected of cheating. My reading of these suspicions builds upon criminologist Alison Young's contention that how onlookers imagine deviant bodies to look is more telling than the criminal acts that those bodies may (or may not) commit. Young explains that such "outlaws" are fashioned through a series of "linguistic turns and tricks, the framing and editing devices."[81] Doping in sport appears a criminalistic offense—even though it is not illegal in all jurisdictions—in part because public narratives condemn doping as criminal and dopers as criminals. In signaling who is not an appropriate athlete subject, the bodies condemned as deviant expose the limits and terms of athlete citizenship. Though athletes may be subject to testing and surveillance in ways that render their bodies suspect, some groups of athletes are portrayed as inherently deviant. In the pages that follow, I argue that postcolonial understandings of race and gender profoundly influence these differential framings of athletes.

While distinguishing insiders from outsiders may seem like a simple task through testing, this book considers how the changing terms of sport and regulation render the delineation a complex process that has scientific, legal, gendered, and postcolonial dimensions. Because sport is girded by globalized dynamics alongside historical legacies, the particularities of anti-doping regulation in action reflect the normative orders through which they have taken shape. In some cases, explicit inconsistencies emerge, which this book aims to unveil and unpack. For instance, as chapter 4 discusses, even though anti-doping regulation claims to protect against athletes using artificial enhancements, some natural bodies deemed to have too much testosterone for women's events, even those not contaminated with doping substances, can be banned from competition and even prescribed drugs or hormones that may reduce their athletic abilities. The official rationale is that it protects fair play in women's sport; however, it also communicates gendered messages that women's physical capacities are limited if not inferior. This practice, referred to as gender-verification testing or "sex testing," shares its origins with anti-doping regulation and points to contradictions embedded in attempts to protect the ideal of fair play, which I discuss further throughout this book.

The contradictions underlying anti-doping regulation can be difficult to detect in part because of its technocratic veneer. Within anti-doping regulation, law and science are closely aligned partners. Policymakers refine rules, and scientists innovate testing in order to better assess which bodies transgress the normative orders of athlete citizenship. In other words, they are intertwined technologies mobilized via anti-doping regulation. Although preoccupied with detecting doping agents and methods, regulatory technologies conjoin with normative systems, including those with evident gendered, classed, and racial contours. In fact, the regulatory regime has never been solely about doping in sport despite the beliefs and intentions of the public and regulators. Stories from past and present featured in this book demonstrate how regulation incorporates other agendas and interests not directly related to WADA's stated cornerstone principles of deterring the use of performance-enhancing substances, protecting athletes' health, and preserving the spirit of sport, a concept vaguely defined under anti-doping rules.

In attending to the technocratic character of regulation in this space, I examine the technologies of science, law, and social control as symbiotic and agentive actors. These technologies are not simply tools leveraged by regulators; rather, their deployment fundamentally shapes anti-doping efforts. Technoscience and law provide the evidence and the means of punishing athletes deemed to be offenders while reinforcing the normative claim that doping is a transgression of fair play. More generally, legality aids in producing and assimilating subjects, usually as members of a national body. By legality, I do not solely mean formal acts of lawmaking and enforcement, but "the meanings, sources of authority, and cultural practices that are commonly recognized as legal."[82] Legality, although pluralistic in relation to anti-doping regulation, operates in its own interest. According to Allen Feldman, law acts to "(m)other bodies in order to engender itself."[83] In other words, by claiming bodies as subjects, regimes perpetuate their own existence.

In this context, the detection and punishment of doping athletes reinforces the presumed need for a regulation and the continual innovation of technologies to catch transgressors. Detection, in particular, relies on forms of bodily policing that are becoming increasingly visible in other social contexts and juridical settings.[84] The fundamental characteristics of WADA's jurisdiction are thus not territorial, but biopolitical. As Lupton notes, "The techniques and strategies of governmentality emerge not simply from the state. While the state is important as part of the power relations, so too are the myriad of institutions, sites, social groups and interconnections at the local level, whose concerns and activities may support, but often conflict with, the imperatives of the state."[85] In other words, the biopolitical aspects of anti-doping regulation are a point of convergence between the concerns of legality and biomedicalization; however, this convergence can signal both complications and contradictions.

Sport draws offers an excellent site through which to investigate how legality contributes to understandings of our bodies and our selves. Athlete citizenship is not bound clearly to the nation-state, as the mechanisms targeting athletes' bodies do not emerge as a "uniform trend of State intervention," but are instead deployed through "a multitude of sites" and other "collective control measures."[86] This closely reflects what Nikolas Rose and Carlos Novas refer to as "biological citizenship," which has taken "shape in the age of biomedicine, biotechnology, and genomics."[87] As a concept, biological citizenship captures "projects that have linked their conceptions of citizens to beliefs about the biological existence of humans."[88] Anti-doping regulation explicitly does this kind of work through the policing of athletes. Similarly, scholarship on obesity attests that both rhetoric and regulation around bodies operates as a form of social control in ways that reveal biological citizenship.[89] Analyses of obesity attest that medicalized discourses carry very real consequences for those labeled obese and thus "abnormal," which have direct bearing on their treatment as stigmatized citizens. In the case of anti-doping regulation, adverse analytical findings can lead to the loss of athlete citizenship, not simply being stigmatized (as in obesity).

While athlete citizens are considered abnormal compared to other citizen subjects, there are usually positive associations with their abnormality. Their bodies occupy a distinctly different position compared to people labeled obese, many of whom are often imagined to be lazy, inefficient, and even morally abject. In contrast, athletes are celebrated through sport and often associated with bodily discipline and a superior work ethic. Elite athletes inhabit a privileged space within a broader discourse that "configure[s] virtue as an open-ended condition: a state of excellence."[90] Such virtue discourses, according to Christine Halse, operate across many societies. Indicators of health, such as regular physical activity and lean body frames, align "with self-discipline and moral fortitude and a high BMI [Body Mass Index] (overweight and obesity) is the binary 'Other'—the physical manifestation of self-indulgence and a lack of self-discipline and moral fortitude."[91] Special regulation aimed at athlete citizens reflects a desire to ensure they are virtuous subjects, at least in a bodily sense. When athletes fail to meet requirements, they are often vilified as frauds.

As a distinct caste of subjects, elite athletes serve a broader biopedagogical function in which their performances and the narrations of their accomplishments serve as lessons about life and how "to be 'healthy' (and good) citizens."[92] The athlete citizen symbolizes a kind of optimized body attributed to an ethic of discipline necessary to achieve this stature, the benefits of which often justify the heightened policing of athletes. Unpacking how these policing mechanisms are employed to protect these ideals enables a fuller explanation of the social, technocratic, and legalistic components that aid in naturalizing beliefs about athletes, including presumptions that they can be pure bodies.

Naturalness is a normative expectation to which elite athletes are held, and regulation reinforces the idea that naturalness is possible. The expectations about athletes' bodies are aesthetic in nature: their bodies are to be accessible. If they appear unnatural, their spectacular qualities can be passed off as an abnormality that is not a purely human feat of excellence. The athlete body, however, is inherently unnatural. As a category, the athlete is dependent upon bodily modification and various technologies to achieve these changes, a dependency that repudiates anti-doping regulation's attempts to purify sport. In addition to body modification, the other constant of being an athlete is an explicit relationship to the guidelines of competition. Within sport—whether it is professional, Olympic, or recreational—there are a host of requirements that athletes must abide by, including sport-specific rules, codes of conduct, and limits around performance enhancement. These requirements and the ideologies from which they spring invariably shape how athletes live and pursue their competitive objectives.

Considering that athletes are the products of their biological capacities, their desires, and the physical pursuit of their aspirations, there are various factors at work in the formation of athletes' identities and bodies. Biological, technological, and subjective factors are interconnected and inseparable. Race, gender, sexuality, nation, class, and a gamut of physical, social, and technological appendages all play some role in shaping an athlete's body. Various technologies, be they prohibited or permitted, are also integral to the creation of athletes and their programming.

Feminist scholars have argued that analyzing these bodies as "cyborgs" can help us develop more robust understandings of the embedded nature of science in relation to embodiment.[93] Extending Donna Haraway's work on cyborgs, they provide detailed accounts of how the athlete body is a "hybrid of machine and organism, a creature of social reality as well as a creature of fiction" living in and among other cyborgs that are always already contaminated, far from pure biological forms.[94] In this book, recognizing that the athlete body is a cyborg enables a deeper exploration into how seemingly external factors, including regulation and technology, become embodied parts through the biopolitical practices of discerning transgressors from athlete citizens as well as the resulting tensions.

Among these tensions are how technologies contribute to naturalizing social differences through factual assertions, an ongoing concern for much of science and technology studies scholarship. Although leveraged to preserve bodily (and presumably moral) purity, anti-doping regulation's deployment of scientific and legal technologies falls short of its stated mission and does a very different kind of work, which Bruno Latour describes as the symptom of *purification*.[95] Amidst continual processes of innovation, purification perpetuates myths of modernity to which subjects within the regime subscribe. These myths include divisions that Latour describes as "Two Great Divides": one between science/culture and nature, the other between the so-called pre-modern and modern.[96] Science, as a valued method of empiricism, can produce and interpret findings in a ways that present such myths as if they were truths.

Modern sport does not escape Latour's critique. Innovations in anti-doping technologies reveal an enduring commitment to diagnosing impure subjects. The rational veneer of technoscience can convince observers that regulatory findings provide proof of deviance and immorality, even though such innovations are simply creating new categories and distinctions that become classified as evidence of doping. Through a series of a priori claims and scientific tactics, the regime presents bodily purity as the natural condition of athletes despite the impossibility of bodily purity. Categories of doped and pure bodies—or "dirty" and "clean" to use anti-doping rhetoric—are imagined as facts. In sum, the science of testing helps us believe that purity is a reasonable expectation to have of athlete citizens. The myths of bodily purity and a level playing field, combined with the scientific and legal tools used to maintain them, feature prominently in the maintenance of athlete citizenship. The resulting tensions are the empirical focus of the fieldwork that informs the pages of this book.

Fieldwork: Tracing Anti-Doping Networks

This book offers a genealogical account of anti-doping regulation by questioning the meanings we take from sport. Informed by ethnographic and archival research, the basis of this analysis is the findings obtained through a multi-sited study, which consisted of "refunctioning ethnography" so as to follow objects of inquiry as they travel beyond localized domains across realms of time and space.[97] It is, like most qualitative studies, as much a product of chance as of calculated research. Both the accidental and planned encounters informing this book are a direct outgrowth of my position as an athlete and as an interlocutor in the field. Accordingly, this narrative balances personal insights from athletic playing fields alongside those obtained through more traditional forms of fieldwork such as conducting interviews and participant observation. The formal research for this book took place between 2007 and 2013, but my twenty-five years of sport participation contribute to my perspective and thus the book itself.

My immersion and familiarity with sport-specific settings comes as much from my personal exposure to sport as it is from the research process itself. I have competed in organized sport at an elite level, though my international experience is short compared to many successful athletes. As an active rugby union player, I have had the opportunity to participate in sport in many parts of the world, including my field sites. Beyond being a participant on the field, I have served in administrative roles that oversee competitive athletes and, at times, acted as a rule-enforcer charged with ensuring compliance with eligibility requirements. Most athletes take up such duties after they finish competing in sport, but given the (mostly) amateur status of women's rugby in the United States, I am among the many active athletes who have taken on these roles while still being subject to the rules as a competitor. This background directly informs how I came to know and relate to the participants who enabled this research.

Given my history as an athlete, it is perhaps not surprising that I set out to do research on the regulation of sport. It is an outgrowth of my situated position as an athlete and researcher. By situated, I mean how I fit into the framing of this project in relation to the collection of the raw data, analysis, and the writing of this text. Following Haraway, I evoke "situated" to flag that this book is composed of "partial, locatable accounts of the world that are both accurate and explicitly embedded within the contexts of its own production."[98] In writing this, I admit that I am skeptical of platforms concerned with protecting fair play, and my perspective stems in part from my own experiences in sport. This is also a direct outgrowth of the "body cultures" I have occupied as an athlete. Body cultures, writes anthropologist Susan Brownell, encompass "everything people do with their bodies" as well as "the elements of culture that shape their doing."[99] Although an array of cultural inputs informs athletes' beliefs and behaviors, the formation of body cultures is important because "the horizons of an athlete's world can never stray far beyond her body."[100]

Although regulators on the ground often mediate various body cultures by working with athletes, anti-doping discourses often dismiss the power and influence of such cultures, assuming that the power of law and punishment can override them. Throughout my research, it was at this disjuncture where I would find athletes in problematic positions, often resulting in anti-doping rule violations that ended their sporting careers—and changed their entire worlds.

By focusing on changes in regulation and on the bodies rendered suspect under its terms, this book unpacks how myths such as fair play have come to carry very real consequences. In taking this approach, the picture painted here is not a complete depiction of international sport or its global regulatory structures but an account of anti-doping networks. While other scholars have presented significant historical analyses of international anti-doping efforts,[101] my focus here is specific to the tensions in and around regulation and how they evidence a formation of citizenship that interacts with other forms of belonging and exclusion. This concentration required conducting research in various sites and in various ways, which I describe in the appendix. This book is not a traditional ethnography that required staying in one locale to become immersed in its cultural conditions. Instead, my fieldwork took a circuitous path that mapped the travels of anti-doping regulation in and across local spaces and globalized spheres. Since 2007, my research has straddled locations in Europe, North America, and Australasia in order to get a better sense of changing regulatory contours and how actors in the field come to understand and negotiate them.

In addition to speaking with athletes, I pursued Laura Nader's suggestion[102] to "study up" by taking an in-depth analytical look at how a relatively small group of elites came to legislate and construct global rules around doping in sport. The tasks that this portion of the research entailed are a stretch from my own upbringing: I grew up in a rural part of the United States, often balancing school with work in my father's general store and weekends at my grandparents' farm. A more labor-intensive than bucolic upbringing, my sports of choice reflect these roots. I always drifted toward contact sports: martial arts and later rugby. In a curious move, I found myself studying a group of (mostly) men[103] who shared similar ethnic origins (Anglo-European) but came from distinctly more privileged socio-economic positions. Coincidently, we often had similar athletic interests, having played rugby union, which is often seen as the upper-class code of rugby in many parts of the world and usually associated with male, rather than female, participation. This shared appreciation of sport often served as the basis of our rapport and ongoing communications.

In order to meet with those particular interlocutors, I navigated their international travel schedules, finding myself in various cities: Madrid, Montreal, Lausanne, Los Angeles, San Diego, Colorado Springs, Auckland, Wellington, and Canberra among them. Through this process, it became clear that was that there was a small, yet influential group of international anti-doping regulators who had close ties to New Zealand (or Aotearoa New Zealand[104]), a small country with a well-established national sports tribunal. During the research for this book, both the director general of WADA and the UNESCO program specialist for anti-doping first obtained professional experience in New Zealand. In addition, the chief executive of the New Zealand national anti-doping organization served on the WADA Foundation board and as the president of the Association for National Anti-Doping Organizations. The author of the first significant legal guide book on the Code worked on various anti-doping rule violation cases heard in New Zealand, and there are high-level athletes from New Zealand who have served in different anti-doping roles. Although small in number, these experts' perspectives helped me to make sense of how they understood the advantages and shortcomings of anti-doping regulation. Because of these connections, I dedicate chapter 5 to a case study analysis of New Zealand's anti-doping system, which illustrates the significance of nation within the transnational regulatory regime.

While keeping in contact with those interlocutors, I interviewed local sport administrators and international officials based in Europe working with and for UNESCO. I have also observed important anti-doping events, such as the World Conference on Doping in Sport held in Madrid in November 2007, in order to gain insight into the international regime. The Madrid conference, for instance, included my attendance at formal hearings and sessions, and also enabled me to interview athletes, scientists, and administrators at various levels. During the summer of 2009, I conducted archival research at the Olympic Studies Centre in Lausanne, Switzerland, to better grasp the historical origins of regulatory and drug-testing practices at the international level. From 2007 to 2010, when I lived in California, I observed California State Athletic Commission meetings to better understand how it adapted anti-doping rules for disciplinary hearings involving athletes who committed violations. As a comparative reference point, this helped me to analyze the dissemination of anti-doping regulation, its intentions and partial applications, as well as the distinctions of New Zealand's anti-doping system. I also interviewed (and kept up a conversation with) a number of active and retired Olympic, national-level, and professional athletes in order to better understand how athletes have negotiated regulation and changing rules over time.

In August 2008, I undertook my first research trip to New Zealand to meet with sport administrators and returned in early 2010 to observe how the agencies charged with overseeing sport and recreation in New Zealand carried out their work. There, I interviewed sport administrators, athletes, members of the Sports Tribunal, and other legal representatives. I also accepted regular invitations to observe and interact with athletes in sport settings. This allowed me to gain a better understanding of New Zealand's cultural dynamics, particularly in its largest and most diverse urban center, Auckland. Completing my fieldwork in August 2010, I went back in 2011 during the Rugby World Cup to follow up with participants, and since relocating to Australia in 2011, I have been fortunate to speak with administrators working in the field who are willing to share their insights into regulatory changes. Moreover, as 2012 and 2013 were eventful years in terms of doping scandals in Australia, my presence here has proven invaluable and timely in terms of making contacts and observing reactions to events.

Informed by these various sites and persons, my perspective is that of a researcher (a presumed outsider) and an athlete (a kind of insider). In this book, I occasionally evoke my own experiences, but I mostly rely on the insights of the many policymakers and athletes who shared their expertise, their desires, and their ambitions in sport. For this I am both humbled and grateful. These individual contributions vary as greatly as the people who offered their time and thoughts. Some athletes became coparticipants during many aspects of this research, especially as I could not observe testing protocols firsthand. During my stay in New Zealand, members of West Auckland's Samoan community shared their homes with me as well as many aspects of their lives. They also translated certain communal values to me and explained how they navigate life in New Zealand, allowing me to glean insights into how their own values can conflict with national sport agendas and anti-doping requirements.

Representatives of regulatory bodies were also generous in sharing their knowledge. Admittedly, the regime that they support bears the brunt of critiques found in this analysis. In being forthright about the critical stance I take in this book, I found that many regulators, especially those who were former athletes, explained how they often straddle a tenuous space, balancing their sympathies with athletes and their roles as overseers. My hope is that their willingness to support this analysis reflects their own commitment to improving regulation by further examining and reconsidering the contradictions I observed during my research.

The Outline of This Book

Given the multiple levels and overlapping considerations examined in this book, each chapter focuses on a distinct context in which these dynamics play out in the quotidian practices of the regulatory regime and how they capture the emergence of athlete citizenship. Because I draw from data obtained through archival and ethnographic research, the contents of this book reflect the strengths and weaknesses of those sources. Primary sources housed in the IOC Archives in Lausanne, Switzerland, offer unique perspective to the analyses in chapters 2 and 4; however, there are noteworthy limitations in relying on these texts. There is a twenty-year embargo on most IOC documents, which, given the time frame covered in those chapters, is not significant. There is, however, no guarantee that documents containing contentious, disconcerting, or humiliating information about the IOC or its members are available to researchers. Chapters 2 and 5 are framed ethnographically, making them confined primarily to observable relationships: those between the rules of sport and athletes' corporality, interactions with regulators, reflections expressed by various actors on anti-doping regulation and ideals. Although the chapters are mere snapshots of the worlds occupied by athletes and administrators, they highlight important interstices within the international anti-doping regime's stated objectives and the practices on the ground. My hope is that this analysis, which puts findings from these data in dialogue with public discourse, sparks an interest for further socio-legal inquiry into sport.

The first three chapters of this book detail the emergence of regulation aimed at preserving fair play and how earlier depictions of deviant athletes compare to contemporary depictions and rhetoric. They illustrate how the terms of athlete citizenship have taken shape. Specifically, in chapter 2, I address how changes to rhetoric and policies since the initial use of scientific testing in the 1960s reveal distinct cultural and regulatory shifts that lead to the embrace of biomedicalized technologies. In chapter 3, I examine the rhetoric and tactics used to mobilize support for the UNESCO Convention against Doping in Sport, which is the first international convention ratified in this field, and those devices are legalistic and ideological in ways that disregard—and, in turn, uphold—ever-present inequalities. In order to examine the differential treatment of athlete citizens in an overt sense, chapter 4 explores the gendered dimensions of upholding fair play by examining the close linkages between anti-doping rules and gender-verification practices. Looking at the impetus for regulation and the changing justifications for gender verification reveal a series of naturalized beliefs that inform ideals of fair play, which directly inform the anti-doping regime. In fact, feminist scholars have condemned the WADA Code and its regulatory predecessors as "gender policing tools."[105] The contradictions analyzed across these three chapters highlight how anti-doping regulation's embedded subscriptions to bodily purity are, in fact, themselves impure ideas.

Chapter 5 stands out as a distinct case study that illustrates how these globalized practices converge in a national context. Through a focus on policies and practices in New Zealand, it describes how anti-doping campaigns related to sport couple with nationalistic agendas, their imbued postcolonial dilemmas, and biomedicalized changes. It also examines how actors in the national anti-doping system adapted legal instruments at the domestic level to comply with international requirements, focusing on how they go about carrying out their regulatory duties. The interplay yields a curious case that departs from the rhetoric of anti-doping regulation, even as national regulators continue to use such language. Administrators spend much of their time developing strategies to ensure that athletes comply with the array of internationally mandated requirements and to help them avoid inadvertent instances of doping. Despite these efforts, the use of marijuana, a drug that likely hinders athletic performance in many cases, is the reason for the majority of anti-doping offenses. This development frustrates both athletes and administrators alike, with the dynamics between actors revealing the constitutive boundaries of who can and cannot become a national athlete representative as rooted in both formal regulation and postcolonial inequalities. In sum, chapter 5 demonstrates how international rules and national values shape the terms of athlete citizenship in practice.

In the conclusion, I build upon the dilemmas highlighted in the New Zealand case study and ask how they draw attention to broader issues around the inflexibility of anti-doping regulation and how it instills a risk-laden belief that renders athletes as inherently suspect subjects. It reflects on the questions that drive the analyses in previous chapters: How has the pursuit of an unattainable purity in sport given rise to a complex global regulatory regime? How has this regime contributed to the ways that the traditions of sport and beliefs about embodiment are understood in a global context? Now that anti-doping regulation is codified under the UNESCO Convention against Doping in Sport, what challenges does the regime face, and how will it adapt? In addressing these questions, the conclusion aims to address both practical and analytical concerns presented by this regulatory space.

Though focused on the anti-doping regime, the observations and encounters detailed in this book provide insight into a range of orders that inform global sport. It unveils how certain governing bodies contribute to ideologies of fair play while also offering an example through which to reflect critically on the conditions of citizenship in a globalized world. Through a discussion of the myths about what athletes should be, this book seeks to enhance knowledge of the technologies of regulation in this field and to illustrate how paying further analytic attention to issues of embodiment can advance scholarship on biomedicine, law, and regulation. The importance of the body is undeniable in the context of sport, but it is also central to many other relationships between law and society. Shorn of cultural attributes, the body, as a corporeal *tabula rasa*, can be subject to various interpretations. It serves, according to Foucault, as the "surface on which events are inscribed," situating the basis of genealogy "at the point of articulation of the body and history. [Genealogy's] task is to show a body totally imprinted with history."[106] In pursuing this point, this book is an attempt to extrapolate how the meanings and bodies that circulate through sport attest to broader issues related to globalization, surveillance, and the status of citizen subjects, arguing that any discussion of fair play cannot be separated from gendered and postcolonial considerations.

2

Diagnosing Doping

The Institutionalization
of the Moral Crusade

The contemporary contours of anti-doping regulation are the outgrowth of a history that took shape primarily during the latter half of the twentieth century. That history reveals how earlier forms of technocratic regulation aided in instilling and institutionalizing suspicions of athletes' bodies. As I will explain further in chapter 3, suspicion has become codified in the World Anti-Doping Code. To illuminate how such values took hold, this chapter explores how formal anti-doping regulation began as technocratic rules that later gave way to a biomedicalized form under the World Anti-Doping Agency. In particular, I examine the historical development of drug testing by the International Olympic Committee in order to explore how the interplay between science and ideology constitutively informed regulation, attending to how historical developments have shaped the stratified nature of contemporary athlete citizenship.

Although WADA was established in 1999, international drug testing preceded it by nearly forty years. Although there is evidence that the IOC banned doping as early as 1938, most historical accounts focus on the development of drug testing in the 1960s.[1] At the 56th IOC session in 1960, doping as an issue arose in relation to concerns around the proliferation of seemingly "unnatural" competitors, those athletes perceived to rely too strongly on artificial enhancement. The regulation that emerged from those concerns reflected a commitment to Olympic values associated with amateurism, particularly beliefs that equated bodily purity with ethical integrity, amid the wider professionalization of sport in the latter half of the twentieth century. Interestingly, as John Gleaves and Matthew Llewellyn document, there was a longstanding general recognition of stimulant use among professional sports, such as cycling and prizefighting. In the early part of the twentieth century, the general perception was that such stimulant use was "contrary to the gentlemanly amateur code that governed middle- and upper-class sport," but was generally acceptable among the working class, particularly in relation to manual laborers.[2] Thus, the use of stimulants in the pursuit of profit not only was distinct from the notion of amateur sport for moral cultivation, but also served as a way to debase the value of professional sport and the athletic accomplishments of working-class participants.[3] With the introduction of the modern Olympics, Pierre de Coubertin recognized that tensions would emerge, as the international stage would fuel a push toward what he referred to as "excess."[4] In fact, the Olympics included sports that many onlookers felt were not suitably amateur sports, such as cycling and the marathon. These tensions persisted, and as the IOC clung to an image of pure sport bolstered by the formal embrace of amateur values, doping became a concern to target. In sum, the regulations developed in the 1960s responded to broader anxieties around the ethics of professional sport as something antithetical to the Olympic values.

The origins and subsequent changes made to anti-doping rules offer an opportunity to unearth how particular ethical concerns became embedded in the regime. While many historical analyses recognize how political and ideological agendas had an influence on scientific testing and procedures in anti-doping regulation, the cultural influence of science sometimes goes overlooked or under-interrogated. Technologies are not simply things shaped by social processes; they are cultural objects that also shape social processes. Scientific pursuits of objective, seemingly "law-like" truths are, in fact, "historical artifacts of instrumental reason."[5] The use of technocratic tools as a response to cultural problems—like doping—hinges on an underlying belief that there are diagnosable truths.[6] The regulation of doping in sport demonstrates a convergence between the cultures of science and the cultural beliefs justifying science's intervention.

The embrace of technological innovation has significantly shaped anti-doping regulation, which Jin-Kyung Park refers to as a form of "technology-driven governance."[7] By this, Park means that anti-doping regulation hinges upon science and technology. A commitment to innovation anchors and drives the regime and its pursuit of athletes using doping agents and methods. The acceptance of scientific innovation has profoundly shaped the nature of anti-doping rules (i.e., their reliance on testing and surveillance mechanisms) and the framing of doping as a problem (i.e., as a dangerous cycle of innovating performance-enhancing methods). The history of this technological embrace reflects the movement toward a biomedicalized regime, revealing how ideologies of fair play, global politics, and science coalesce to inform IOC policies toward doping in sport. Anti-doping regulation came to reflect an arms-race mentality, the Cold War strategy employed by the West to anticipate pre-emptive strike from rival powers. This mentality was the driving force in early anti-doping efforts. Here, I describe and reflect on how an arms-race logic became manifest in regulation through the IOC Medical Commission's embrace of scientific rationalities. In doing so, these tactics not only defined and redefined what constituted doping but also shifted the stratified terms of athlete citizenship.

Recognizing that technologies have influenced IOC policies on performance enhancement expands upon scholarly suggestions that "moral entrepreneurship" has played—and continues to play—an important role in the development of drug testing and anti-doping policy.[8] Moral entrepreneurs, explains Howard Becker, promote their own normative values by ascribing a social label to a behavior or a practice through the creation or enforcement of rules that reflect and reinforce their own ideological disposition.[9] This concept has been employed usefully in relation to other anti-drug campaigns and illustrates how such lobbying can influence the institutionalization of a particular group's agenda.[10] It also helps to explain how a group of mostly European medical doctors shaped the foundations of anti-doping regulation.

As historical research on doping in sport attests, anti-doping practices and beliefs have taken shape as part of—and response to—broader transformations in modern sport. Fuelled by intense Cold War politics, the rise of highly developed national sport systems, accompanied by the professionalization of sport and athletic performance training, relied strongly on scientific advances.[11] Even though the arms race of the Cold War era no longer persists, there remains an arms-race logic built into anti-doping regulation. Regulatory development is so closely linked to scientific innovation that it is often characterized as a competition between those developing (illegal) performance-enhancing substances and methods and those developing instruments to detect them.

Drawing primarily from sources housed in the IOC Archives in Lausanne, Switzerland, this chapter revisits how anti-doping regulation took on a *scientistic* disposition and how developments in drug testing evidence it as a cultural shift.[12] This shift precedes the later embrace of biomedicalization under WADA's leadership. In this chapter, I focus primarily on the foundational years of the IOC Medical Commission's existence and how it oversaw the development of testing protocols and technocratic policies. As advances in testing have driven developments in anti-doping policy, this chapter offers historical insight into events that paved the way for contemporary anti-doping practices implemented by WADA, paying close attention to how its members, most of whom were scientists and medical doctors, acted as moral entrepreneurs. Their moral crusade not only made a practice (doping) into an issue of broad moral concern, but it also aided in reframing how authorities condemned doping. The condemnation superseded its origins in class divisions as sport professionalized. In doing so, regulation came to reflect the desire to protect foundational Olympic beliefs attributed to amateurism, even though sport increasingly became a venue for financial profit and entertainment—the very values against which amateurism originally stood.

Caught in the middle of these tensions, the IOC Medical Commission laid the regulatory and ideological foundations of the contemporary global anti-doping regime. Scientific developments, however, serve as more than tools leveraged by moral entrepreneurs against doping in sport; they are themselves actors that influenced moral entrepreneurs in this field as the rules developed.[13] In fact, the Medical Commission's embrace of science in its pursuit of detecting "cheats" who dope eventually overshadowed a key moral impetus for anti-doping regulation: the protection of athletes' health. The resulting changes to regulation attest to the convergence of science, ideology, and politics in underpinning the institutionalization of the moral crusade against doping as well as the terms of athlete citizenship.

The Origins of the IOC Medical Commission and Its Role in Anti-Doping Regulation

The IOC Medical Commission introduced formalized drug testing at the 1968 Olympic Games, making it a distinct kind of moral entrepreneur. "Rule creators," a category of moral entrepreneur described by Becker, are often portrayed as "crusaders" championing a cause that they deem to be a social threat.[14] Their work is typically to persuade others in society to accept their perspective. If their crusade is successful, these values become institutionalized through the creation of new rules. Archetypal rule creators are ardent and sanctimonious, although they often see their cause as being for the greater social good. They, in turn, are not so much concerned with the details of the rules, but about pushing a reformist agenda, and in extreme cases, the end results can serve to justify any means necessary.

Paul Dimeo has similarly characterized some members of the IOC Medical Commission during the 1960s and 1970s as "proselytizers as well as fanatics" who sought to protect the purity of sport, not simply the health of athletes.[15] This coincided with a broader effort by Olympic officials to lobby for the international acceptance of sport as a distinct sphere on the basis of its presumed purity.[16] Ian Ritchie has described their presumption of purity as a "foundation myth" that helped to galvanize support for the Olympic Movement.[17] This notion of purity, however, was itself a contaminated ideal, one that morphed as Olympic sport abandoned ideals of amateurism and as anti-doping regulation became more sophisticated.[18] The history of anti-doping regulation reflects how changes to rules are constitutively related to changes in international politics as well as the accompanying corporatized shift in Olympic sport, what Peter Donnelly refers to as "Prolympism," which, simply put, is the "merger of professional sport and corporate Olympic sport."[19]

At the time of the Medical Commission's establishment in 1961, Olympic sport had not yet embarked on this corporatized path. The IOC and the Olympic Charter "directly opposed the most extreme manifestations of the forces of scientific rationality and the cult of victory that increasingly threatened to undermine and debase the Olympic project."[20] In essence, this stance assumed that practices of doping embodied the values of pursuing winning at all costs, undermining the Olympic principles of camaraderie and moral development cultivated by amateur sport. Although the impetus for anti-doping regulation was to protect such Olympic foundation myths, the rise of anti-doping regulation—alongside the competitive climate of Cold War sport, increasingly sophisticated scientific tools, and the wider professionalization of sport—would coincide with the erosion of amateurism.

In addition to the Olympic ideals, personal correspondence by members of the IOC Medical Commission evidence their own moral reasons for condemning doping, even though their enduring acts of moral entrepreneurship took on a technocratic form.[21] In clinging to objective measures, formal Medical Commission recommendations seemingly disavow cultural factors; however, this erasure is an important aspect of science's cultural influence: those developing and deploying these tools have an "unmarked" power "to see and not be seen."[22] By leveraging drug testing to preserve bodily (and presumably moral) purity, regulation has rendered the cultural tenets of amateurism as tangible truth-claims, not as a forthright ideological stance. In other words, the basis of testing suggests that bodies *can and should be* natural; however, recognizing sport as a technological process reveals that drug testing actually only distinguishes some methods of performance enhancement as beyond the moral order. In a very basic sense, science influences how anti-doping regulation levies its moral claims, doing so in ways that are often discursive and not always rendered explicit.

Well before scholars such as Dimeo characterized the Medical Commission as a group of moral entrepreneurs, critical commentators referred to their work as a "crusade" with moralistic underpinnings. For instance, in describing the anti-doping crusade, sports doctor Lan Barnes explained that Medical Commission policies were flawed, yet nonetheless growing. Dominated by European doctors, the anti-doping effort, he argued, used a variety of reasons to justify its cause, including that doping caused "physiological damage, addiction, psychological deterioration, and progressive moral degradation."[23] Pointing to the limitations of regulatory tactics, he stressed that "the list of banned drugs and practices they recommend is only limited by the availability of tests for the substance."[24] Barnes highlighted an underlying tension: relying on scientific testing would only address elements of the doping problem. Rules were only as robust as the science that underpinned them, which perpetuated a cycle of innovation in order to detect more doping products and agents. This limitation, now an embedded feature of anti-doping regulation, was the outgrowth of the Medical Commission's early interventions, which had taken on a distinctly technocratic focus as early as 1967.

Depending primarily upon drug testing was not the evident course of action when the IOC began formal discussions of taking action to regulate drug use in sport in the 1960s. In addition, although Olympic drug testing began while Avery Brundage was at the helm of the IOC, he is not remembered as a strong advocate of drug-testing protocols, even though he is attributed with authoring one of the first strong IOC statements against doping.[25] Brundage was more concerned with championing amateurism, even amid pressures to remove the requirement from the Olympic Charter, and resurrecting Coubertin's original values of Olympism. In fact, Brundage arguably defended amateur requirements more vehemently than Coubertin.[26] Characterizing sport as a field beyond governmental or political intervention, Brundage contended that the Olympic Games should highlight "'true internationalism,' that is, respect for and celebration of national cultural differences, rather than 'cosmopolitanism,' the extirpation of such differences."[27] Despite this purported vision, Brundage's tenure as IOC president is better known for permitting, and arguably endorsing, race-based discrimination in United States and international sport under the guise of being apolitical.[28] It is perhaps not surprising, then, to find that the Medical Commission operated fairly autonomously while Brundage engaged with other issues, including threats by African nations to boycott the 1968 Olympic Games in Mexico City if South Africa and Rhodesia participated.

The story of how anti-doping efforts came to fit into Brundage's notions of Olympism is more complex than that of neglect, though. At the IOC session in 1960, Brundage raised the issue of athletes using amphetamines, better known then as "pep pills."[29] During the meeting, the prospect of endorsing the scientific examination of doping arose but was not pursued. Instead, members received encouragement to "speak of this matter in their respective countries."[30] Months later, however, the death of Danish cyclist Knud Jensen during the Rome Olympics emphasized the need for more regulation. Jensen reportedly had taken stimulants prior to the race and his death became symbolic by seemingly demonstrating that athletes needed to be saved from the dangers, both moral and physical, inherent in the "winning at all costs" mentality promoted by professional sport.[31] Further, as cycling was a recognizable professional sport, it was not a surprising target for anti-doping reforms.

Calls for regulation underscored what became construed as a need to save athletes from the dangers posed by such competitive conditions. Although this rationale is distinct from the idea of cheating to undermine fair play in sport, this initial justification for regulation nonetheless was imbued with a distrust of athletes. It presumed their inability to know what is—or should be—in their own interests or for their own good. Coincidentally, and discussed in more depth by Dimeo, there is no public evidence that Jensen's death was the direct result of drug use.[32] Some reports attribute his death to doping, but the actual autopsy findings were not publicized.

Even though these developments prompted the IOC executive board to call for sanctions, the IOC again failed to take direct action.[33] Accompanying the aversion to professional sport and its technologies of performance enhancement was also a hesitation by the IOC executive board to embrace—and fund—scientific testing to enhance its regulatory response to doping.[34] Instead, in the aftermath of the controversy, it endorsed the establishment of a medical commission with a doping subcommittee to focus on the emergent concern of drug use in sport. This body would later come to serve as a regulatory gatekeeper of Olympic athlete citizenship, ultimately deciding which athletes were or were not eligible, but it did not take immediate steps in this direction. In fact, the IOC Medical Commission did not began its work on scientific testing and protocols until 1967, which was after its first chairperson, Sir Arthur Porritt (who had accomplished little in terms of policy) had stepped down to accept his appointment as the governor-general of New Zealand. Around that time, another high-profile cyclist, British champion Tom Simpson, died, his death attributed to the use of stimulants during competition.

Porritt's position on what constituted doping and how to counteract it is notably different from contemporary rhetoric.[35] Defining doping, he argued, "is, if not impossible, at best extremely difficult, and yet everyone who takes part in competitive sport or who administers it knows exactly what it means. The definition lies not in words but in integrity of character."[36] Porritt did, however, acknowledge doping as a consequence of sport's modernization, writing that "the highly competitive nature of modern sport, often associated with the factor of national prestige" as well as "the far greater rewards" accompanying athletic success, encouraged taking drugs and additional risks to enhance performance.[37] For Porritt, those who used doping agents had "an inferiority complex" and were similar to a "'dope' in the American sense—the mentally, physically, and morally dulled individual."[38] He stressed that "only a long-term education policy stressing the physical and moral aspects of the drug problem" would prevent and deter athletes from using ergogenic aids.[39] Connecting the physical and the moral aspects of sport reflected foundational Olympic principles. As Rob Beamish and Ian Ritchie write, "The overly competitive zeal represented by the use of performance-enhancing substances fell outside the Movement's moral code. This was the educational message Porritt wanted conveyed to the athletes of the Games."[40]

Porritt's tenure as chairman of the IOC Medical Commission is marked by inaction. He was not simply hesitant to act, but perhaps uninterested as he sometimes failed to attend meetings and submit reports.[41] The Medical Commission did not deliver its first report until 1966, over five years after its establishment. It suggested the following recommendations as the basis of anti-doping efforts:

1) National Olympic Committees (NOCs) should begin work on general education;
2) the inclusion of entry forms signed by competitors with a statement that he or she did not dope (which would pave the way for testing and examinations);
3) international federations should prohibit the behavior in their own rules;
4) the IOC should formally condemn doping and sanction either National Olympic Committees or individual athletes if found guilty of an offense during the Olympic Games; and
5) it should ensure that testing can take place when deemed necessary.[42]

While this early articulation of the Medical Commission's position embraced fundamental tenets of moral entrepreneurship by promoting the broader condemnation of doping in sport, its initial lack of follow-through made it far from a fervent crusader.

Beyond Porritt's reluctance, the IOC did not participate in the first conference on the subject of doping, which was held by Council of Europe (CoE) in 1963. Taking action without the IOC, the CoE commission worked out a distinctly different notion of doping, one that Porritt had described as difficult, if not impossible, to do. The CoE commission defined doping as: "the administration to or the use by, a competing athlete of any substance foreign to the body or any physiological substance taken in abnormal quantity or by an abnormal route of entry into the body, with the sole intention of increasing in an artificial and unfair manner his performance in competition."[43] This definition married moral and physiological concerns. It made the direct connection that the presence of a "foreign" (and presumably unnatural) substance in an athlete's body marked an ethical transgression. Interestingly, the definition did not explicitly address physical well-being, even though health risks served as a direct impetus for developing anti-doping policy. Nonetheless, this act labeled doping as an act of deviance, providing the grounds to justify drug testing as a way to obtain evidence of an athlete's transgression. This definitional act did more than condemn doping; it set the stage for rules and sanctions based on the findings of testing. It enabled technology to serve as the mechanism through which to inscribe a cultural belief in bodily purity that was already supported by values of amateurism. Through the ability to detect a substance, testing practices would offer an empirical mechanism to bolster an ideological stance.

The IOC Medical Commission later embraced the tenets of the CoE commission's definition under the chairmanship of Prince Alexandre de Mérode of Belgium. In pursuing this narrow, albeit still vague, definition of doping, the Medical Commission's work took on an explicitly technocratic focus under de Mérode. This approach was perhaps expected given that seven of the other members appointed to the Medical Commission were specialists in either medicine or pharmacology. In fact, other than de Mérode, only Arpad Csanadi of Hungary lacked training in these fields. The other members were Dr. Arnold Beckett of Great Britain; Dr. Albert Dirix, vice president of the Belgian Olympic Committee; Dr. Roger Genin of France, who was also on the organizing committee of the 1968 Olympic Games in Grenoble; Eduardo Hay, the medical director of the 1968 Olympic Games in Mexico; Professor Giuseppe La Cava, the president of the International Federation of Sports Medicine; Professor Ludwig Prokop of Austria; and Pieter Van Dijk, president of the Medical Commission of the International Cycling Union.[44] Dirix and Prokop had been part of a group that had met and arranged small-scale testing at the 1964 Tokyo Games, while Beckett had aided in the development of procedures and rules for the 1966 football World Cup.[45]

Many appointees to the IOC Medical Commission also expressed strong anti-doping sentiments, some of which focused on the issue of athletes' health, others on ethical concerns. For instance, la Cava had written that amphetamines' performance-enhancing effects were both "illegitimate" in terms of ethics and dangerous in terms of health.[46] Prokop too had cast doping as an immoral act while attending the CoE commission conference. Having encountered amphetamine use among cyclists he had treated, he had denounced the sport's resistance to anti-doping efforts and later argued that sports doctors often enabled drug use.[47] Attributing Jensen's death to doping, Dirix appealed, "We doctors wish to prevent such tragedies." Characterizing doping as a widespread "evil," he explained that "nothing could be more criminal than to destroy the health or life of a young athlete."[48]

Although many members justified their work in moral terms, a series of technocratic priorities that "placed a particular emphasis on medical controls concerning both doping and the establishment of sex" emerged from the Medical Commission's first meeting in September 1967.[49] The five areas of the concern were:

1) the need for entry forms requiring athletes and NOCs to consent to medical examinations "thought necessary in the interests of both his health and future";

2) the development of a list of banned substances as well as sample collection and laboratory testing procedures;

3) the random selection of athletes for anti-doping testing and mandatory sex testing of the three winning female competitors in an event;

4) the obligation of international federations to disseminate information in order to ease implementation; and

5) the provision of medical assistance to any country that does not have adequate staff at either the 1968 Grenoble or Mexico City Games.[50]

Of these revised goals, the second and aspects of the third became the central focus of the Medical Commission's work, especially in its early years, and chapter 4 discusses "the establishment of sex" through testing in more depth than I do here. Overall, the direction of the Medical Commission's work would follow a decidedly scientific path, and the implementation of medical protocols required the involvement of commission members, which Porritt's earlier recommendations had not endorsed.

As a collective, the Medical Commission acted as both a "rule creator" and a "rule enforcer," which are two distinct categories of moral entrepreneurs under Becker's original explanation. In fact, Becker described rule enforcers as part of the development of organizations and rules that resulted from successful moral crusades led by reformers.[51] Because of its members' medical expertise, the Medical Commission wore both hats, often simultaneously. As rule creators, members gave credence to anti-doping guidelines because their collective social status and scientific training lent credibility to regulatory claims and tools. They were also sometimes rule enforcers who carried out the tests and made decisions on punishment (although this would change later as anti-doping regulation expanded). The rules and membership of the Medical Commission would fluctuate in the years that followed; however, de Mérode and Beckett would directly influence anti-doping policy for more than three decades. While Beckett's suggestions for testing procedures and methods impacted the actual protocols carried out, the prince was the more active lobbyist—at least early on. In fact, de Mérode—who has been criticized as an ineffective chairman by some[52]—made up for his lack of formal medical training by advocating on behalf of the Medical Commission. His contributions, which I explain in the next section, ensured that it became a recognized voice within the Olympic Movement.

Early Drug Testing under the IOC Medical Commission

Focusing on the technical aspects of outlining the methods of testing and analysis, the Medical Commission agreed to use thin-layer and gas chromatography.[53] Members also decided upon five classifications of banned substances, which is remarkably few compared to the thousands of individual substances currently banned by WADA. They were sympathomimetic amines; stimulants of the central nervous system (strychnine) and analeptics; narcotics and analgesics; antidepressants, imipramine and similar substances; and major tranquilizers.[54] Recognizing the limitations of this list, the members of the IOC Medical Commission included a clause acknowledging, "We have concentrated on products which are detrimental when used by healthy athletes in competition, but which on the other hand are used for therapeutic reasons."[55] The initial list of banned substances therefore reflected concerns around athletes' health and well-being, and as the sophistication of testing protocols improved, the Medical Commission added more substances to the list.

Early on, the development and oversight of testing protocols took precedence; however, the process of implementing protocols, or even establishing the Medical Commission's credibility, was not smooth. As Steven Epstein acknowledges, credibility is itself a process, one that is "both a stake and a weapon in the skirmishes between all those who are in competition" as well as a "mechanism for forging durable relationships within which knowledge can reliably be exchanged."[56] In essence, it is contested. An early battle regarding the role of the Medical Commission offers an illustration of this point: the prince faced direct challenges from President Brundage who, concerned with the IOC's finances (or lack thereof), did not feel that the IOC should shoulder the responsibility of implementing drug-testing procedures. Specifically, in a curricular to international sport federations, NOCs, and IOC members dated August 27, 1968, Brundage (without consulting de Mérode) announced that the commission's role was merely advisory in nature.

Before Brundage's letter, the IOC Medical Commission had already developed testing protocols that required the direct involvement of Medical Commission members. In fact, the Medical Commission had delineated its duties:

[to] carry out the taking of the urine samples on a random basis and the laboratory analysis. In addition, in the case of doubt, they must decide whether a misuse has been made of the dope substances and, each time, a positive result is obtained, advise the authorized disciplinary department accordingly in a strictly confidential manner. The Medical Commission should meet every two days [during the Games]. Should positive results be obtained during the dope test or other questions, such as those pertaining to the sex tests for example, arise, it should meet as soon as possible.[57]

With responsibilities and testing procedures outlined, de Mérode rebuffed Brundage, copying all parties who received the original memorandum. Calling Brundage's letter "a serious blow to the work we are trying to achieve," he wrote that the role of commission had been defined and "cannot be changed unilaterally without first consulting the qualified authorities who decreed them," adding that "these extremely delicate matters concern the moral responsibility of the IOC and go far beyond technical questions, if we still wish to remain loyal to the fundamental principles of the Olympic Spirit."[58]

De Mérode's argument is important to note because it highlighted that technical procedures should not overshadow or erase the normative reasons for anti-doping regulation. In fact, he contended that they could be complementary. Not only did this mark an attempt to assuage IOC members' anxieties around technology, it actually refigured Olympic values in a way that rendered them compatible with scientific pursuits. Although disagreeing with and defying Brundage, he did so by appealing to Olympic agendas. This development emerged as part of a broader shift within the Olympic Movement, which began to move away from the formal doctrine of amateurism toward principles that reconciled ongoing changes in sport sparked by professionalism and increasingly competitive sporting systems.[59] De Mérode's words struck a balance by articulating the place of the Medical Commission within the values upon which the Olympic Movement hinged. This prompted Brundage to clarify his position, writing that he had "no intention whatsoever . . . to undermine the Medical Commission." He specified, "If there is any testing done in Mexico, it will be done under the supervision of this Commission and according to its regulations and procedures. *However, it must be done at the written request of the International Federations concerned.*"[60]

Although members attempted to establish clear rules, the process of determining testing protocols and procedures did not start off as hoped or anticipated. With anti-doping rules drawn up by Professor Beckett and colleagues for the 1966 Fédération Internationale de Football Association (FIFA) World Championship hosted by England, blueprints for testing protocols and procedures were readily available. Early sample collection procedures were as follows:

1) It would be carried out in the presence of a doctor;
2) sample collection from female athletes would be overseen by female doctors;
3) the presence of a Medical Commission member was desirable;[61]
4) the sample would be placed in two bottles and sealed with wax in the presence of the doctor and athlete;
5) a report would be competed, including the athlete's name, and signed by the athlete, doctor and, if desired, by the official accompanying the athlete;
6) to preserve secrecy, a code number would be placed on the labels of the two bottles;[62]

7) a sample of at least 10 milliliters was to be in each bottle; and

8) the bottles would be kept at a temperature of $-4°$[Celsius].[63]

These protocols, on the one hand, were to ensure standardized procedures and presumably the equal and fair treatment of all athletes. On the other hand, they demonstrated that many regulatory actors would have to observe the sample collection process—and the bodily exposure it required—to ensure that athletes would not try to manipulate or alter the process. Even though framed in scientific terms, bodily scrutiny was a central focus of testing, both through scientific techniques and through observations of those overseeing these processes.

Difficulties arose during the 1968 Olympic Games in Grenoble. French laboratories, for instance, could not manage all of the analyses, having only been reminded five days before the beginning of competition that they were to carry out tests, "and of course, in this minimal time, they were not able to establish a sufficiently equipped laboratory to deal with the technical requirements of these tests."[64] It was also not possible to countercheck samples on site. In other words, if a athlete suspected of doping had requested his or her second sample be tested (as it was not compulsory at that time), Beckett would have had to conduct the analysis at his laboratory in London.[65] With no positive tests, this was not an issue, but the lack of findings would cast doubt on the effectiveness of testing. Reporting on the Games, Dr. Jacques Thiébault indicated, "This is the first time such action has been taken at the Olympic Games, which accounts for certain imperfections on the practical side of these controls, which should, however, be easily eliminated in the future."[66]

Despite improvements in Mexico City, the Medical Commission was still aware it needed to improve protocols and ensure that more athletes were tested. In fact, capacity building was important. There was only one three-room medical facility at the Mexico City Games (with a room dedicated to reception, administration, and testing respectively), and the report filed on both Grenoble and Mexico City Games suggested the need for more on-site help from trained medical staff.[67] Beyond issues regarding the ineffectiveness of the actual testing, outlining procedures were also a concern. Given the sensitivity of these issues, some Medical Commission members felt confidentiality was of the utmost concern. Others felt the random selection of participants for testing was more important. For example, in correspondence with de Mérode, D. T. P. Pain, the secretary general of the International Association of Athletics Federations, made the following point: "May I say here that our object is not to find positive tests but to abolish doping and it is for that reason that I would ask that the incidence of testing be kept completely confidential, as the element of surprise is the best deterrent."[68] Pain's comments stated clearly that the effectiveness of anti-doping policy relied on the fact that testing must be random and kept secret. Others cited random selection was necessary, for the "fear of the law frightens away the criminal."[69] Thus, even early on, regulation relied on an embedded suspicion of athletes, even though ideally they were pure in physical and moral intent.

Determining punishments was another area of debate. Early on, recommendations included anything from short bans and the removal of medals to the dismissal of all of an offending athlete's prior records and lifetime bans.[70] Pain, in the same letter calling for random testing, prescribed, "Incidentally, the penalty for having been found guilty of taking dope will be life suspension from athletics," a sentiment that was not as widespread as his language suggests. Others, including de Mérode, favored an approach of "balance and understanding," which would give athletes a "second chance" after a temporary suspension.[71] As the Medical Commission proceeded in its work, the sanctions for failed tests became more streamlined and standardized, eventually aligning with a "use-proves-intent" logic that equated detection with guilt.

The shift to use-proves-intent, which is referred to as the strict-liability approach today, did not surface immediately. First, in an attempt to standardize procedures, the Medical Commission published its first pamphlet in 1972, which contained clearer rules, procedures, and sanctions, as well as a direct statement on the Medical Commission's purpose. The pamphlet articulated a message that now underpins anti-doping rhetoric: science would protect the showcasing of athletes' natural abilities, a value previously guarded by the Olympic Charter and its amateurism requirements (which were struck from the charter's text in 1974). Competitors also received "green cards," which, like the US naturalization documents of the same name, essentially allowed them to "legally" enter the Olympic Games. They enabled athletes to compete because testing had found them to be worthy of Olympic status. This documentation, itself a technology, certified a competitor as an athlete citizen as opposed to an alien body—or a body containing foreign contaminants. Testing and documentation certified them as eligible competitors, providing technocratic mechanisms to enforce the Olympic Charter's explicit condemnation of "the use of drugs or artificial stimulants of any kind." On a very basic level, it distinguished between athletes deemed to be tainted from other competitors. In essence, it codified the bounds of athlete citizenship, doing so in a way that held bodies physically accountable, vis-à-vis testing.

Questions still remained regarding what substances (and reasons for using such substances) warranted punishment, even as the Medical Commission moved toward more standardized protocols and stricter rules. One notable example from the 1972 Games was the case of Rich DeMont, a seventeen-year-old white American swimmer who was asthmatic. After tests revealed ephedrine in his urine, the IOC stripped DeMont of his gold medal, prompting international criticism. Observers agreed that the substance was in his system, but did this mean that he was cheating? The rules at the time—and today—hold an athlete liable for an anti-doping offense irrespective of their intent to use a substance to enhance performance or cheat. Even if the athlete does not intend to ingest the substance (which DeMont clearly had, presumably for his asthma), he or she is still held liable for an anti-doping rule violation if tests reveal the presence of a banned substance.

Writing in the aftermath of the DeMont controversy, Doctor Barnes declared that the case highlighted how "the use-proves-intent approach was already causing problems," and there "was enough furor over DeMont's case that the IOC specifically permitted beta-2 bronchospasmolytics (e.g., salbutamol, terbutaline) for asthma at the Montreal Games in 1976."[72] Brundage too acknowledged "that some distinction would have to be made between medicine and doping," even though IOC reports suggest that the concentration of ephedrine found in DeMont's urine exceeded the amount he claimed to have taken.[73]

Brundage's recognition of this problem, however, did not result in the restoration of DeMont's medal, even though it provoked American outrage and widespread sympathy. It paved the way for the later implementation of an exemption process for therapeutic use. This process enables athletes to use some medically prescribed substances if there are no other alternatives available and they complete the proper paperwork in advance. More generally in relation to the terms of athlete citizenship, the use-proves-intent approach to these rules modified what constituted a contaminated body as transgressive: no longer was intent a concern; instead, the mere presence of a banned substance was grounds for sanctions. This development further inscribed athletes as suspect, essentially changing the terms of athlete citizenship.

With increasing attention paid to suspicions of athletes using drugs in a growing number of sports and other than amphetamines, an endorsement of the Medical Commission's importance came from Brundage's successor, Lord Killanin, who described "doping as one of the greatest problems of the Olympic Movement." He framed the purpose and goals of the Medical Commission as striving "as far as it can against the creation of the artificial man or woman."[74] This statement, explain Paul Dimeo, Thomas Hunt, and Matthew Bowers, marked a shift in thinking about doping in which androgenic anabolic steroids "presented the new problem of altering human physiology."[75] Construed as not simply cheating, but as "playing God," the stakes appeared much higher and the need for swift and severe action seemed pressing.[76] Androgenic anabolic steroids were a notable absence on the prohibited list. Amphetamines had been the primary focus of the Medical Commission's work prior to de Mérode's chairmanship, even though, as Beckett later stated, members were aware of steroid use as early as 1960.[77] The drive to develop a test that could detect steroids marked the beginnings of an accepted arms-race mentality in anti-doping regulation.

The technological arms race emerged from the cultural conditions of scientific mobilization as well as the competitive sporting regimes of the Cold War era. As sport seemed to increasingly rely on science and technology for enhancement so too did anti-doping regulation, reiterating the importance of both testing and sanctions. In essence, anti-doping efforts presented two kinds of competing technologies: one used unfairly to modify athletes' bodies—a kind of bad, unethical science—and one leveraged to regulate these forms of enhancement—a presumably good, counteractive science. No longer was the campaign about the protection of purity in sport; it had come to be about preserving the natural human body. A notion of purity rooted in bodily and moral integrity still justified anti-doping protocols, but the discourse had shifted, overshadowing the moral concerns around athletes' health. Doping was no longer a crime against athletes, as Dirix had once explained; rather, doping athletes emerged as unnatural, making them deviant, even arguably criminal, under revised anti-doping rules. The institutionalized suspicion aimed at athletes' bodies had thus actually altered the underlying rationale for regulation, even though it still reflected tropes of amateurism through its valuing of natural bodies.

Given the limitations of science, the Medical Commission's certification process did not ensure that all competitors were uncontaminated by foreign substances. Rumor, speculation, and anecdotal evidence supported fears that anabolic steroid use had become widespread. The reason attributed to the growth in doping was to catch up with East German athletes, who were suspected of systematically doping.[78] With the Soviet Union replicating the German Democratic Republic's centrally planned approach to elite athlete development and both communistic countries providing financial support for athletes to train full time, there was additional pressure for Western countries to better organize their athlete-development programming—and for their athletes to use doping methods to remain competitive.[79] The Medical Commission, in turn, strongly condemned steroid use, but it could not test for the metabolites at the time of the 1968 and 1972 Games.

How Testing for Steroids Changed Anti-Doping Regulation

With the rules themselves—not just their enforcement—dependent on science's ability to detect banned substances, the development of an effective test for steroids became a growing concern in light of evidence suggesting there was widespread steroid use by the late 1960s and at the 1972 Olympics, including an unofficial poll finding that two-thirds of athletes from a variety of countries (the United States, USSR, United Kingdom, Canada, Egypt, New Zealand, and Morocco) and sports had used steroids during the lead-up to the Games.[80] Dimeo explains that prior to the introduction of a test, there was "little ethical debate" about athletes using steroids.[81] Further, and in part "due to the sportive nationalism catalyzed by the Cold War," according to Thomas Hunt, Paul Dimeo, and Scott Jedilicka, "neither side of the Iron Curtain wanted to cause a disadvantage to their athletes by pushing for an effective anti-doping regime."[82] In other words, there were evident disincentives for improving methods of detecting anabolic steroids.

Smaller countries too had become swept up in the sports arms race. For example, the New Zealand team doctor, T. R. Anderson, contended that the use of anabolic steroids was especially common in strength sports. Writing to IOC director Monique Berlioux, he explained, "[Steroids'] harmful effects are known, but not yet fully understood, and I would suggest that while champion performance depends on these drugs, participants in these events be excluded from future New Zealand teams."[83] In short, Anderson appealed for the banning of his own nation's strength athletes under the presumption that every one of them used anabolic steroids. Strong suspicion alone, however, could not justify such a ban.

Writing on behalf of the IOC Medical Commission, Beckett reflected that "the banning of the use of anabolic steroids was considered to be necessary even in 1967," but there was no test to enforce the prohibition.[84] When the UK Sports Council announced in late 1973 that a research team had "progressed to a stage" at which they could test blood and urine samples to detect whether athletes had taken anabolic steroids, the Medical Commission welcomed the development.[85] To justify a ban on anabolic steroids, Beckett evoked health-related concerns:

> By 1974, sufficient progress [in terms of testing] had been made for the IOC Medical Commission to include anabolic steroids in the list of prohibited drugs at the Olympic Games. Anabolic steroids are compounds which represent chemical modifications of the male hormone testosterone in which the anabolic effect, i.e. the muscle building actions are enhanced. . . . The reason for banning them is not only because their use contravenes sporting ethics but because it constitutes a definite danger to females and also to the growth of young people; furthermore, the use of some anabolic steroids in large doses may cause liver damage, affect spermetogenisis and there are reports of their use constituting a cancer hazard.[86]

Other experts did not universally support Beckett's statements about the effects of steroids, at least not to the extent that his language suggests. There were ongoing scientific studies about how to discern the physiological effects of anabolic steroids use, many of which resulted in mixed findings, especially in relation to health consequences.[87] In fact, one of the scientists who worked on the UK Sports Council–funded project that developed detection techniques,

Professor F. T. G. Prunty, acknowledged that the risky side effects were likely few and reversible after discontinuing use.[88]

There were also questionable tactics being employed to deter the use of anabolic steroids, even by medical professionals aligned with the IOC. US medical doctor Daniel Hanley (who had become a member of the IOC Medical Commission) reportedly told athletes that steroids had a placebo effect. In a published interview, US high jumper Chris Dunn criticized Hanley's method: "How are athletes supposed to take the drug problem seriously when the alleged 'experts' like Dr. Hanley tell all the Olympic weight men to their faces that steroids only help psychologically—when every weight man on the US team took them? Steroids are wrong, but you can't curb an athlete from taking them by lying to his face."[89] Not only did Dunn reject Hanley's claims, but his language suggests that he was also insulted by Hanley's "lying" about the widespread recognition of anabolic steroids' performance-enhancing benefits.

Despite these concerns, the UK Sports Council announced in 1973, after four years of research, that a team led by Professor Raymond Brooks at St. Thomas's Hospital Medical School in London had developed a screening test that could detect anabolic steroids, adding a caveat that for "conclusive evidence of the particular drug it might be necessary to use mass spectrometry techniques."[90] Following the news, the chairman of the Sports Council, Roger Bannister, provided additional information, stating, "Professor Beckett accepts that this test is a satisfactory screening-test but his Commission has always required back-up proof of identification of the precise chemical (in this case it could be one of some 15 variants on the anabolic theme) before they would ban an athlete. This is possible for some drugs by the rather expensive technique of mass spectrometry (equipment costing £50,000) and some research yet to come."[91] He concluded that "with international backing, these tests could most certainly be developed over the next year or so, well in time for Montreal."[92]

Even without compelling evidence of a threat to athletes' health, the IOC Medical Commission sought to implement the test. As other scholarly accounts illustrate, Cold War rhetoric and anxieties around the growing number of seemingly unnatural athlete bodies, particularly those competing in women's events, coalesced to fortify its justifications.[93] This instance of innovation marked how foundational moral claims had begun to shift in relation to social changes and scientific developments. With the introduction of the test in 1974, the IOC amended its rules not only to ban competitors found to have doping agents in their system, but also to ban "any athlete refusing to take a doping test."[94] This rendered any athlete resistant to compliance a transgressor. In 1975, the IOC supported a formal stance that "doping is forbidden," adding that it was responsible for developing the banned substances list and that the Medical Commission was to develop rules of application and implement them.

Technological development had therefore actually contributed to changing the definitions and meanings of what it was to be an eligible Olympic athlete. These changes coincided with the "watershed" of the Olympic Movement— that is, according to Beamish and Ritchie, "the constitutive practices of world class, high performance sport were finally, and resolutely, undermining de Coubertin's cardinal principles."[95] High-performance sport had changed the Olympics; and the rules, which were supported by scientific techniques, reflected the shifts. The terms of athlete citizenship too came to reflect this embrace, even as the rules clung to preserving an ideal of naturalness.

The Medical Commission did endorse the procedures for the 1976 Olympic Games after a trial of random testing at the 1975 Commonwealth Games yielded nine positive results for steroids out of fifty-five samples (two of which were randomly selected for a more detailed examination using gas liquid chromatography mass spectrometry, which confirmed them as positive).[96] In total, there were 2,001 tests conducted at the Games held in Montreal, 268 targeting anabolic steroids,[97] an expansion that would become the norm as the regime expanded and embraced biomedicalization.

There were some expressed reservations regarding the implementation of specific tests for anabolic steroids metabolites. James Worrall, a Canadian IOC member, wrote directly to de Mérode, arguing, "Present evidence would appear to indicate that testing for steroids is quite inconclusive and the effect of the use of such drugs could be very easily circumvented by any athlete who has been taking them, by merely discontinuing the use of them for a reasonable period prior to competition. It is also indicated that the technical requirements for setting up a depot for steroid testing are going to be extremely expensive, both from an equipment and personnel requirement standpoint."[98] This challenge was distinctly different from Brundage's attempt to limit the activities of the IOC Medical Commission in 1968. Instead of questioning the Medical Commission's authority or the place of testing, Worrall accepted both. Instead, his concern focused on doubts that testing was accurate or sophisticated enough to justify the financial burden. Thus, even in protest, Worrall's words revealed a tacit acceptance of the future capabilities of anti-doping technologies, not questioning whether innovation would eventually deliver an accurate test for steroids metabolites worth the associated financial costs. In short, his words evidence a shift in attitude toward science in this regulatory space.

Overall, testing at the 1976 Games in Montreal yielded findings that resulted in eleven disqualifications: three resulting from the use of various substances (competitors in weightlifting, shooting, and yachting respectively), eight stemming from the detection of anabolic steroids use (one in athletics, seven in weightlifting), and three resulting from the use of other substances (competitors in weightlifting, shooting, and yachting respectively).[99] There were lingering problems with regard to results management, some of which were grave administrative errors. One, in particular, led to the mishandling of the positive tests. In fact, the press reported the names of five athletes prior to them being informed that they had tested positive. As recounted by the then-president of the International Weightlifting Federation (IWF), Gottfried Schödl:

> On the late evening of the 10th of August 1976 I was phoned by Mr. Oscar State [former IWF general secretary] from London. He informed me that there are five weightlifters with positive results on anabolic steroids in the first analysis of doping. He gave me the names. . . . On the 12th of August 1976 I could read the names of those five weightlifters in a German paper. The same day I was informed with cable by Mr. Dirix [of the Medical Commission] about these doping cases but without names. This was the correct way. According to the rules there is only one person who has to be informed in cases of positive doping results: the President of the competent federation.[100]

At the time, Oscar State was not an IWF official, and Schödl expressed his disappointment in the Medical Commission members' "indiscreetness," which caused "damage not only to five weightlifters' reputation before an official IOC decision but also to IWF's reputation."[101]

Over the next two months, controversy ensued around the events that led to the information's disclosure and how to handle the athletes' cases in light of the indiscretion. The respective national governing bodies of three of the accused weightlifters filed complaints, alleging that sample containers had been opened in transit as well (which was denied).[102] At the Medical Commission meeting held later that October in Barcelona, members resolved the issue. Because the tests were positive, the athletes would be disqualified despite the petitions claiming procedural irregularities. These developments reflected the recognition that the Medical Commission had decision-making, even quasi-juridical, authority embedded in its technocratic role. Even though members had violated of their own stated commitments to confidentiality and endured challenges from governing sports bodies, the Medical Commission's decision still held. Irrespective of its shortcomings, the Medical Commission occupied a much more secure place within the Olympic Movement than it had ten years prior, in large part because of de Mérode's early lobbying efforts and the influence of scientific testing. Moreover, this development marked a clear instance where responsibility fell squarely onto the bodies of athletes, not officials.

This close look at the Medical Commission's early history highlights how technocratic rules and technological practices directly informed—and were informed by—cultural shifts in sport, including developments in athletic performance enhancement and its policing. In this case, the ability to see athletes suspected of doping with the naked eye, but not the actual biological impurity (presumed to cause the visible abnormality) reinforced a dependency upon sample collection and testing that supported the Medical Commission's moral crusade. To counteract more effective doping, testing innovations were required to detect more doping agents. In doing so, they substantiated the need for enhancing technological instruments to provide evidence that supported suspicions of athletes' impure behaviors. Following 1976, a decidedly different regulatory environment would emerge, one that embraced more scientific testing practices.

The Era of Anti-Doping Regulatory Expansion

Following the 1976 Olympiad, the Medical Commission continued to expand its capacity. Considering that it took place against the backdrop of an increasingly corporatized Prolympic sport, it is perhaps not surprising that the Medical Commission sought to devise more ways to scrutinize these bodies. Not only were there more professional athletes, but with a growth in sponsorship, there was also growing corporate incentives for sport authorities to preserve the Olympic image of purity as a marketable brand. As described further in chapter 4, contemporary anti-doping regulation has evident features of "regulatory capitalism"; that is, it leverages a number of partners and resources to expand its regulatory scope. As early as the 1976, however, the numbers of banned substances—and budgets for testing facilities—began to increase as technological developments enabled testing for more compounds.[103] Commenting on these efforts, Dimeo, Hunt, and Bowers suggest that "an implied fear of change, modernity, and over-use of technological forms of enhancement" underpinned these developments, even though there was "no evidence of widespread usage and no challenge to the ongoing obsession with winning."[104] It would appear, then, that an emergent embrace of scientific development had a clear, arguably agentive, role in setting the anti-doping agenda.

In the short term, improving on-site testing facilities to meet the new requirements increased costs and burdens to international federations and hosts, most urgently for Lake Placid and Moscow, the sites of the 1980 Games. Possibly because of financial considerations, there was little information dispersed about testing following those Games. There were no positive tests reported in Lake Placid, even though it is speculated that 440 tests were conducted, 350 targeting anabolic steroids.[105] There were also no positive tests at the 1980 Summer Games in Moscow, even though 2,488 tests were conducted, 800 targeting anabolic steroids.[106] As a result, de Mérode declared the 1980 Moscow Games to be the most "pure" in Olympic history, even though it was more likely a case of regulatory failure.[107] Moreover and despite this claim, he and the Medical Commission continued to outline additional needs, which included provisions to unify testing procedures and rules among international federations and to establish a network of accredited laboratories.[108] These proposals would become integral components of the current anti-doping regime under WADA. These developments also paved the way for a professionalized anti-doping bureaucracy. As the institutionalized embodiment of the moral crusade during the 1960s and 1970s, new rule enforcers would begin to enter this regulatory environment, which I discuss further in the next chapter.

The rise of more biomedicalized regulation coincided with a rise in corporate investment in Olympic sport. Throughout the 1980s, the IOC began to partner with corporate sponsors, and the Medical Commission increased the number of banned substances as scientific developments enabled testing for more compounds and ergogenic aids. With more available research, improved testing procedures, and further review, the banned substances list grew and became more specific. Notable among these additions were caffeine (which was later removed); testosterone, which many believed East German athletes had used immediately prior to competing to avoid steroid detection; blood doping; beta blockers (added in 1985); and diuretics (added in 1986).[109] Even though tests to detect testosterone were available in 1982, the Organizing Committee for the 1984 Olympics in Los Angeles expressed fears that athletes who tested positive for the substance could legally retaliate.[110] Despite some resistance, discussions of implementing testing during training phases, not simply competition, began in 1987 in response to suspicions of athletes masking the use of performance-enhancing substances.[111] Accompanying the expansion of testing was a growth in bureaucracy. Three new committees emerged: Anti-Doping, Biomechanics and Physiology of Sport, and Sports Medication. Also, the Association Olympique Internationale pour la Recherche Médico-Sportive was established to develop research and practical measures based on scientific data. By 1987, there were twenty-one accredited laboratories; of the 38,000 samples analyzed (2.25 percent testing positive), anabolic steroids accounted for 56 percent of positive tests.

With these procedures strongly established and accepted, one of the first public spectacles involving the sanctioning of an Olympic "hero" for doping came about in 1988, when 100-meter gold medalist runner and notable Canadian Ben Johnson was stripped of his medal for testing positive for the anabolic steroid, stanozolol. Although previous Olympians had lost their medals when testing yielded evidence of banned substances, John MacAloon argues that there had never before been "a case so celebrated."[112] Subsequently, Johnson is not remembered as a Canadian national hero but condemned as "the Jamaican immigrant" who at first denied his guilt.[113] Because of advances in drug testing, the famous image of Johnson running that graced the cover of *Sports Illustrated* in October 1988 emerged not as evidence of physical superiority, but as the muscular embodiment of deviance.

The condemnation of Ben Johnson is significant in terms of athlete citizenship, for it highlights the convergence of national dimensions of citizenship with those of sport. Athlete citizenship embodies both facets. The rhetorical devices used to frame Johnson's deviance are not limited to Olympic ideals of purity or evidence that he cheated. They also take on racialized and nationalistic contours, the dimensions of which, writes Steven Jackson, are multilayered in nature. Johnson becomes refigured as a racial foreigner in terms of Canadian national identity, as a "cheat" and "fraud" that disappointed many spectators who expected him to (fairly) win an Olympic gold medal. He also appears as an outsider in terms of the norms of purity in sport. Johnson, as an embodied symbol of doping, marked the first, but certainly not the last, athlete to emerge as what Jackson describes as an "anabolic apparition," a figure that haunted international sport for many years after the scandal broke.[114] As I explain in the next chapter, anabolic apparitions continue to inform anti-doping regulation, especially as other such racialized bodies who represent the Global North in sport are rendered suspect and sanctioned for doping.

The lasting image of Johnson as an anabolic apparition marks a departure from the image of Eastern Bloc athletes thought to be doping. Even though his body represented the first world as an athlete citizen, its disavowal by international and Canadian authorities rendered him as not one of their own. Instead, he became an evident Other. Johnson's condemnation and punishment, including the Dubin Inquiry launched by the Canadian government in the aftermath of his positive test, aimed to distance the Olympics and the nation from his polluted body. This, an elaborate melodrama, not only labeled Johnson deviant but, and perhaps more importantly, preserved the appearance of national and Olympic purity. The process maintained and reinforced the first-world suspicion of non-Western bodies, taking aim at a body once celebrated as a representative of Canada's strengths as a multicultural nation. As the remaining chapters of this book describe, this kind of distancing continues today, often with other racialized bodies.

The 1988 Olympics were notable for more than the legacy of Johnson's positive test. The Calgary Games marked a record amount of funds allocated for medical controls—1.3 million US dollars—and the move toward more standardized punishments.[115] At that time, de Mérode proposed the following guidelines for anti-doping violations: "two years for a first offense; a lifetime suspension in the event of a second offense (for the use of anabolic steroids, stimulants or sedatives of the central nervous system); a maximum of three months for a first offense; two years for a second offense; a lifetime suspension for a third offense (in the case of convictions for the use of prohibited substances such as sedatives, narcotics and decongestants, among others)."[116] There was, however, speculation regarding the extent to which standardized guidelines were enforced.[117] Under the presidency of Juan Antonio Samaranch, who

FIGURE 2.1 *Sports Illustrated* cover following Ben Johnson testing positive for stanzolol. Photo by Ronald C. Modra/Sports Illustrated/Getty Images.

took over in 1980 and prioritized the commercial growth of the Olympics, de Mérode's direct influence on anti-doping regulation waned with his inconsistencies becoming more evident, although he did contribute to expanding international partnerships to work against doping in sport.[118] As such, an curious relationship between capitalism and anti-doping surfaced: capitalist desires incentivize doping and enable its growth through the demand and supply of more doping products; however, with the IOC's corporate growth, capitalism also enables it to invest in additional anti-doping techniques and partnerships. In essence, the Cold War logics of the arms race gave way to an expansion fueled by capitalism.

While there is evidence of corruption under Samaranch's watch as IOC president,[119] he, like de Mérode, did make some notable contributions to anti-doping regulation, even considering his inconsistencies. Specifically, he maintained that there were two central concerns: the protection of "the health of athletes" as well as respect "of the egalitarian principles inherent within the Olympic spirit."[120] He also recommended a commitment to athletes' "rights" by giving them an opportunity for a hearing before the final determination of guilt or innocence. Taking the position that more than sanctions were required and that athletes should have more information (regarding health risks and how doping violates sport integrity), he called for the First Permanent World Conference on Doping in Sport, which was held in Ottawa in June 1988, and successive conferences followed in 1990 (in Moscow), 1991 (in Bergen), and 1993 (in London). An outgrowth of the initial conference was the approval of the International Olympic Charter against Doping in Sport, which also received UNESCO support and served as a precursor to the World Anti-Doping Code and WADA's partnership with UNESCO.

Though at times Samarach was criticized for not taking a stronger stand on the issue of doping, his presidency began the legacy of transnational partnerships, which WADA relies upon today. In 1993, he recalled that "the IOC had fought almost entirely alone for two decades against doping," but in light of the actions taken against Ben Johnson following the Seoul Games, "the wind changed and it was an important and positive day for the history of Olympism, as the National Olympic Committees, the international federations and even governments—including that of Canada—as well as the media, joined our cause."[121]

Thus, and in part because of the scandal around Ben Johnson, the anti-doping landscape continued to change into the 1990s. Erythropoietin was added to the banned substances list, and because it was only detectable via blood testing, the Medical Commission approved this form of sample collection, even though the executive was reluctant to do so.[122] Appointed to advise the executive board on this matter, then-IOC vice president, Judge Kéba Mbaye, brought forth two primary concerns, one oriented around human rights—specifically that one cannot be forced to provide proof of one's own guilt—and the other in relation to health; that is, the principle of the inviolability of a person's physical integrity.[123] While the IOC did not conduct blood testing during the 1992 Summer Games, the International Ski Federation took the initiative to do so on its own for Nordic skiing and biathlon sports, and this practice would later become an accepted part of anti-doping surveillance. Though these strategies crossed new physical boundaries, they emerged as yet another product of the longstanding interplay between capitalistic expansion, scientific surveillance, and a culturally engrained suspicion of athletes' bodies, which continue today under WADA and which attest to the arms-race mentality embedded in the anti-doping regime.

Under these conditions, athlete citizens endure heightened levels of risk, as they not only are rendered suspect and held responsible for maintaining bodily purity, but are also monitored by additional forms of surveillance and held accountable for a growing list of banned substances. WADA has established the Anti-Doping Administration and Management System, which is an online database management system that is to simplify the daily activities required to maintain compliance; developed the Whereabouts Program in order to collect samples from athletes without providing advance notice; introduced the Biological Passport, an electronic record of athletes' blood profiles to assess changes that may indicate possible doping; and encouraged a preemptive strike on prospective gene doping, which is the non-therapeutic use of cells, genes, or gene therapies in sport. The combination of scientific progress, institutionalized protocols, and large global networks, all of which solidified under Samaranch's presidency, in turn, have paved the way for WADA's establishment at the end of the twentieth century and the anti-doping regime's expansion in the twenty-first century, which is the subject of chapter 3. The motivation of the regime no longer arises from Cold War nationalisms. It is now driven by perpetual innovation in detection and surveillance techniques justified by the claim that athletes have access to newer, undetectable substances and methods.

Accompanying the anti-doping regime's growth is a proliferation of costly scientific techniques aimed at detecting newer substances. Preoccupied with the desire not to repeat the failings of the IOC Medical Commission, the arms-race mentality that has ensued carries with it unexpected consequences. Among them is the exorbitantly high price tag for regular testing. The U.S. Anti-Doping Agency, for example, has reportedly spent over $50 million on drug testing since its establishment in 2000.[124] Further, athletes remain at greater risk of getting caught for using over-the-counter supplements, many of which are not clearly delineated as being on the prohibited list. There are also concerns that even if their ingredients do formally indicate that they contain banned substances, they could be contaminated, especially as many athletes have attempted (often unsuccessfully) to argue when testing positive for a banned substance. Not being able to detect dope with a naked eye—or at least prove it, as the appearance of many athletes' bodies have rendered them suspect—reinforces the regime's dependency upon sample collection and testing. The presumption that scientific tools can be developed to catch suspect athletes continues to drive the anti-doping regime today.

Thus, moral entrepreneurship in this context has yielded a cyclical process: as anti-doping regulation deployed more technological techniques in response to growing pressures, rules and discourse shifted, requiring the nature of the Medical Commission's advocacy to also adapt. Originally posited as a defender of athlete's health and sport's ethics, regulatory techniques have refigured the notion of bodily purity (as an engrained value to protect) into the pursuit of a detectable impurity in the form of doping metabolites. This embedded belief has come to anchor the justification for regulation and perpetual scientific development. Suspicion is built into the logic of anti-doping regulation. No longer preoccupied with the bodies who represented the Eastern Bloc, regulation takes aim at bodies suspected of being sporting frauds posing as athlete citizens.

The fact that many athletes targeted by anti-doping regulation are bodies already considered suspect is not coincidental, but it is also not conspiratorial. As workplace opportunities are smaller for people of color in North America, it is not surprising that many male athletes of color look to sport, a field that grew significantly in terms of lucrative opportunities and visibility in the latter part of the twentieth century, as a source of social status and economic benefits. Further, as Michael Messner describes in depth, sport is central to the cultivation of American masculinity, with a strong emphasis on athletic success as evidence of "true" masculinity.[125] Against this cultural backdrop, more people of color are visible in Olympic sport than previously. Drug testing is not simply out to get bodies of color; it has institutionalized suspicion of athlete bodies more generally. But, as athlete citizenship intersects with national citizenship, other inequalities map onto regulatory mechanisms and outcomes in both overt and insidious ways. In this case, the deployment of science through regulation provides a seemingly objective basis on which to justify suspicions aimed at such athletes.

As this chapter describes, the moral crusade against doping and the drive for scientific innovation to catch more offenders go hand in hand. On the one hand, doping and its regulation constitute a tale of medical experts and rule creators leveraging science to accomplish a moral crusade against the impurities of sport. On the other hand, it is a narrative in which a group of moral entrepreneurs' commitment to innovation serves a performative function that continues the regime but also clouds the social conditions and class-based anxieties that enabled the condemnation of doping in sport. Even though health and well-being still serve as justifications, anti-doping regulation orients around punishment as a form of condemning polluted bodies and distinguishing them from so-called pure ones.

Technological innovation is a compelling actor that has helped to script the current anti-doping regime; however, it comes with consequences. The resulting arms-race logic shifts attention away from the moral impetus of protecting athletes' health to a more narrow preoccupation with detecting evidence of doping—as a physical impurity presumed to be symbolic of a moral impurity. What began as the protection of foundation myths linked to ideals of Olympism has actually fostered a process that generates significant risks, even as it claims to prevent and counter doping in sport. Anti-doping technologies operate in the service of ideology, even though they veil it as the pursuit of a truth-claim. The history of anti-doping regulation evidences the cultural power of these technologies, revealing a cycle reliant upon innovation and suspicion. In addition, politics, both global and national in nature, play an important role in its maintenance. Drug testing, initially intended to catch unnatural athletes using doping agents, continues to secure a particular set of privileged first-world values, as evidenced by its longstanding preoccupation with professional and Eastern Bloc athletes. With suspicion of athletes institutionalized through the biomedicalized tools, the targets of anti-doping regulation have come to encompass a broader range of bodily impurities. The bodies most publically condemned for transgressing the terms of athlete citizenship, however, are those already seen as suspect to a Western gaze, particularly non-Western bodies and bodies of color. Building upon the account of anti-doping regulation provided here, the next chapter addresses how WADA continues to embrace these values, even as it aims to defend fair play in sport.

3

Codifying the Code

————————————————————●

The Legalization of
Anti-Doping Regulation

Moral underpinnings of the global campaign remain relevant today, albeit articulated in different ways than earlier efforts that condemned professionalism. Society, argues Richard Pound, the first chairman of the World Anti-Doping Agency, "is built on an ethical platform, as is sport." The foundations of both, he says, "should be sturdy."[1] WADA, he explained, is a necessary partner in work aimed at counteracting what he refers to as the "wave of misconduct at the end of the twentieth century and the beginning of the new millennium."[2] In essence, his words suggest that doping in sport is symptomatic of a broader moral degradation nurtured by unbridled capitalistic values. Pound's contention that sport has succumbed to a kind of ethical decay serves to justify WADA's purpose: to protect a level playing field in sport that is under attack by not only doping, but a broader "winning at all costs" mentality.

Under Pound's leadership from 1999 to 2008, WADA and the campaign against doping in sport explicitly articulated a concern for the "far darker" moral issues underlying practices often "attributed to nothing more than greed."[3] While this agenda has roots in the history outlined in the previous chapter, WADA's current efforts reflect additional legalistic, biomedicalized, and neoliberal dimensions that are not as evident in earlier forms of regulation. Despite WADA's condemnation of the evils of capitalism, the anti-doping regime reflects an embrace of what scholars refer to as "regulatory capitalism."[4]

In other words, the regime encourages and leverages a proliferation of instruments in order to expand its regulatory scope and jurisdiction, often through partnerships with governments, legal authorities, and private actors, including sport organizations and pharmaceutical companies.[5]

Under WADA, the anti-doping regime has taken a decidedly legalistic approach to the issue of doping in sport, which this chapter examines by paying particular attention to how WADA representatives and stakeholders have lobbied for the global condemnation of doping. In essence, they have endeavored to *legalize* anti-doping rules in order to effect moral change. Although most discussions of legalization and drugs focus on decriminalizing or permitting the use of illicit substances, legalization in this case marks an attempt to do the opposite by harnessing the power of law. WADA's efforts have sought to compel governments to hold their citizens accountable to anti-doping rules. It has successfully achieved legal backing for its regulatory regime, codifying athletes' obligations to the regime's terms, which it also enforces through biomedicalized techniques.

Legality in this field is inherently pluralistic. It is a constitutive formation, which can yield complications for the goals that law and lawmakers assert. Because law is "nested" in society, there is often a gap between "law on the books" and "law in action."[6] As this chapter describes, WADA and its stakeholders put forth a series of promises presented as realities guaranteed by law, negating the complex social conditions that undergird them and the embedded complexities of anti-doping regulation that took shape under the International Olympic Committee. In particular, even though Pound and colleagues recognize that structural conditions enable and incentivize doping, regulation adopts a biomedical gaze that largely negates these factors by holding individuals liable for anti-doping rule violations. This is perhaps expected given that many corporate actors interact and coordinate to help develop regulatory tactics. In doing so, regulation fails to attend to how social differences and inequalities inform anti-doping agendas and practices. Here, I explain the resulting consequences, addressing how WADA continues to champion older Olympic principles without critically attending to the impurities imbued within those values and the arrangements that inform regulation's limited focus on athletes.

Given the historical influence of Olympic ideologies and practices, it is not surprising that the IOC sponsored WADA's establishment and continues to provide half of the agency's funding by matching governmental contributions. By defining what substances are unacceptable under this framework, WADA plays a specific role in the IOC's broader institutional objectives of promoting Olympism, which the IOC characterizes as "a way of life based on the joy of effort, the educational value of good example and respect for universal fundamental ethical principles."[7] By upholding Olympic principles as integral to sport and establishing regulations to police athletes' bodies, WADA's role has symbolic and material dimensions. By discouraging doping as a form of cheating, WADA serves as a gatekeeper of athlete citizenship, and it supports broader messages endorsed by the IOC that privilege bodily purity and hard work.

Just as importantly, WADA's practices render athletes' bodies visible to scrutiny, particularly those characterized as deviant, but do not take aim at corporatized sport structures that can incentivize or cause individual doping offenses. Through its narrow focus on athletes, regulation posits discursive messages that reinscribe culpability onto the athlete. By looking at the legalized aspects of the regime, this chapter examines current lobbying efforts and regulatory tactics utilized by anti-doping advocates at the international level. It describes the scientific and legal tools employed by the regime while also addressing how the justifications for such interventions reveal postcolonial and racial underpinnings. In analyzing how advocates explain and narrate which athletes are suspected of being polluted or contaminated by doping, this chapter also draws attention to how anti-doping tools and rhetoric implicitly index the Global North as "clean"—or the normative space of (white) persons worth protecting—while the Global South is a source of pollution (doping).

The Architecture of the Global Anti-Doping Regime

The anti-doping regime is a complex arrangement of rules, actors, and stakeholders. Although spearheaded by WADA, a private law foundation with its headquarters located in Montreal, support for anti-doping regulation comes from a range of sports organizations and governments.[8] Over 175 government signatories, 150 regional and national anti-doping organizations, and 600 governing sports bodies contribute to anti-doping efforts.[9] The various partnerships between these private (e.g., many, albeit not all, international sports organizations) and public actors (e.g., governments, law-enforcement agencies) enable the widespread adherence to the World Anti-Doping Code. International ordinances, such as the UNESCO International Convention against Doping in Sport and its predecessor, the 2006 Copenhagen Declaration on Anti-Doping in Sport, outline the terms of the regime, but they do not capture the full extent of the regulatory instruments at work and the scope of their influence.

To achieve this level of international support, the anti-doping regime leverages "synergies between binding and non-binding mechanisms," making it a unique "hard/soft hybrid."[10] Specifically, the World Anti-Doping Code, a nonlegal document produced by WADA, provides coercive incentives for governments to become signatories of the UNESCO International Convention against Doping in Sport—the first international treaty focusing on doping in sport—and to pass legislation that supports anti-doping efforts. The Convention, which came into force in February 2007, states that governmental and sport authorities "have complementary responsibilities to prevent and combat doping in sport" in accordance with the rules found in the WADA Code.[11] In essence, these agreements bind governmental, nongovernmental, and private actors to a common cause.

Although the UNESCO Convention is a notable accomplishment, only forty-one nation-states had ratified it when it came into force.[12] In response, WADA added clauses to the 2009 version to ensure that more countries became signatories. These changes introduced contingencies that, if not met, result in sanctions and the revoking of sport-related privileges. As expressed in article 22.6 of the Code, "failure by a government to ratify, accept, approve or accede to the UNESCO Convention by January 1, 2010, or to comply with the UNESCO Convention thereafter may result in ineligibility to bid for Events," which "may result in additional consequences."[13] Penalties include "ineligibility or non-admission of any candidature to hold any International Event in a country, cancellation of International Events; symbolic consequences and other consequences pursuant to the Olympic Charter."[14] The IOC gave teeth to the clause because it determines which cities receive successful Olympic bids and invites, thereby providing WADA a unique form of bargaining power with public authorities. With the inclusion of article 22.6, the number of state parties—that is, countries that have ratified, accepted, approved, or acceded to the UNESCO Convention—has surpassed 160. The Convention endorses and expands WADA's influence in legally defined territories (e.g., nation-states, international legal authorities) and nonlegally defined spheres (e.g., the Olympic Movement, international sport federations).

Many of these developments crystallized at the 2007 World Conference on Doping in Sport, a meeting that marked the end of an eighteen-month consultation process that yielded over 1,800 changes to the Code. Looking back on the actual events at the 2007 World Conference reveals additional dimensions of WADA's legal aspirations and the values to which regulators appealed. In particular, the debates at the conference capture how WADA officials justified the expansion of their moral crusade against doping, evidencing their tacit acceptance of values once associated with amateurism.[15] Lobbying for the protection of the ideal of fair play (as if it were a real verifiable kind of truth), they presented law as a path toward stronger global enforcement, but negated possible side effects of doing so.

The consequences of these actions revealed two important dimensions of how anti-doping regulation informs athlete citizenship. On the one hand, many advocates tacitly accepted punitive tropes by calling for stronger law-enforcement interventions and legal punishments, which carry over into the treatment of those suspected of doping offenses. On the other hand, they evoked ideals about what athletes should be to support their appeals, revealing how they perceived and distinguished elite athletes as subjects who should embody moral values. The exceptional status of athletes thus served to justify increased bodily policing and greater governmental action. Taken together, these observations illustrate how claims to protect an ideal athlete citizen justified an expanded regulatory scope.

Within these narratives, law emerged as a way to protect athletes from not only doping, but also the evils of sport embodied by athletes who cheat; however, in practice, law rendered them more visible to scrutiny and increased their risk of being caught for intentional or unintentional doping. Moreover, by characterizing doping as an agentive act of deviance, conference participants located the evils of capitalist greed primarily onto athletes, reflecting the focus of biomedicalized techniques employed in this field. The stories of these deviant bodies operated as forms of evidence that the analytical findings from drug testing substantiated. Particular athletes, or anabolic apparitions such as former gold medalist Ben Johnson, symbolized the social ills at which law can take aim. They served as evidence that many more athletes were suspect, even those who had not yet tested positively for doping. Law and biomedicalization thus anticipated doping in ways that reiterated and manufactured risk among athletes.

The 2007 World Conference served as a venue where stakeholders could express the practical and performative reasons for governments to legally back the regime. In a practical sense, the conference afforded stakeholders the opportunity to approve the final version of the WADA Code and assess its potential impact in relation to the goal of ensuring that more countries ratified the UNESCO Convention against Doping in Sport. Symbolically, it provided a space to articulate how the mobilization of law advanced the broader condemnation of doping as an impending social ill. Although advocates argued that the threat of doping was clear and present, they did not use the opportunity to clarify the arguably vague criteria used to determine if a substance constitutes doping. A substance can be considered doping if it meets two of the following conditions: (1) it is performance enhancing, (2) it is a risk to the health of the athlete, or (3) it violates "the spirit of sport."[16] Of the three criteria used to evaluate whether a substance or method should be banned, the "spirit of sport" criterion is problematic because it is largely undefined and open to interpretation. According to Ian Ritchie, the "spirit of sport" requirement is a remnant of Olympic foundation myths that upheld the essence of sport as something morally distinct.[17] In current practice, the clause enables the banning of many substances that presumably do not enhance athletic performance, such as illicit drugs like marijuana, or do not cause physical harm to athletes. What common threat, then, does doping in sport pose if it can include a host of substances that are not necessarily harmful or performance enhancing? This slippage reveals how older Olympic ideologies continue to influence regulation.

A closer look at how anti-doping advocates framed these issues at the 2007 World Conference on Doping is quite telling. There, doping emerged as a scourge so prevalent that new kinds of innovation were necessary, even though testing had resulted in a comparatively low number of positive findings.[18] In fact, the limited findings were an important concern given the presumption that doping was widespread. The nature and scope of the threat posed by doping took on multiple dimensions, some of which surpassed sport. A central element in their narrative was that of crisis, or at least, an effort to substantiate doping as a crisis in sport. This crisis narrative, according to Jin-Kyung Park, has perpetuated a continual need for innovative technologies to catch athletes who presumably have access to newer and previously undetectable substances.[19] Park characterizes this an effort led by the First World, an observation that the conference rhetoric illuminated.

Against this backdrop, law emerges as an important technology to counteract doping, one that would hold unethical athletes and drug traffickers to account. The language employed at the 2007 World Conference evidences how stakeholders employ various imaginings of athletes, both innocent and deviant, to lobby for further regulatory interventions. Specifically, professional athletes in the Global North would come to occupy the ranks of the deviant, as many regulators cast them as subjects preoccupied with self-aggrandizement, winning at all costs, and financial gains rather than the ethics of fair play in sport. Thus, some, yet not all, professional athletes still embodied the values condemned by authorities. Calls to protect true athlete citizens who do not dope and to condemn, to use their language, the "imposters" who do dope reflect discursive forms of belonging and exclusion, many of which retain postcolonial and racialized contours.

Promises of Law

The specter of law was an eerie presence at the 2007 World Conference on Doping in Sport, at least to me as an outsider looking into this world. After proceeding through security checks and metal detectors, I walked into the room reserved for invited observers and members of the media. The popular song, "I Fought the Law," by the Bobby Fuller Four streamed through the sound system. Its message was striking in that it presented a simplistic narrative of law and order. This version of the song, released in the 1960s, evoked a past in which so-called bad guys got what they deserved, and the good guys won out in the end. As I walked upstairs to the balcony overlooking the auditorium, the chorus lingered. From this purview, I could see sport administrators and government officials from across the globe take their seats, a scene that reflected the aesthetics of international lawmaking: auditorium seating and microphones at the participants' seats, which were marked by bronze nameplates. They faced a stage where a separate podium, reserved for select members of WADA's executive board, stood under a spotlight. Bustling delegates filled the space over which I looked.

Although marked by a kind of cosmopolitan elitism, the scene, set to the soundtrack of "I Fought the Law," appeared a mere caricature of lawmaking. It also reflected an underlying concern: anti-doping regulation was not "real law" in the traditional ways we often think of government lawmaking, even though it makes similarly authoritarian claims. In this setting, advocates lobbied to add law to the existing repertoire of regulatory technologies in order to advance the moral crusade against doping. To do so, WADA embraced the formal aesthetics and messages of law to the extent that its lobbying efforts—at least as captured in this environment—dismissed transnational complexities in favor of more simplistic messages of law enforcement in order to condemn athletes suspected of doping. This simplistic presentation, however, aimed to expand a complex hybrid regime.

Law emerged as a promise of bigger, stronger, and ultimately more powerful form of regulation. Figuratively speaking, it offered the possibility of a WADA *on steroids*. As acknowledged by the then-chairman of the Australian Sports Anti-Doping Authority, Richard Ings, merging the traditional use of drug testing with the "strong investigative and intelligence management capabilities" of law enforcement agencies "is the future of protecting the integrity of sport."[20] Spain's secretary of state for sports, Jaime Lissavetzsky Diez, offered a similar sentiment: "We want a World Anti-Doping Agency which is a strong agency, an agency which is fully committed, an agency which takes into account the needs and has as much scientific backing as possible, as much *legal* backing as possible, in any of the decisions taking into account the sportsmen—and the sportswomen. Prevention, control and sanctions."[21]

Emphasizing this point, conference participants revisited what they characterized as WADA's most notable accomplishments: its partnerships with legal authorities. They focused specifically on the agency's contributions to successful police stings and raids of steroid trafficking rings. WADA director general David Howman cited the infamous Festina affair at the 1998 Tour de France, which led to findings of mass quantities of doping substances. The scandal itself initially centered on the police raids of cyclists' hotel rooms and belongings, which prompted a subsequent sit-down strike staged by riders and the arrest of a Festina team member. The race, sometimes referred to as the "Tour of Doping" (Tour du Dopage) or "Tour de Shame," did not resume until after Tour officials negotiated with the police to end the impromptu searches. By that point, however, police had made additional discoveries in the lodgings of the Dutch team, TVM, and later, they found more.[22] The Festina Scandal and the inquiry into the Bay Area Laboratory Co-operative (BALCO), a company that supplied banned substances to athletes across a variety of sports in the United States, were central examples, but they also emerged alongside lesser-known examples from other jurisdictions.

Among those other examples were Australian customs' "confiscation of prohibited substances from a team of swimmers that were living in the country"; Operación Puerto in Spain, which unearthed revelations about blood doping among a group of professional road cyclists; and Operation Gear Grinder, which targeted and tracked illegal steroids produced by eight major companies, 82 percent of which were of Mexican origin.[23] Howman also pointed to an inquiry into Australian weightlifting, which "led to the first sanctions being made against athletes for the use of HGH [human growth hormone]," and the Signature Pharmacy[24] bust, which resulted in "the naming of a number of professional baseballers" who were allegedly doping. Subsequent speakers at the conference validated these examples as testaments to the need for more intergovernmental partnerships. A range of countries, including Finland, Indonesia, Italy, Korea, New Zealand, and the Netherlands among others, gave pledges of support to ensure many more such successes in the future.

Partnering with law-enforcement agencies was the primary way that stakeholders said law could be used to get tough on doping under the UNESCO Convention. According to the chair of WADA's Athlete Commission, Viacheslav Fetisov, "Governments are obligated to restrict the availability, to prohibit the substances and methods in order to restrict their use in sport. This includes measures against production, movements, importation, distribution, sale[s], and trafficking."[25] Fetisov went on, stating, "Ministries of sport can't do this alone. They have to ask for the help of the police and customs. . . . When all of these parties work together, considerable progress can be made." The kind of progress to which he directly spoke was clear: "Further arrest and prosecution [is] expected from increasing governments' involvement in anti-doping." Such promises implied that law would deliver punishments that testing athletes in and out of competition could not, appealing to a desire for more investigative power than WADA and subsidiary anti-doping agencies leveraged at the time.

Advocates lobbied for law as a way to expand to the tactics of detecting and counteracting doping, arguing that traditional modes of sample collection testing and detection could not catch the most insidious offenders. They cast the force of law as a necessary means to stop a broad social threat posed by doping, and their presentations rendered athletes as more likely to dope because of the increasing financial incentives of sport (e.g., lucrative sponsorships for top athletes). Justifications for governmental involvement came alongside claims that relying on drug testing had clear limitations: "Faced with a reality that athletes can and will engage in forms of doping that are difficult or indeed impossible to detect through traditional testing, anti-doping strategies that made us successful in the past may not translate into success in the future. . . . The challenge here is not hypothetical, nor is it limited to any one nation or any one sport. BALCO has taught us the lengths that athletes will go to dope, the relative ease which they can do it, and the fame and fortune that can be reaped from such fraud. It is a challenge that we ignore at the peril of clean sport."[26]

When speaking on behalf of WADA, Howman emphasized, "We know now that some athletes are resorting to the use of veterinarian substances. They are available. We all know how easy it is to obtain banned substances through the Internet. It is *so* easy."[27] This and other such appeals reveal how many stakeholders had appropriated Pound's earlier point that the problem of doping had been fueled by unethical capitalist pursuits. In contrast, law seemed a corrective tool to harness the uncontrolled market for performance-enhancing drugs and to shift advantages from illegal, amoral traffickers to legal, moral authorities.

Instead of questioning how the corporate investments into sport have enabled or contributed to these markets, a desire for punishing individuals for doping took center stage. This was evident in conference discussions about the need for proper legal procedures. Participants described tribunals and judicial proceedings as necessary to ensure efficiency and regulatory oversight with no consideration given to the issue of procedural justice for individual subjects. For example, Howman explained, "We cannot and should not rely on a simple system of sample collection and analysis to find the cheats. We must use all the tools that might be available to us to ensure that evidence is gathered in a proper and an appropriate way, tended before a tribunal, again in a proper way, to ensure that disciplinary proceedings can be conducted against those who commit anti-doping violations. This leads into the issue of conducting investigations and—and developing investigation protocols."[28] His words were, in part, a direct response to the prospect of costly, drawn-out litigation and the growing number of appeals by athletes before the Court of Arbitration for Sport, which had more than doubled between 2006 and 2007.

Howman's statements revealed some of the established practices and norms of the anti-doping regime, particularly around the issue of intent, which is not considered in the evaluation of most anti-doping violations. In other words, athletes can be sanctioned even if they did not intend to take a doping agent; the very presence of a banned substance implies guilt. The grounds for an athlete's guilt do not require *mens rea*, or a "guilty mind"; instead, testing provides alternative forms of proof that substitute for evidence of the workings of a guilty mind. Stakeholders, including Howman, in turn, did not ask questions about whether or not athletes were innocent. Instead, they presumed guilt—and that law would also detect, prove, and punish those tainted athletes. Athletes' suspect status had become ingrained through the WADA Code, and advocates did not intend for law to correct or shift that regulatory orientation.

Leveraging Legal Hybrids to Catch Suspect Athletes

An embedded suspicion of athletes drove the logic for regulatory reforms. For example, the strict-liability standard, which is the "use-proves-intent" approach used to evaluate evidence detected through testing, prevents athletes from providing nonscientific explanations for the presence of banned substances in their bodies. It reflects a codified presumption that athletes will lie. Taking this a step further, anti-doping regulators at the conference expressed that athletes had a duty to undergo testing and adjoining forms of surveillance in order to provide proof of their purity and to distinguish them from cheaters. They also argued that law would bring about new forms of scientific evidence to substantiate the guilt of athletes engaged in doping. They did not reject testing measures in favor of law per se, but they did argue that current methods could not keep up with emerging challenges. Again, Howman's presentation directly addressed this point: "We must catch up with the rest of society and use forensic science. On a daily basis, in our criminal and civil courts, it is forensic science that is used. Why don't we do this for our anti-doping tribunals? We must, as we move forward, use the benefits that we can get from those people who have already put into place systems and information that will assist our tribunals reach proper conclusions."[29]

Note that Howman called for tribunals to include different forms of evidence beyond findings from scientific testing, such as those commonly accepted in legal courts and obtained by law enforcement agencies, but did not argue for the use of formal legal courts. A common sentiment within anti-doping circles is that legal courts are too slow and expensive. A hybrid, a tribunal that maintains certain aspects of a court, often utilizing legally trained professionals, offered a preferable alternative. Although they emphasized that adapting aspects of law would enable WADA to meet emerging challenges head on, the details were largely left ambiguous. In fact, the only concrete examples of law's influence were instances where traditional forms of sample collection and testing had not caught athletes. Further, even though earlier panels stressed the need for education as a cornerstone strategy against the proliferation of unethical values in sport and society, no presenters expanded upon the potentially fruitful relationship between education, law, and stronger modes of enforcement. Instead, WADA representatives favored deploying a more punitive rhetoric to make their appeals.

Despite demands to "get tough" on doping in the same way other legal authorities have targeted illicit drug use, participants still asserted WADA's hybridity as a necessary feature of anti-doping regulation, implying that

WADA would not forfeit its power within the regime as more governmental actors became directly involved. Law emerged instead as an innovation, a new technology that would enable WADA to expand into uncharted territories. Law's most attractive promise for WADA was that of a truly global jurisdiction, something it has actively pursued throughout the 2000s. Beyond having an anti-doping presence on every continent, law seemed to ensure that people across regional divides came to support WADA's mission and ways of thinking—that is, recognizing doping as a transgression of the fundamental tenets of sport.

The lobby for legal interventions marks a move to expand and shore up the boundaries of the regime, but it also speaks to the contours of athlete citizenship. Participants were quite clear about who they sought to punish, immoral subjects depicted as on par with criminals, and who they sought to protect, a kind of pure, innocent body. The distinctions between these two kinds of subjects took shape over the course of the World Conference, which I describe further in the next sections. One point stakeholders used to justify expanded surveillance was that the athletes using performance-enhancing drugs who *look* as if they were innocent posed a particularly insidious threat. Such deviant athletes, they argued, were often popular sportspersons playing the part of ethical Olympic-caliber athletes. Conference participants reflected on how these elusive figures were markedly different than professional athletes who were often openly deviant or visibly detectable. Scientific testing retained an important place in the movement, as it was to provide proof of doping that enabled the condemnation of suspect athletes. Substantiating the crisis of doping in sport was, therefore, an integral part of the strategy to gain legal backing, which, in turn, also highlighted the operative function of categorical (and imagined) distinctions among athlete subjects.

Capitalizing on Crisis and Crime

The crisis narratives used to substantiate concern for doping in sport have prompted some to call it a moral panic—that is, an issue presented as a threat to the current social order, which also displaces blame by scapegoating marginalized groups.[30] WADA representatives actively contribute to sense of hostility, calling for doping in sport to receive the same punitive response used against illicit substances. Despite well-documented criticisms that the current international prohibition regime is largely ineffective and problematic, WADA encourages countries to criminalize doping and the actions that enable it.[31] Such strategies are necessary "in order to target not only athletes but also the entourage, and to enhance the effectiveness of the fight against doping in sport."[32] In short, the moral-panic reasoning required the anticipation of higher rates of doping and an emphasis on the severity of the threat more generally.

The beginnings of WADA's calls to criminalize doping were evident at 2007 World Conference. Crime-control discourses and images substantiated the grounds cited for more legalistic tactics in a way that reflected what Jonathan Simon refers to as "governing through crime." Governing through crime, Simon explains, is a rhetoric that induces "the technologies, discourses, and metaphors of crime and criminal justice" to frame a social problem and its remedy.[33] Stakeholders explicitly evoked a "culture of fear" mentality to garner support,[34] while also claiming to guide "subjects through the socially valorized pursuit of security and justice," which, according to Simon, is another attribute of governing through crime.[35]

Such appeals were pervasive in the formal conference proceedings, and they also relied on images of athletes as either idealized citizens or agentive criminals. When conference speakers criticized authorities, it was for their leniency toward doping. For instance, in justifying the expansion of their regulatory purview, WADA representatives focused on the shortcomings of earlier tactics, primarily those overseen by the IOC Medical Commission, which WADA replaced in 1999. They pointed to the Festina Scandal at the 1998 Tour de France as evidence of the previous regime's ineptitude and the beginning of drastic changes in the global climate around doping and its regulation.[36] The police intervention in the Festina Scandal, many have argued, exposed the pervasiveness of doping in cycling. It also brought to light the bigger problem of governing sport bodies turning a blind eye to performance-enhancing drugs. In fact, as Pound has written elsewhere, while arrests ensued and several governments—Spain, Switzerland, and Italy—took investigative actions, the IOC president at the time, Juan Antonio Samaranch, "blurted out that, for him, this was not doping and that the IOC's list of prohibited substances and methods was too long."[37]

Overall, conference delegates concurred that the Festina Scandal was a low point within international sport and also acknowledged its silver lining: it had prompted the first World Conference on Doping in Sport in 1999 with both sport and government representatives involved, where WADA was created. The agency's establishment came about, to use the words of one stakeholder, because sport representatives, at the behest of governments, "*finally* realized more was needed" to combat doping in sport.[38] With an independent international agency in place, legal authorities would not alone dictate how this war on drugs played out, and governing sport bodies would remain active participants in the regulation of doping.

The shadow of the 1998 Festina Scandal still loomed over the 2007 World Conference, and participants continued to cast doping as an impending threat to sport and society that required a multitude of regulatory actions and collaborative partnerships to achieve some level of deterrence. Deterrence, however, was not the primary justification for WADA's multifaceted approach; rather, it was the elimination of doping. In fact, during the opening remarks of the conference, host representatives aligned themselves with WADA's pursuit of eradicating a practice described as "incompatible with sports," one that not only "denaturalizes the actual essence of sports," but also "attacks the dignity of athletes and sports competition . . . and it attacks the health of these athletes taking these banned substances."[39] In appealing to this governing-through-crime rhetoric, athletes emerge simultaneously as subjects of suspicion and citizens worth protecting.

Calls to action drew attention away from the consequences of higher levels of surveillance in favor of allusions to protecting an imagined group of pure subjects.[40] Advocates highlighted how doping was a divisive peril facing modern sport, its participants, and the well-being of both. IOC president Jacques Rogge characterized doping as "one of the most serious threats the Olympic Movement has ever seen." And he stated further, "It undermines all we stand for. It endangers the health of the athlete. It undermines the credibility of results. It risks drying out the recruitment of sport, as, one day, parents might refuse to send their children to sports clubs."[41] This is not to say that their appeals did not show concern for the well-being of athletes. In fact, Rogge aligned WADA's mission with international public-health agendas, stating that its efforts seek to protect the "youth and weekend warriors." He rallied for increased action by repeating a genuine concern for promoting healthy and ethical athletes, citing an (unsupported) statistic that over 20 percent of recreational athletes are doping today compared to the 5 percent who did twenty years ago. His speech thus emphasized another dimension of governing through crime: in claiming to protect innocents, discourses can actually perpetuate idealized notions of certain groups of citizens. In this example, innocent "youth and weekend warriors" emerge as the subjects threatened by doping. These representations of innocents serve as symbolic capital in the push for stronger regulatory interventions. In fact, one need not look further than WADA's website to see how the regime uses their likeness in its campaigns.

In light of these concerns about children, not just elite athletes, anxieties over a future contaminated by doping abounded. For instance, according to Spain's minister of sport and science Mercedes Cabrera Calvo-Sotelo: "Any tolerant attitude toward [doping] by the sports federations, by the public authorities will lead to a very rapid spread of this threat beyond—far beyond—high-level competitions, and this has already been said, it can be turned into a very dangerous threat to public health, and it could spread among international organized criminal organizations. It could lead to the deterioration of our social living together, because it would basically help those who do not enjoy fair play, people who do not believe in fair play. And, in the end, this would lead to a situation in which anything is possible."[42] Akin to Gayle S.

Rubin's analysis of the "domino theory of peril" with regard to sex, this statement places heightened significance upon doping, presuming a need "to draw the line" around such behaviors so as to preserve order as distinct from chaos.[43] Fearing an escalation toward societal deterioration, such statements actually call for only a limited number of behaviors to be classified as "safe, healthy, mature, legal, or politically correct."[44] Moreover, while this characterization of the threat posed by doping seems unrealistic and overstated, many stakeholders took similar liberties, describing doping as a problem reflective of systemic moral decay. Collectively, these appeals to broader public concerns aimed to justify the importance of WADA's mission but did so by taking particular action against doping as a form of deviance in ways that neglected the possibility of limiting other corporate practices and incentives in sport that also encourage such values.

WADA representations played upon anxieties around doping in order to substantiate collective calls to action. Again, extreme depictions continually surfaced alongside calls for new and improved tactics to combat doping. For instance, Pound's introductory speech reiterated doping as an epidemic: "Recent events tell us that doping is much more pervasive than some of even the most cynical observers could have ever imagined. . . . The risk of this epidemic is not theoretical. It is a certainty for society at large, and it results in an all too horrible human tragedy for some. There are no short cuts. There are no magic bullets. There are none of the quick fixes. . . . It will take new and bold thinking."[45] Building upon his statements, another presenter offered a high-stakes scenario in which the anti-doping movement was at a pivotal point: "Either we win the fight, or we lose it. If we lose it, the greater loser is the sport movement in the world . . . because doping does not only kill athletes, it kills sport."[46] Such representations linguistically captured the arms-race mentality that became embedded within anti-doping regulation during the twentieth century. In this case, the arms-race mentality substantiates the crisis that WADA seeks to counteract.

Consequently, these calls also substantiate the perceived need for the agency. In many ways, this logic reveals the inherent tensions of WADA's position as a "rule enforcer," which Howard Becker has described as marked by a competition between two drives.[47] The first is to justify its role, and the second is to prove its capacity to be effectual. Ironically, the pursuit of one can undermine the other: that is, if WADA is too effective, it may no longer seem necessary; however, if WADA appears incompetent, some may call for its abolishment or replacement. WADA's survival is thus bound to its own performance as a regulatory entity and the balancing act inherent in being a rule enforcer on a global scale.

Following this reasoning, it is perhaps not surprising that participants left open the question of whether their war against doping could be won. They sometimes characterized it as a doomed, even impossible effort. In fact, in one of his speeches, Chairman Pound, adopting a skeptical disposition that Becker states is common among rule enforcers, attributed the root cause of doping to "human nature," a problem "exacerbated by other incentives" offered in contemporary sport and its promises of wealth, status, and fame. His allusion highlighted the quasi-religious, even missionary, undertone of the many speeches delivered. Doping was seemingly impossible to overcome, yet still worth valiantly fighting against. Reforms emerged as necessary to save athletes from their inherently deviant, arguably sinful, disposition. These claims revealed an underlying contradiction: in seeking to combat doping in sport, WADA simultaneously normalizes and sustains doping as a perpetual state of emergency. The campaign against this crisis has actually substantiated, even arguably created, the very panic that anti-doping regulation seeks to counteract.

Imagining the Outlaws of Sport

Amidst crisis-laden calls to action, the question of who was the threat to sport became ambiguously referenced as an abstract foe, an Other that could only be detected through scientific testing or police investigations. Suspect athletes represented a threat to the moral order of sport that would come to justify regulatory innovations. In addition to the many references to cycling, often considered a sport with a culture of doping,[48] individual high-profile athletes in other sports often occupied this condemned role. Keeping in mind that in 2007 Lance Armstrong had not yet been formally accused of doping or stripped of his Tour de France titles, the most notable figure was Marion Jones, a former gold medalist in track and field who admitted to using performance-enhancing drugs during the BALCO investigations. As presented by WADA officials, Jones was symbolic of the many other deviant athletes who, tempted by fame, fortune and the desire to win at all costs, regularly break the rules. Her criminal prosecution, they contended, illustrated the need to expand efforts beyond current testing practices to more expansive forms of monitoring. Following their reasoning, it seemed impossible to apprehend, yet alone punish, individuals like Jones—who, according to WADA representatives, made up an increasing number of athletes—without legal backing. As stated by one participant, the legal recognition of doping as a problem would finally "remove the veil of silence around doping that has led to its proliferation."[49]

Additional governmental support, participants argued, was a key long-term strategy, because it could catch elusive athletes who mislead the public by presenting themselves as true athlete citizens. Specifically, they highlighted that legal authorities' investigative and punitive powers were of necessary assistance. According to WADA representatives, Jones's case crystallized how law could supplement the agency's authority. They claimed Jones was willing to do anything, including dope and lie to the public about it, to reap the benefits and rewards of sport. For anti-doping advocates, her criminal prosecution for perjury (specifically, for making false statements to a federal agent about her steroid use) marked an unprecedented success that illustrated the need to expand investigations beyond current testing practices.

According to Howman, Jones was an example

> of *how* an athlete can beat the system of sample collection. 160 samples were taken from that athlete. Not one resulted in an adverse finding. The evidence that was collected from BALCO was sufficient to lead to charges of perjury being brought against that athlete in federal court, and it was only during the plea-bargaining during those charges that she admitted that she had been cheating for seven years. So, it was only when faced with the inevitable prospect of going to jail for a long time that the athlete conceded that she had cheated and relinquished her results.[50]

Jones's story, and references to others like it, served a specific purpose: to lobby for further governmental involvement and to demonstrate how many athletes who are doping were sinful to the point of being criminal. The take-home message was that legal enforcement and policing were the next necessary steps to ensure that such athletes were condemned, not rewarded.

WADA's platform echoed the linguistic appropriations of campaigns that declared wars against illicit drugs, perpetuating a suspect class of athletes who bear an increasingly criminalized stigma. Delegates paralleled doping athletes to other athletes who they rendered as evidently deviant, most of whom were US professional athletes.[51] In light of the BALCO scandal, many high-profile US athletes had been condemned for doping and, sprinkled alongside references to saving the future of sport, were allusions to them as "lost causes." Falling in line with Pound's earlier condemnation of the spoils of capitalistic greed, many advocates characterized US professional sports leagues as bastions of unethical behavior. Most explicitly, they referred to particular leagues, Major League Baseball (MLB), the National Football League (NFL), and the National Basketball Association (NBA). Though recognizing that such "leagues are not just in the United States of America," one WADA board member argued, "We always come back to those leagues. We have been in discussion over the past 18 months with each one of them."[52] As the doping controversies linked to the MLB and BALCO had not yet fully materialized at the time of the conference, WADA representatives championed their "recent success" in convincing professional golf to adopt an anti-doping program. At the time, getting golf to accept the conditions of the Code was its primary victory within the realm of professional sports. Apart from hopes that professional golf would "come around to [WADA's] way of thinking," many delegates condemned the NBA and the NFL as hopeless, unyielding strongholds for doping as well as other kinds of unethical behavior.[53]

Casting those professional leagues as evidently deviant, WADA representatives were preoccupied with raising awareness of immoral athletes who seemingly appeared and acted "like us," those athletes posing as pure athlete citizens but who were cheating without being caught. They emerged as a kind of sport-specific "criminal genius," which, according to Alan Sekula, is a long-standing "invention" used to demark a deviant body that is "indistinguishable from the bourgeois, save for a conspicuous lack of moral inhibition."[54] While formal presentations focused on the issue of how doped athletes mislead the public by appearing pure and ethical, one-on-one encounters with conference attendees often highlighted an equally pressing concern for other kinds of deviance, particularly as associated with professional US athletes. Their stories were oriented primarily around African American athletes, emphasizing the regular—and not always flattering—media attention that such athletes command as celebrities.[55] Black men, explain Earl Smith and Angela Hattery "are disproportionately likely to be reported, arrested, charged, convicted, and imprisoned," and because they are often at the center of US sport, their offenses are also more visible.[56] Mediated images of such athletes thus come to reinforce presumptions of their deviance. The dynamics are cyclical, according to Suzanne Marie Enck-Wanzer, making the black male athlete a "convenient villain" to onlookers who are accustomed to seeing them "cast repeatedly in the media as naturally more aggressive."[57]

Along these lines, at the time of the World Conference, the majority of athletes accused of doping during the BALCO investigation were African American. Overall, the coverage of "the steroids problem" in the United States, explain CL Cole and Alex Mobley, drew heavily upon the accepted cultural linkages between race, drugs, and black bodies, perceptions reinforced by the US war on illicit drugs. Accordingly, by rendering many professional athletes of color as "alien, brutal, and threatening" and performance-enhancing drugs as an "organic component of the game" that they play, Cole and Mobley contend that these narratives extend this racialized trope to sport.[58] The coverage of doping scandals in the United States was not simply concerned with bodily integrity or athletes' health, but also the "anxiety about the racialization and hybridization of America's favorite 'pastime.'"[59] The past, one without racial difference, came to signify a better time for sport, rewritten as less corrupt than the present. Similar to the song, "I Fought the Law," it harkened back to a time where boundaries, particularly racial boundaries in the United States, were more clearly defined.

This nostalgic longing referenced an imagined past, disregarding the forms of exclusion and corruption that plagued both sport and society. For instance, even though former IOC president Avery Brundage championed pure sport as morally grounded, he also enabled overt race-based discrimination in US and international sport under the guise of being apolitical. Conference participants, however, evoked a desire for a traditional sport as if it were more pure than contemporary sport. While the racialized imagery to which Cole and Mobley refer did not explicitly surface in the formal language used by conference speakers, questions about professional athletes and racialized beliefs about their abilities and behaviors did emerge in my one-on-one interviews and conversations with conference attendees.[60]

Many interlocutors were curious about professional US sport, often asking for my perspective on these sports. Such questions included, "How are professional leagues managed?"; "Who does the anti-doping testing and how?"; "How much money do athletes actually make?"; "What other illegal activities do those athletes do?" Disdain often accompanied these questions, as many participants were open about their own presumptions about US sports leagues. They felt they were mismanaged and corrupt, had ineffective drug-testing practices, and overcompensated athletes. They regularly stated that these leagues were "not *really* sport," but "just a kind of entertainment."[61] Many dismissed these athletes' accomplishments as inauthentic, even unreal, because their bodies did not "*even look natural*," and their performances appeared "contrived for the audience."[62]

This skepticism of professional sports reflected the longstanding differences in the ethical expectations of amateur and professional athletes. Historian John Hoberman describes this division as a "cultural apartheid" that "separated drug-free amateurs from professional athletes, whose right to use drugs was taken for granted."[63] Amateurism was concerned with maintaining middle- and upper-class social positions. In fact, John Gleaves convincingly argues that the distinction between professional and amateur sports was not strictly enforced, suggesting that the division was actually about preserving class divisions.[64] With the professionalization of sport more generally, bodily purity has become more strictly policed. This shift reflects Mary Douglas's observation about dirt as a social condition: the need to "cleanse" sport emerged when the existing normative orders became challenged.

Professional sport's distinct ethics around doping are historically linked to the prevalence of working-class participants, and the suspicion of professional sport participants remains embedded in regulation. The desire for doping, however, can also be understood in rational and earnest terms. As one former professional cyclist reflected, "You know, [road cycling] is an opportunity for people, guys like me who come from small towns like mine in France, to do something with themselves. It's better than working in the mines or something like that, that's for sure. Yes, there is a lot of doping, but that's the culture. That's the culture. [The athletes] see everyone doing it to get ahead, and people are willing to do it. It's part of the training really. It's really about the ethics. There are plenty [of] good people doing doping. For a lot of people, it's just an opportunity, and there are tradeoffs with any opportunity."[65] Despite the well-documented divisions between amateur and professional sport, WADA's campaign aims to spread ethics historically associated with amateur sport to professional endeavors, especially in light of many more sports professionalizing in the late-twentieth century. In essence, regulation seeks to refashion a class division into a truth-claim backed by science and law, universalizing a normative stance of bodily purity that has never existed.

The divisions between professional and amateur sports and the ethics attributed to them are not limited to issues of class. They maintain racialized undertones as well. Over one hundred years ago, IOC founding father Pierre de Coubertin disparaged the 1904 Olympic Games in St. Louis for its inclusion of the Anthropology Days, a separate two-day, eighteen-event exhibition reserved for "Native" peoples to showcase their athletic abilities.[66] Coubertin saw them as "inauthentic" sideshows and uncivilized spectacles that should not share the same stage as the Olympics, a celebration of pure amateur sport and human ability. Other documented accounts revealed that many participants and spectators viewed this kind of Native inclusion as a spectacle of Native inferiority, especially as the participants selected to represent the symbolic Others (as distinct from Anglo, amateur athletes) did not often know the rules of engagement.[67] Similarly, although not formally referring to these athletes as uncivilized, many interviewees at the 2007 World Conference suggested that commercialized professional sports had an inauthentic quality. In this case, professional athletes appeared unnatural, even fake, because they appeared well trained, even *too* well trained—as if their performances were too good and therefore had to be staged. The suspicion of professional athletes and (in many cases) people of color in particular remained.

One encounter that best captures how ideas about race and ability came to bear on these discussions occurred during the conference-sponsored bus ride from the Palacio Municipal de Congresos to the social hosted at the World Conference. Seated beside a Swiss-born lawyer, I struck up a conversation about basketball, a game he loved to play despite his own "lack of height and athletic ability." Jokingly, he stated that he was "no Thabo Sefolosha," a member of the national Swiss basketball team, who at the time of our conversation had recently been drafted into the NBA. He said that he felt Sefolosha deserved his iconic status in Switzerland for being the first Swiss player to "make it" in the NBA (even though Sefolosha was not considered a marquee player). The lawyer, gesturing to his own stocky physique and face, suggested that his whiteness was definitive marker that he lacked the natural abilities that Sefolosha—whose father is a black South African—possessed.

This racialized recognition took an unexpected turn when the lawyer reflected on what he had heard about other NBA players: that their decadent consumption of commodities, women, and drugs (namely marijuana) indicated their ethics, or lack thereof. Drawing a stark comparison between Sefolosha and other NBA players, he rhetorically asked me if I honestly believed that NBA players did not use performance-enhancing drugs. (I say rhetorically because he did not give me an opportunity to respond.) Surely, he asserted, they could not be that naturally talented, especially given his impression of Stefolosha's athleticism and his knowledge of other NBA players' amoral behavior. Perhaps blinded by his own national pride in a Swiss player's success, he elaborated upon how he had been told that NBA players knew when they would be tested for drugs during the season so as to avoid detection, presenting this as evidence that they lacked both ethical principles and athletic ability.

For other participants, US professional sport demonstrated the problematic emulation of the unethical and selfish values manifest in unregulated neoliberal pursuits. In other words, they condemned how these athletes seemed to have a "winning at all costs" mentality toward life, not just sport. Distinct from the condemnation of professional cycling in Europe, racist implications that often coincide with images of criminality entered into imagery evoked by many interlocutors when discussing professional US sport. Despite some gestures of political correctness, many of the conference attendees expressed strong concerns about what they referred to as "gangsta culture"; that is, they explained, the glamorization of "rapper types" and "criminals," especially by athletes donning markers of deviance, such as tattoos and material excess, such as "bling," the flashy and sometimes ostentatious diamond jewelry often visible in US popular culture and rap music. In condemning these excessive displays, however, those with whom I spoke would often jokingly use a condescending vernacular, as they criticized athletes' "low class" displays of their wealth. Their concerns were oriented not so much around athletes' success, but a certain kind of reprehensible demonstration of that success, a public performance that also revealed athletes' disdain, even disregard, for authority.

This narrative of black athletes is not new. In fact, when pugilist Jack Johnson became the first African American heavyweight champion of the world in the 1910s, W. E. B. DuBois described Jackson's "crime" as his "unforgiveable blackness."[68] By this, DuBois referred to punitive treatment and derision of Johnson in light of his success and blatant disregard for society's designated place for him as a black man born to formerly enslaved parents. Johnson drove fast and expensive cars, wore finely tailored suits, owned nightclubs, and openly slept with (and married) white women.

In 2007, this association with black professional athletes, particularly from the United States, still resonated. For many participants I spoke to at the conference, this trope of unforgiveable blackness appeared threatening because it flew in the face of ethics instilled by Olympism, amateurism, and anti-doping efforts. Further, participants in many cases tried to prove to me that such professional athletes were likely doping by invoking rumors as evidence of their immoral behavior.

One story in particular had taken on seemingly mythic qualities as three different participants conveyed it to me over the course of the conference. The details varied by narrator, but the crux of the account oriented around one of the US Olympic Dream Teams, which has included some well-known NBA players since the original Dream Team won the gold medal in the 1992 Barcelona Games. According to participants, there was an unofficial deal struck between NBA players and IOC officials, which ensured they would not be drug tested during the Games. In one account, the narrator specified that the players did not want to have to curb their use of marijuana (which is a banned substance in competition), but the other two renditions provided no such specification. An unknowing listener might thus assume that the bargain concerned performance-enhancing substances. As told, the conflict peaked when one US player received a notice to be tested. Instead of appearing before doping control officers, he packed his bags to leave the Olympic Village and encouraged his teammates to do so as well. This story concluded, at least as presented, at the airport with the IOC president asking them to stay and promising them immunity from testing.

The story served as a critique of the athletes and the previous IOC administration. One person conveyed it as a justification for stronger anti-doping enforcement and anticorruption reforms. Another argued that no athlete should ever feel entitled to behave that brashly toward authorities regardless of his income or national origin. A third participant emphasized that the kind of banned substance—that is, recreational or performance enhancing—did not matter in this case: all drugs are bad, and athletes as role models should be prohibited from ever using them. Within these narrations, however, an unforeseen transnational twist emerged in which the longstanding scrutiny of professional athletes conjoined with the heightened visibility of black (male) bodies through the globalized coverage of professional sport. Because of their presumed deviance, these athletes' physical abilities became the subject of scorn, skepticism, and even disbelief. A paradox in turn surfaced: even though there are widespread beliefs asserting that black athletes are naturally physically superior compared to other racial groups (even to the extent that their pursuit of sport as their "natural" career impedes success in other professional fields[69]), authorities still cast these athletes as too immoral for "pure" sport. In this case, their pre-existing suspect condition, reinforced by cultural and national rhetoric, rendered them as not worthy of athlete citizenship.

While these depictions are perhaps more telling of how interlocutors imagined the behaviors of professional athletes than of actual acts of deviance, there was some grain of truth embedded in participants' criticisms, at least in terms of the impact of the corporatization of sport. Sports are a big business, which has encouraged forms of corporate corruption and has contributed to the heightened visibility of professional athletes in both positive and negative ways. The perceived cultural entitlements of being a high-profile male athlete, irrespective of race, have reinforced evident displays of the chauvinism commonly instilled by male-segregated fraternities.[70] As one participant explained, these issues spoke to a deeper problem—only "athletes, drug dealers, and CEOs" can afford life's luxuries.[71] These insinuations often came up alongside discussion points condemning American commercialism and its role in international sport, despite the fact that commercialization is a notable source of the Olympic Movement's financial sustenance and arguably a cause for the expansion of anti-doping regulation.[72] More generally, there was open resentment toward the reliance upon corporate interests in sport, and many participants expressed concerns over professional football (soccer) in Europe, which they saw as following suit in terms of commercialism and the adjoining moral degradation.

Despite expressing concerns that this moral degradation stemmed from structural conditions fostered by capitalistic incentives and greed, regulatory solutions and rhetoric focused on individual athletes and drug traffickers. Neoliberalism went unchallenged; in fact, by focusing on particular bodies, it was reinforced. Accordingly, many participants described science (in the form of drug testing) and law (in the form of investigations such as the one into BALCO) as the only ways to prove that some athletes are deviant and deceitful. The expansion of WADA's campaign to clean up sport may have expressly embraced the ethics associated with amateur sport—that is, of bodily purity— and applied them to spheres of professional sport; however, in doing so, it did not escape the consequences of the cultural apartheid between professional and amateur sport. In fact, it actually exacerbates these stratified conditions by positing a catch-22: regulation holds professional athletes accountable to ideals of bodily purity not previously expected of them; however, in doing so, it anticipates and expects their failure, emphasizing that they are inherently suspect. Further, not all athletes are portrayed as equally suspect. As the depictions of professional African American athletes evidence, some professional athletes emerge as polluted, even without proof of doping, because of racialized difference.

Postcolonial Implications of Anti-Doping Rhetoric

While condemning a subgroup of athletes as deviant, presenters also claimed that "clean" athletes were "under attack" by the athletes who chose to dope, not the broader capitalist structures that incentivized doping. Specifically, WADA representatives reflected on interventions to prevent these so-called innocents from emulating deviant athletes in professional leagues. Their anxieties were thus as much concerned with acts of doping as they were with apprehensions that children, even their own, would emulate the professional athletes they viewed as unruly, uppity, and deviant. Overall, their vision for the future land-scape was to adapt a series of technologies—law, science, and education among them—to instill values congruent with ideals of fair play. This, they argued, was necessary to "deter and counter this epidemic," which had enabled the normalization of doping in sport across the globe.

Amid the calls for more global anti-doping regulation, postcolonial tropes surfaced, particularly around calls for a stronger anti-doping presence within the Global South. Such dynamics, argue Anna Agathangelou and L. H. M. Ling, are features of neoliberal governance. By cultivating an enlightened persona that seeks to aid people the Global South, these governance strategies reflect "older traditions of colonialism and patriarchy that valorize unequal treatments of race, gender, class and culture."[73] Director General Howman's presentation on the future landscapes of anti-doping regulation offers a case in point. He stated that it was necessary to intervene in these states of lawlessness: "In many countries so unregulated that this is a scourge that must be addressed urgently by us all. We know there is more money to be made in the trafficking of banned substances such as steroids than there is in the trafficking of what we loosely refer to as recreational drugs such as heroin and cocaine. Why? Because in many countries, there are no rules prohibiting it."[74] This specific statement emerged in relation to Operation Gear Grinder, which he charac-terized as "a significant advance in the closing down of a number of labora-tories in Mexico that were producing and providing anabolic steroids to the United States and other countries." Reiterating a black-market relationship in which the Global South served as the source of banned substances that flowed into the Global North, law and education were necessary counter-active measures. These countries were characterized as the inevitable pro-duction sites of the doping products trafficked into industrialized nations, not actors fulfilling the consumer-based demands from the Global North. The Global North's purity went unchallenged. Instead, there was a desire to control and enlighten nation-states in the Global South, a rhetorical maneu-ver that dismissed the imperial legacies that influence and shape globalized inequalities and their enduring problems.

The narrow focus of anti-doping regulation was not simply about con-trolling individual bodies to avoid contamination; it was about controlling nations deemed to be the source of such pollution. The condemnation of dop-ing and the adjoining calls for law enforcement interventions aids in reinscrib-ing these judgments onto states and regions, not simply individuals. Following Howman's identification of "lawlessness" in the Global South as a threat to the normative and moral orders (of the Global North) that anti-doping regulation sought to protect, he concluded,

> In many countries, therefore, [the trafficking and making of banned drugs] is legal. There has to be a change. There has to be some regulation. When you add to that the fact that many of the substances that might be sent . . . from plants that produce the raw material, the composition of the final product is undertaken in kitchens, in underground laboratories, where there is no sanitation, no health regulation, no policing, and these are the substances which are then made available to *our* youth. Not only is there a danger to *their* health from taking them per se, it's an extraordinary danger to *them* in terms of the lack of sanitation under which they have been prepared, and *we* must take steps to stop this as soon as *we* possibly can.[75]

Cast in a paternalistic frame, his language conveyed binary distinctions between "them" versus "us," which evoked an explicit division between areas of the world seemingly without regulation—that is, the areas characterized as the producers of banned substances in the Global South—and the threat they posed to *our* (presumably innocent) children, those consumers in the Global North. The linguistic appropriations of governing through crime, which had primarily targeted individual athletes, had become transposed onto these global relations.

Howman's statement also articulated that it was the responsibility of the anti-doping movement ("us") to ensure that that these regions ("them") received preventative measures in the form of ("our") law. Again, the postcolonial tendency to characterize the Global South as Other in need of saving underpinned this rationale, even if it was unintended. UNESCO deputy director-general Marcio Barbosa concurred with Howman's point, stating that the UNESCO Convention against Doping in Sport "filled a normative void that needed to be dealt with urgently," requiring a "redoubling of efforts to strengthen ethics, personal responsibility, and integrity," all Western values upheld by anti-doping rhetoric.[76] The resounding applause following his statement attested to stakeholders' support. Neither man's language criminalized the Global South in the ways that contaminated professional athletes from the Global North had been, though. Instead, the Global South symbolized a place of unguided countries and persons in need of aid and assistance. Outreach to the Global South appeared necessary in order to protect the innocents of the Global North who may be enticed to take drugs. The imagining of innocent athlete-subjects thus revealed a group bifurcated along globalized distinctions.

Discussions about doping among athletes living in the Global South also reflected postcolonial underpinnings. D. M. Stofile's intervention on behalf of the South African government characterized the growth of doping in the Global South as a trickle-down effect of modern sport:

> Representing a region where, not too long ago, the concept of anti-doping was foreign and unknown, we are beginning to witness a significant change. We are experiencing a revolution in the way issues of doping are no longer perceived as being out of reach for African athletes or, as a First World phenomenon. African sport has also experienced the numbness and displeasure when our athletes succumb to cheating through doping. We have also witnessed how lives are destroyed and how families and communities are shattered because of the actions of an unscrupulous few who defied the rules and integrity of sport in an attempt to achieve their own selfish and ill-gotten gains. We realize that no country is immune to doping. We have also realized that we need to be sharp and decisive and we are conscious of the necessity for swift and uncompromising intervention.[77]

The relationship that he highlighted between the Global South and the Global North was not one in which the Global South provided raw materials for illicit global markets, but one that was oriented around the importation of beliefs that seemingly flowed from the Global North to the Global South. His words also revealed a subscription to WADA's vision for addressing these changes. Rather than dismissing concerns about doping in his country or blaming Western countries for the doping problem in Africa, he instead skirted around causation through his reference to cultural tides shifting in a way that rendered doping to be a cause for concern, an impetus to join the campaign. Thus, the debate did not create a space in which the Global North emerged as culpable or suspect.

One can speculate the reasons for Stofile's characterization. Even though his intervention maintained altruistic features, more pressing motivations accompanied them. Stofile alluded to them at the end of his remarks: "Yes, as a continent we [African countries] have been slow off the mark in ensuring that we join the global fight; Yes, we have so many other challenges that require our attention and scarce resources; Yes, we still have a lot of catching up to do, but, we are committed to ensure that we join the international fray and we are steadfast in our resolve to contribute and play a significant role in the unfolding processes."[78] In short, the need for resources was evident. UNESCO had already earmarked support to provide aid to such countries pursuing compliance, which totaled 1.3 million US dollars in 2008.[79]

With the possibility of hosting international events linked to complying with the terms of the anti-doping regime, countries with limited resources and goals of hosting major sporting events—like South Africa, the host of the 2010 FIFA World Cup—have little to no choice in taking a stance on anti-doping regulation. Global inequalities encourage compliance in terms of both language and practice. Stofile's words, although performing an official function within the conference, revealed certain conditions of anti-doping discourse and his country's double bind within it: even if doping was not an evident problem in his region, it had to receive recognition as such so as to ensure that South Africa could take advantage of the other symbolic and financial benefits of sport as specified by the Code. In this way, economic coercion appeared a successful international tool for the expansion of the anti-doping regime, at least in terms of achieving buy-in from many countries. It also ensured that South Africa played the part of a dutiful citizen in this context, condemning doping as an evil, but in need of resources from the Global North to do so.

Other anti-doping advocates expressed that doping was a legitimate concern in developing countries. Reflecting on an earlier conversation with an African doctor, one anti-doping regulator stated, "We [in the Global North] have top training facilities and methods. The Third World has steroids. That's an important perspective to consider."[80] Framed in this way, inequality of access and resources drove the need for other performance-enhancing methods. The Global North could afford anti-doping regulation, because its more affluent athletes presumably had enough resources to not need doping products in order to be competitive or by using substances or methods that could elude detection.

There were also expressed concerns that biomedicine could aid in proving and verifying that successful athletes representing countries in the Global South were, in fact, pure athletes. One notable perspective, although not formally endorsed by the anti-doping regime, crystallized around an unsettling conversation that I had with a medical doctor who was from northern Europe.[81] It began with a question as to why some athletes from certain regions seemed to be naturally superior in specific sports:

MD: So, why do *you* think [East] African athletes are so competitive in long distance running? They don't have the best training facilities. They don't usually have equipment, so why?

ME: Well, I think their performances show just how committed they are as athletes . . .

MD: No, what I mean is so many of their runners come from really poor, I mean totally impoverished, conditions. Their food is nowhere near the nutritional quality we have or even the quantity in many cases . . . that we think athletes should have. They don't have access to doping—unless there's some native plant we don't know about yet, but I really doubt that . . .

ME: Yes, so it really does speak to their hard work and fortitude.

MD: Well, that's only part of it when you think about it. You see, a team of doctors actually conducted research there, you know with them as [human] subjects. We wanted to know why they are superior . . . as compared to the rest of the world.

Taken aback, I tried to ask politely when and how so, but he began explaining before I finished my question. He recounted how a group of doctors visited various parts of the region, including remote areas, to do empirical tests. Upon hearing the word, "tests," I asked him what kinds he meant. He responded simply, "Oh, just pretty standard stuff," explaining that their focus was on empirical factors, such as the athletes' diet and schedule, as well as measures of body composition and proportionality, even taking bodily samples for testing. In this case, it was not for doping substances per se, but other physical indicators of advantage discernable through biomedicalized scrutiny.

Although anti-doping authorities were not responsible for these tests, anti-doping regulation shares a common desire to scientifically prove which athletes are natural and which athletes are artificial. Although I was well aware that physiological testing is the norm in most elite training facilities in the Global North, the idea of going to African people's homes to take tissue samples and physical measurements evoked thoughts of early positivist criminologists like Cesare Lombroso and phrenologists who used bodily dimensions to explain deviant bodies. The doctor's explanation did not quell my unease. He stated that East African runners have longer shins than "us" (people of Anglo-European descent), and as a result, their hamstrings did not tire as easily over long distances. In this case, his aim was to prove their bodily purity, but the intrusion it entailed was evident. Whereas sport and science had historically worked hand in hand as sites to test theories of racial logic, often with the goal of proving white superiority,[82] his testing was intended to prove the opposite. In this case, it served to "prove" that such athletes were pure. By demonstrating that East African runners of a particular ethnic lineage had physical proportions that made them more efficient, science he argued debunked any suspicions that African runners doped. Their bodies were nonetheless cast as initially suspect. As representatives of the Global South, their abilities to surpass the feats of their counterparts in the Global North were still questioned, that is, until Western science provided an explanation.

Later, well after the World Conference on Doping in Sport, I read an account by anthropologist John Bale that offered a different reading of a similar research project (likely even the same) conducted by an institute on the science of East African running.[83] The mission of the institute, an interdisciplinary endeavor with social scientists, biologists, nutritionists, and geneticists, was to unearth and explain these runners' natural advantages through comprehensive study. While visiting Kenya, according to Bale, these researchers had "examined hundreds of runners, taken blood and DNA samples, undertaken genetic analysis, established whether the boys they interviewed ran or walked to school, and checked the athletes' diets. The runners' bodies were measured and analyzed."[84] Admitting his own unease, Bale reflects on a comment made by an elite African runner during a conference hosted by the institute, where members had presented their findings. She asked: "Why are you studying me? Why don't you study the British world-record marathon runner, Paula Radcliffe?"[85] Providing a voice not present during my conversation with the doctor, her words, according to Bale, drew attention to how this use of science echoed "the anthropometrical antics of the nineteenth century explorers."[86] In other words, these efforts continued the (white) Western gaze that has historically taken aim at non-Western peoples.

Likewise, my discussions with participants point to persisting postcolonial logics embedded in sport and anti-doping regulation. Athlete citizenship and the desire for physical purity do not escape the material conditions of inequality in which these discourses operate. The findings of science combined with the desire to preserve the ideals of amateurism, particularly as expressed through hard work without the achievement of wealth, aided in explaining these East African bodies as appropriate athlete citizens. Although evidently fitting within the scope and bounds of fair play, their status as others still made them susceptible to additional forms of scientific scrutiny. This "discovery" of a biological advantage did not extend to discussions of professional African American athletes in the United States, even those of similar ethnic descent, for their open pursuit of financial rewards cast them as decidedly different subjects who represented ethics that anti-doping efforts sought to disavow.

Side Effects of the Anti-Doping Regime

The postcolonial dimensions of anti-doping regulation are notable, arguably unforeseen, side effects, especially to readers in the Global North. There are other concerns and consequences that emerge, particularly with the formal embrace of governmental and legal intervention. One such issue crystallizes around practices of punishment. Left unsaid during conference proceedings were the actual punishments endured by athletes investigated by governmental authorities. While the WADA Code establishes standardized guidelines regarding sanctions for violations, it does not and cannot dictate what happens within legal courts. Jones, for example, in admitting to perjury before two grand juries during the BALCO investigations, was actually subject to two forms of punishment. For perjury, she received a six-month prison sentence followed by a two-year probationary period and life as a disenfranchised felon. Her other punishment, the stripping of the five Olympic medals she won during the 2000 Sydney Olympic Games, though limited to the realm of sport, would have resulted in the loss of stature and income even without the additional criminal prosecution.

Jones, once an international icon revered for her athleticism, is now a felon who lacks full citizenship rights in the United States. Although WADA advocates rendered her punishment as a success story, she cannot vote in her home state, endures the combined stigmas of fallen athlete and ex-convict (not to mention the memories of trauma that accompany incarceration, including solitary confinement), and has had to overcome the burden of significant financial debt. She did manage to resurrect her athletic career as a professional basketball player in the Women's National Basketball Association.[87] Excluded from other forms of work because of her status as a felon, Jones, a mother of three children, returned to sport with a starting salary of approximately $35,000 per year, a number seemingly insignificant compared to the average $70,000 to $80,000 per race (not including her endorsements) that she made at the peak of her track career. Despite making this comeback, her story emerged at the conference not as one of resilience and redemption, but as one of just deserts.

Other rulings related to the BALCO investigations did not necessarily result in punishments like those endured by Marion Jones. Victor Conte, the founder and former president of BALCO, the force behind the ring, served only four months in prison and another four on house arrest in exchange for his guilty plea and a list of the athletes he supplied with performance enhancing drugs (twenty-seven in total). After his release, Conte, claiming to have reformed, started a new sport-supplement company. His case seems a stark contrast to stakeholders' claims that law would ensure harsh punishments for suppliers and remove them from markets. In April 2011, baseball legend Barry Bonds was found guilty on only one of four charges—for obstruction of justice, not by lying but by giving evasive answers while testifying under oath, not for using steroids or performance-enhancing substances. The jury could not agree if the remaining counts had been proven beyond a reasonable doubt. Though this felony conviction can result in up to ten years in prison—federal guidelines call for fifteen to twenty-one months—he has yet to serve any time.[88] In contrast, his former trainer Greg Anderson—having already served three months in prison for pleading guilty to charges of distributing steroids and money laundering—was detained and found in contempt of court for refusing to testify in the trial of Bonds, his long-time friend and client. Others charged in the BALCO investigations have also received differing levels of punishment: In 2008, cyclist Tammy Thomas spent six months in home confinement after being convicted on three counts of perjury and one on obstruction of justice, and Trevor Graham, a former Olympic track coach, received one year of home confinement on grounds that he lied to investigators. These disproportionate outcomes reveal how legal jurisdictions can ultimately carry with them a varying degree of impact on athlete citizens as national subjects held accountable to their country's laws, justice systems, and adjoining punishments.

These contradictions do not paint the same harmonized picture described by WADA representatives. Instead, they reveal that the anti-doping movement cannot dictate the terms of punishment—or even the ideals of athlete citizenship—in practice. These developments, however, do speak to how technologies of regulation, be they legal or scientific, are institutionalized features of protecting fair play in sport. Symbolically, law emerges as an important mode of codifying regulation's normative claims by compelling subjects to its terms. In need of new innovations to catch those bodies suspected to be cheats, law materializes as a path toward substantially enhancing the agency's regulatory power, an enticing technology to add to WADA's existing arsenal in its war on performance-enhancing drugs. These practices also reveal how various groups of athletes are perceived and treated differently, as some are presumed to be model citizens, while others are inherently suspect or deviant. The excess not captured by the formal language of anti-doping regulation—in this case, the postcolonial and racialized dimensions of these power relations—nonetheless shapes regulatory practices in action.

The legalization of anti-doping regulation is therefore not simply about dissuading cheating in sport but about sustaining the anti-doping narrative as a means to make sense of the ethics of sport in a globalized world where professional sport has proliferated. On the one hand, it promotes an imagined notion of fair play by condemning a particular group of athletes as "sporting frauds," to use one conference participant's words. On the other hand, by rendering many more athletes as suspect, regulation and rhetoric draw attention away from the shifting expectations targeted at professional athletes. Instead, anti-doping regulation instills earlier values associated with amateurism as enduring values for sport more generally, no longer limiting them to certain classes of athletes.

Such developments demonstrate a globalized example of the process that Eric Hobsbawm describes as "inventing tradition," which involves appealing to and leveraging ideals in order to foster a strong sense of communal belonging.[89] The term "inventing" is not to suggest that regulators are inauthentic in their claims, but to highlight the constitutive power of their ideological claims. "Invented traditions," writes Allan Hanson, are often "ordinary event[s] in the development of all discourse," which require unpacking.[90] As this chapter illuminates, anti-doping advocates have clung to and recited values attributed to sport's past in order to justify present and future regulation, regulation that embraces neoliberal values and protects capitalistic interests, even as it condemns these ethics in individual athletes. In doing so, regulation also perpetuates a discourse that embraces tropes of Olympic sport as if the past was more pure than the contemporary moment. Law in turn becomes mobilized in order to uphold and protect these myths of a purer kind of sport, ones that claim to embrace and celebrate athletes as untainted vessels embodying the moral vitality achieved through discipline and hard work.[91] Articulated in a modern discourse, these Western values of individuality, persistence, and obedience uphold capitalistic ethics upon which modern sport relies by directing the gaze onto individual suspect athletes.

The consequences of these practices are two-fold: they not only disregard how colonial inequalities informed and accompanied Olympic ideals, they also ignore the lingering postcolonial dimensions that inform these refashioned principles. Anti-doping regulation's formal dismissal does not mean that postcoloniality does not still shape the terms of athlete citizenship. It actually enables these stratified logics to persist behind the objective veneer posited by both law and science. This observation draws attention to the contradictions that permeate the mobilization of law and science in this field, highlighting how the broader international politics continue come to bear on the athletes condemned for transgressing the terms of athlete citizenship. Chapter 4 further explores the gendered contours of these contradictions as they surface in the relationships between anti-doping regulation and gender verification in women's sports.

4

Impossible Purities

────────────────────────────●

The Gendered Science
of Fair Play

The emergence of anti-doping regulation marks an instance whereby techno-cratic and legalistic mechanisms are used to police longstanding ideologies about sport and embodiment as if they are tangible truths. Athlete citizen-ship is not about regulation alone; it is a constitutive process of belonging and exclusion in which regulation plays an important role. Citizenship is gendered, and athlete citizenship is no exception in this regard.[1] According to Anne McClintock, there is an "uneven gendering of national citizenship" that draws upon accepted cultural values to justify and naturalize the subordi-nate position of women.[2] Scholarly analyses of sport and nation provide many examples of how female athletes experience different forms of exclusion than their male counterparts and how they navigate these tensions, even as they are upheld as symbols of nation.[3] In fact, women are subject to forms of testing—that is, gender-verification testing—that men are not. Building upon Michael Messner's contention that the female body in sport is a "contested ideological terrain,"[4] this chapter examines the gendered contours of policing female ath-letes' bodies in the name of protecting fair play. Gender-verification testing, working in tandem with the sex segregation of sport, explicitly perpetuates the scrutiny and condemnation of embodied female masculinity; however, as this chapter describes further, anti-doping regulation, too, perpetuates gendered beliefs about physical ability.[5]

The regulation of women's sport employs biomedicalized techniques to evaluate and legitimize whether bodies comply with or transgress the terms of fair play. In addition to drug testing, authorities have employed gender-verification practices targeting competitors in women's athletic events in order to distinguish female competitors from so-called "gender frauds," participants characterized as male, intersex, or transgender.[6] In essence, gender verification in women's sport polices a presumed boundary between women and men as if that binary is a clear biological distinction. This assertion, however, is a gendered claim, not a scientific fact. Gender verification, combined with the sex segregation of sport, enshrines two values: that women are subordinate to men and that the gendered boundary upheld by testing protects the level playing field in women's sport.[7] In terms of athlete citizenship, this offers a conspicuous example of how the use of science operates in the service of gendered hierarchies. In fact, as this chapter describes, both gender verification and anti-doping regulation uphold these hierarchies even as evidence obtained through testing procedures exposes them as a fallacy. Regulation co-constitutively reinforces the presumed divide between the categories of woman and man by levying gender-specific requirements for recognition as a "true" female athlete citizen—requirements that are not uniformly applied.

To explain the distinct regulations aimed at women's bodies in sport, this chapter begins with an overview of the goals of gender-verification practices and the challenges inherent to trying to distinguish a boundary between women and men using scientific testing. It then discusses how gendered concerns about fair play inform both gender verification and anti-doping regulation in women's sports. Considering the circumstances of athletes who have been cast as gender frauds in women's sport alongside developments in gender-verification procedures, I explain how tactics have shifted over time in relation to both scientific developments and international politics. These changes highlight the broader gendered implications of athlete citizenship. Despite the use of different techniques, gender-verification practices, I argue, do not provide evidence of a clear binary between women and men. They only confirm that sex is complex, even scientifically undetectable.

Despite these findings, the IOC Medical Commission continues to implement specific guidelines for women's sport, revealing the powerful influence of normative gender on beliefs regarding human embodiment and physical ability. A paradox thus emerges at the heart of athlete citizenship: despite asserting that it values only natural athletes, guidelines can actually require those athletes deemed too naturally masculine for women's sport to artificially modify their bodies so that they seem less masculine. Certain women are scrutinized or tested when they appear to be "too good" for women's sport and do not look like "natural" women, a sexist rationale that is similar to the insidious forms of racism that rendered the bodies of US professional athletes as inauthentic and suspect. In the case of women's sport, global politics and institutionalized forms of racism and sexism coalesce with biomedicalization in ways that hold non-Western women to heightened levels of scrutiny.

Although the introduction of scientific gender-verification requirements in Olympic sport coincided with that of drug testing in 1968, they are distinct from anti-doping regulation. Drug testing and anti-doping surveillance, at least on the surface, are to discourage the use of artificial substances by banning athletes found to have used them, even though testing protocols do not always yield clear evidence of deliberate cheating. The inclusion of gender verification for female participants does not lend itself to as easy an explanation. "Failing" a gender-verification test stems from naturally occurring biological conditions, not ergogenic aids. According to Susan Birrell and CL Cole, calls for gender verification emerged from the "suspicion that superior female athletic performances . . . were actually accomplished by women who were not truly women," implying that "superior athletic process is the natural domain of men," not women.[8] Gender verification is thus interconnected with women's success in elite sport and how exceptional accomplishments challenge the physical norms that buttress beliefs that women are the weaker sex. Binary notions of sex—and the desire to segregate sport along an imagined line according to presumed biological differences—remain a fundamental part in modern sport.

Anxieties around women participating in sport are longstanding. One of the most successful athletes (male or female), Mildred "Babe" Didrikson, offers one historically notable example that demonstrates how female athletes have challenged norms of femininity.[9] Her athletic dominance in track and field was clear when she won three Olympic medals in the 1932 Summer Games. She later went on to become a successful professional golfer. Her physique, according to Dennis Phillips, became a site where "normality and abnormality" became debated, and "the threat of being *labeled* 'abnormal' was constantly held over the head of women and girls" participating in sport more generally.[10] As many other scholarly analyses attest, women's sport remains a site where the boundaries of abnormality are policed.[11]

Gender verification provides an example of how the objective of protecting fair play couples with other forms of social control aimed at feminine bodies, revealing that earlier Olympic values haunt this form of testing in much the same way that they underpin anti-doping regulation. On the one hand, the regulation of women's bodies in sport highlights tensions between the recognition of women's rights to participate in sport and the desire to maintain their corporeal passivity in accordance with naturalized beliefs about their physical abilities. On the other hand, it highlights how female athletes characterized as gender frauds do significant symbolic work in both challenging and preserving normative worldviews. In addition, these two concerns evidence that not all women are uniformly scrutinized as prospective gender frauds, as non-Western women and women of color often emerge as the bodies deemed suspect.

Gender Verification in Sport Today

Gender verification in women's sporting events has received ample critical attention from feminist scholars.[12] Collectively, their work evidences an important dilemma undergirding gender verification: sex testing cannot prove what it sets out to do, because, as simply put by Anne Fausto-Sterling, "a body's sex is too complex."[13] Sex is not two polarized opposites. Instead, as Rebecca Jordan-Young and Katrina Karkazis explain, sex has "a cultural mode and a lived mode," between which there are divergences. Whereas the cultural mode suggests that bodies should fit into male and female categories, the lived mode reveals sex as "multiple *within* bodies, and . . . not always easily classed *across* bodies."[14] In other words, the desire to have the lived mode reflect the cultural mode is itself a cultural artifact. Despite this observation, gender verification still occurs selectively in sport, as demonstrated by the high-profile controversy surrounding the 2009 women's 800-meter world champion, Caster Semenya, a South African runner who could not compete for eleven months while authorities determined if she was eligible to participate in women's events.

Temporarily setting aside the details of Semenya's case, I first address how a new chapter in the history of gender verification in sport began in April 2011 when the IOC Medical Commission proposed revised guidelines for female participants. The guidelines target female athletes with hyperandrogenism; that is, those who produce high levels of androgens and more specifically, testosterone, the androgen primarily associated with male characteristics and strength-enhancing attributes.[15] According to the press release from the IOC, these rules, were developed for the following reason: "Although rare, some women develop male-like body characteristics due to an overproduction of male sex hormones, so-called 'androgens.' The androgenic effects on the human body explain why men perform better than women in most sports and are, in fact, the very reason for the distinction between male and female competition in most sports. Consequently, women with hyperandrogenism generally perform better in sport than other women."[16]

In response, Katrina Karkazis, Rebecca Jordan-Young, Georgiann Davis, and Silvia Camporesi contend that there is no evidence proving that athletic success depends upon higher levels of testosterone.[17] Why, then, do such regulations around women's participation exist? While some may argue it is in part a response to the controversy around Semenya, it is also part of a longer genealogy that reveals how cultural and gendered norms influence the deployment of gender verification in the name of fair play.

The 2011 press release by the IOC justifies gender-verification testing in a way that is distinctly different from the rationale it presented in 1968. Historically speaking, the original justification for gender verification was to prevent male intruders from fraudulently competing in women's sport.[18] Even though the IOC is no longer preoccupied with finding men masquerading as women, guidelines continue to reflect a hegemonic belief that male qualities are inherently superior to those of females. Sheila Cavanagh and Heather Sykes refer to this subscription as the "advantage thesis."[19] Accordingly, revised gender-verification practices seek to ensure that female athletes who are suspected to have hyperandrogenism and are not androgen resistant (that is, they can recruit the benefits of higher levels of testosterone) do not participate (or are treated before competing again) so that no one would have an "unfair" physical advantage. Although the IOC did not publically announce a specific testosterone limit for women, the policy requires the an assessment of whether one's testosterone levels are below the normal "male range," which is considered 260 to 1,000 nanograms per deciliter.[20] If an athlete is found to be within the normal male range, the policy requires an analysis that demonstrates she is resistant to the effects of androgen to compete in women's events.[21] If an athlete does not meet the requirements, authorities are to notify her and outline "the conditions she would be required to meet should she wish to become eligible again"; however, if she "fails to comply with any aspect of the eligibility determination process, while that is her right as an individual, she will not be eligible to participate as a competitor in the chosen sport."[22] Although public statements by the IOC do not specify what subsequent treatment would entail, there is evidence that women identified under the policy have received hormonal treatments and even the nonessential surgery, including the removal of gonads and clitorises, to lower testosterone levels under the presumption that it would ensure a playing field among seemingly (more) equal women.[23]

Although under this policy relatively few female athletes would be evaluated and treated, some critics, including Hida Viloria, human rights spokesperson for the Organisation Intersex International, argue that such recommendations undermine the impetus for anti-doping regulation. The prospect of requiring some women to take artificial hormones in order to compete, she argues, is problematic. Having lobbied against this requirement, Viloria states that it "seems contrary to the very ethos of athletic competition, which punishes the use of steroids and instead encourages making the most of one's natural talents."[24] Instead, the policy renders higher levels of testosterone in women akin to doping in sport, a violation of fair play, despite the fact that higher testosterone levels occur naturally. In contrast, testing does not target men's sports even though, as Viloria acknowledges, "men with the intersex variation Diplo, a.k.a. XYY, produce higher levels of testosterone than other men and could also be said to have an 'unfair physical advantage' over their peers."[25] Moreover,

FIGURE 4.1 Caster Semenya's celebration following her victory in the women's 800-meter final race of the 2009 IAAF Athletics World Championships in Berlin Photo by Olivier Morin/AFP/Getty Images.

because the IOC has opted to selectively test female athletes on the basis of their appearance, Viloria suggests that the underlying issue involves "some people's inability to accept women who appear masculine." For example, even though Semenya's amazing performances are cast as the cause for suspicion, "Pamela Jelimo, who sports long hair, has outperformed Semenya and was not forced to undergo gender-verification testing." In short, Viloria argues that Semenya's appearance was, in fact, a driving motivation for authorities to recommend that she be examined.

This observation is part of a longstanding trend of suspecting that seemingly more masculine female bodies compete unfairly in women's events.[26] In fact, the current policy focuses on a specific disorder of sexual development, recognizing that previous regulations had limited the participation of many women with intersex characteristics, even in cases where such conditions did not result a comparative athletic advantage. Throughout the history of the modern Olympics, there have been allegations that such women are men, steroids users, or male-female "hybrids." Allucquére Rosanne "Sandy" Stone, a cyborg theorist and influential transgender studies scholar, contends that these assertions rely on "the Duck test"; that is, "if it walks like a duck, quacks like a duck, and looks like a duck, then it's a duck."[27] Stone's charge suggests that Olympic doctors relied upon visual criteria; however, a closer scrutiny of the Medical Commission's technical work reveals that its members took steps to use science as the basis for their claims, making "the Duck test" a more elaborate scheme.

Revisiting the IOC Medical Commission records on testing and the discourses around the women judged to be too transgressive for female-only events marks a unique cross-section of dilemmas linked to heteronormativity, international politics, and scientific practice. To illustrate these dilemmas, this chapter discusses how a particular notion of naturalness, one that is informed by earlier Olympic ideologies, has come to anchor the ideal of fair play. In this case, the desired notion of naturalness is not dependent upon natural physiological characteristics, but naturalized beliefs about how bodies should reflect binary sex categories—themselves gendered constructs—and how those constructs reflect individuals' abilities in sport. Although revised, current gender-verification rules continue the legacies of earlier regulations by perpetuating presumptions about what a natural female athlete should be. Rather than cast these bodies as deviant in an agentive or criminal sense, the medicalized justifications that underpin the rationale for gender verification characterize more masculine female bodies as disordered or flawed.

In the pages that follow, my aim is to divulge the misperception posited by regulatory logics: the assumption that regulation levels the playing field for natural or "true" female athletes. Analyses of public discourses around female athletes reveal how international politics contribute directly to these narrations. Historically speaking, there is a clear disjuncture between depictions of Western women and their seemingly more muscular and masculine counterparts from the Eastern bloc countries during the Cold War.[28] Today, women from the Global South often emerge as the bodies condemned as outlaws. A closer reading of the IOC Medical Commission files on gender verification provides further insight into the authors' beliefs and how they converge with rationales for anti-doping regulation. In sum, both interventions attest to a broader form of gendered boundary work that operates within and through claims of fair play and athlete citizenship more generally.

Sex, Nature, and Fair Play

Longstanding gendered assumptions—and even some medical literature—have purported that "women were *by nature* not athletic competitors."[29] Foundational Olympic ideologies have embraced such claims. According to IOC founder Pierre de Coubertin, women's bodies were inherently inferior. In 1896, he wrote, "No matter how toughened a sportswoman may be, her organism is not cut out to sustain certain shocks. Her nerves rule her muscles, nature wanted it that way."[30] As the Olympics began to formally include women in the early twentieth century, sex-segregated sport aimed to protect the integrity of women's competition. It operated under the logic that women, as the weaker and physically inferior sex, would not otherwise have a fair shot at winning medals.

Other concerns fueled calls for gender verification. The discovery at the 1936 Olympics Games in Berlin that female competitor Dora Retjen, a member of the Hitler Youth, was a man substantiated suspicions that men masqueraded as female competitors in order to win, even though Retjen placed fourth overall behind three women. During those Olympic Games, then-US Olympic Committee president Avery Brundage (who would become IOC president in 1952) vocalized his fear that "hermaphrodites" and athletes with "sex ambiguities" were competing in women's events, making the recommendation that all women entrants be physically examined to ensure that they were truly female. He also reportedly claimed that two unnamed athletes who had competed as women later underwent sex-change operations to become men, conveying the sentiment that they had intentionally cheated.[31] This prompted further public scrutiny of successful female athletes. For instance, questions around the sex of Helen Stephens, an American athlete, surfaced after she upset the legendary Polish athlete Stanislawa Walasiewicz, popularly known as Stella Walsh, in the 100-meter dash in 1936. Because of this speculation, Stephens submitted to a physical examination of her genitals, which served as evidence that she was a natural woman. Coincidentally, autopsy findings published after Walsh's tragic murder in 1980 indicated that she, in fact, had ambiguous genitalia.[32] The legacies of the controversy thus continued to live on well beyond competition, even death. In this case, the anatomical features of Walsh's body—and the assumption that they explained her athletic success—became the subject of public attention, not her accomplishments alone.

The speculative discourse surrounding female athletes and the threat of gender frauds in women's events was therefore well established decades prior to the IOC's introduction of scientific drug and gender-verification testing in the late 1960s. The advent of more systematic testing coincided with the inclusion of a record number of women's events in the Olympics, revealing that sport was no longer only a male domain. Despite being more inclusive, there was still a desire to preserve boundaries between the sexes and the belief that binary division was normal, if not natural. The implementation of gender-verification tests was one of the primary duties of the newly formed Medical Commission, which according to Brundage's successor, Lord Killanin, was to certify who was a natural—as opposed to an artificially enhanced—athlete and to "strive as far as it can against the creation of the artificial man or woman."[33] This statement was misleading, however: while drug testing resulted in the suspension of athletes who had used artificial substances, gender-verification tests took aim at participants' inherent biological characteristics. Women who failed tests were not unnatural, but were judged to be abnormal, even disordered.[34]

Female masculinity has emerged as an aesthetic marker of bodies suspected of being unfairly enhanced (either by steroids or biology). Rebecca Lock contends that such athletes' violation is that they appear grotesque because they embody a "mythical/stereotypical lesbian aesthetic"; that is, they are "offensive to the heterosexual gaze."[35] In short, the absence of normative femininity makes them look unreal, or unlike "true" women. The judgment of female masculinity as either unnatural or a lapse of nature reveals a co-constitutive moment in which "the dislike of the non-heterosexually feminine women" conjoins with the disdain of violating fair play.[36] Moreover, these heteronormative judgments are intertwined with naturalized beliefs about the gendered hierarchies of human capacity—that is, that women are physically inferior to men and should appear as such. Fair play may articulate its values as protecting natural bodies and detecting unnatural contaminations, but its primary preoccupation is not with artificiality per se but with the policing of socialized forms of difference.

The continued justification and inclusion of gender-verification practices under the umbrella of protecting a level playing field highlights how gendered norms around physical ability and embodiment are still influential. Visual judgments of athletes in women's events still have a regulatory function: they serve as the initial screening of who becomes deemed as suspect. To illustrate the continued role of aesthetics alongside the shifting terrains of sport and its regulation, let us comparatively consider two notable cases of athletes who gained notoriety for transgressing the terms of fair play and femininity, Caster Semenya, and Andreas (formerly Heidi) Krieger, a former European champion women's shot putter who testified in the 2000 trial of East German doctors and administrators about systematic doping and his gender identity. Taken together, they evidence not only gendered anxieties around the boundaries between women and men, but also the interrelated concern of how these seemingly transgressive bodies symbolize perceived threats to Global North (or first-world) hegemony.

Two Bodies of Evidence

By the age of eighteen, South African runner Caster Semenya had risen to prominence as competitive middle-distance runner. Because of her masculine physique, rumors circulated around her sex, but visual inspections of her genitals indicated that she was female.[37] In fact, in the hours prior to winning the 800-meter final at the 2009 International Association of Athletics Federations (IAAF) World Championships, she, unbeknownst to other competitors, underwent a gender test. After the race, accusations continued. Elisa Cusma Piccione, the sixth-place finisher from Italy, argued, "For me, she is not a woman. She is a man," while another competitor, Russia's Mariya Savinova, plainly stated, "Just look at her."[38] Commentators even characterized Semenya as "breathtakingly butch" after she crossed the finish line two seconds before the second-place finisher.[39] Although her time was not world-record pace, Semenya had improved her personal best by seven seconds in less than one year. Despite recognizing that she had started working with a world-class coach, the IAAF stated it was "obliged to investigate" further because such advances prompt suspicions of doping.[40]

Doping, however, was not a central concern for authorities. Gender was. The IAAF called for a more comprehensive gender-verification examination that included the analyses of Semenya's biological and psychological traits (although exact details were never made public). Over the next eleven months, during which Semenya could not compete, speculation continued, and news broke that the IAAF had preemptively instructed South African authorities to verify her sex prior to the World Championships. Doctors had conducted tests, but they did not disclose their reasons for doing so or their results to Semenya and had allowed her to compete in Berlin despite their concerns over the findings.[41] When controversy ensued after revelations of administrators lying about their knowledge of the tests, high-level officials were eventually forced to resign from their positions, including Athletics South Africa president Leonard Cheune.

In response to the IAAF investigations, many well-known South Africans came to Semenya's defense, including Winnie Madikizela-Mandela, one of Nelson Mandela's ex-wives and a member of Parliament; Noluthando Mayende Sibiya, the South African minister of women, children, and persons with disabilities; and Julius Malema, the president of the African National Congress Youth League. They publically condemned the authorities for their treatment of Semenya. Madikizela-Mandela announced, "I think it is the responsibility of South Africa to rally behind this child and tell the rest of the world she remains the hero she is and no one will take that away from her. . . . There is nothing wrong with being a hermaphrodite. It is God's creation. She is God's child." Mayende-Sibiya called upon South Africans to speak out, "She is our own. . . . You cannot be silent! The human rights of Caster have been violated."[42] Malema and the African National Congress Youth League issued statements that characterized these actions as a "racist attack," refusing "to accept the categorization of Caster Semenya as a hermaphrodite, because in South Africa and the entire world of sanity, such does not exist."[43] The defense of Semenya was also the defense of nation, particularly Semenya's position as a valued national hero and "true" female athlete citizen who represented South Africa. It was more than a defensive effort; it was an attack on authorities and Western worldviews.

Others drew parallels between Semenya's situation and earlier European preoccupations with Saartjie Baartman.[44] Baartman, better known as the

FIGURE 4.2 A cartoon capturing nationalistic sentiments and international tensions. Cartoon by Zapiro, 25 August 2009.

Hottentot Venus, was a Khoikhoi woman from South Africa who became an infamous human exhibit during the early 1800s because of the public fascination with her large buttocks and the rumors of her long labia. Although Semenya's body was not sexualized, many critics argued that Western observers had nonetheless fetishized her by focusing only on her physique. For them, her case emerged as a twenty-first-century instance of "white foreigners . . . yet again scrutinizing a black female body as though it did not contain a human being."[45] The scrutiny of Semenya's sex became understood as a form of postcolonial voyeurism, one that revealed an intolerance of human difference.[46] Moreover, as Cheryl Cooky, Ranissa Dycus, and Shari Dworkin found through a comparative content and textual analysis, the media coverage of the events diverged significantly between the United States and South Africa. Whereas both mainstream US and South African media privileged notions of binary sex, US media coverage privileged scientific knowledge and affirmed gender verification's legitimacy, and South African media coverage favored voices who evoked binary sex as a kind of defense against the Global North's racist beliefs about African women's bodies.[47]

When the IAAF finally announced that Semenya was "innocent of any wrongdoing" and able to compete again in women's events, it indicated that her medical records would remain confidential.[48] In framing this decision not as an apology but as an investigative finding, the IAAF's language still suggested that her body warranted suspicion. Seemingly cleared to compete without further hindrance, the decision also came with a caveat. IAAF general secretary Pierre Weiss added, "she is a woman but maybe not 100%."[49] In light of these comments, skepticism regarding Semenya's sex remained. When she returned to competition, rumors leaked that she was undergoing hormonal-therapy treatment, even though all information regarding the IAAF evaluation officially remained undisclosed.

Although Semenya's case highlights how aesthetic judgments, particularly those of Western authorities, came to bear on the debate around her participation, it is not the first time in which such an issue in women's sport showcased the interface between international politics and fair play. During the Cold War, female East German athletes were also accused of not being fully female or of being drug users. Their seemingly unnatural bodies appeared to reflect what many characterized as the evils of professionalism and the horrific possibilities of participating in a form of sport that values winning at all costs.[50] The fears of state-sponsored sport reflected critiques that communism had failed to incentivize hard work by providing shortcuts (such as doping), undermined individual enterprise, and repressed free will. To Western onlookers, female East German athletes embodied the unethical stance of communistic pursuits and of women seemingly going against their feminine nature.

The story of Andreas Krieger brings forth additional gendered dimensions to these narratives. As told in the 2008 documentary, *Doping: Factory of Champions*, years of doping as a female athlete had advanced his masculine affinities to the extent that he chose to undergo sex-reassignment surgery in 1997.[51] Other reports indicate that he felt that drugs had robbed him of the choice to determine his gender, which he had begun to question at a younger age.[52] Krieger, like his wife Ute Krause, a former East German swimmer, admits to taking anabolic steroids and other performance-enhancing substances through his athletic career, even though he received them from doctors and coaches without knowing what they were. Both Krieger and Krause testified about systematic doping during the 2000 trial that led to the criminal convictions of Manfred Hoeppner and Manfred Ewald on the grounds both men willingly inflicted bodily harm on athletes, including minors, during their tenure at the German Democratic Republic Olympic Committee.[53] As framed by the published transcripts of the trial, Krieger's testimony portrays systematic doping as the cause of him identifying himself as a man, doing so in a way that dismisses other likely complexities linked to making his choice—if it can be called that in this case—to undergo sex-reassignment surgery. Regardless of whether these narratives fully capture the nuances of his feelings, they point to how intertwined sex, gender, and athletic performance can feel. Steroids emerge not only as an artificial drug, but also as a cultural artifact of maleness that permeated then-Heidi's body.

Krieger's story also attests that doping and its regulation communicate gendered messages. Anti-doping rules are arguably more effective in policing gendered norms because diagnosing women's bodies as either doped or suspected of doping enables a condemnation of excess masculinity under an objective veneer of targeting drugs, not sex or gender. Despite being distinctly different offenses, they both mark instances of gendered excess being construed as an unnatural impurity. Krieger's recitation of his experience crystallizes how ideology becomes real and embodied, a point I will emphasize in relation to how IOC medical doctors have justified gender-verification tests.

Krieger's narrative often emerges as a tragedy in sport, even though he accepts his gender, has overcome severe emotional and physical challenges, and has a fulfilling relationship. There is even an award given to German athletes who combat doping in sport, the Heidi Krieger Medal, which is made from his 1986 European Championship gold medal and serves as a reminder that "she" is no more.[54] Irrespective of whether one reads his story as heartbreaking, enduring, or something in between, its messages draw attention to the extent to which the politics of fair play contribute to naturalizing the gendered categories into which we assume bodies should fit. Krieger is an embodied reminder of the interrelated relationships between sex, gender, and performance enhancement in sport and everyday life. His bodily changes send a discursive message that implies his participation in women's sport was a transgression that he too recognizes. Krieger's body, which came to voluntarily submit to hormonal treatments, emerges as a form of evidence regarding the dangers of excess masculinity in women's sport and communism's promotion of winning at all costs. It symbolizes the extreme that justifies anti-doping regulation.

Putting Krieger's narrative alongside Semenya's story, we can take away other insights. Both drug testing and gender verification enable the condemnation of female masculinity by reinforcing it as a violation of fair play in sport, regardless of whether or not it can be traced to a natural source. Aesthetic judgments, backed by the scientific testing, cast Semenya and Krieger (at least as then-Heidi) as committing a similar gendered violation against the naturalized boundary between women and men. What these narratives neglect, though, is how doctors have sought to police these boundaries through science and how gender verification both reflects and polices the naturalized beliefs about sex and gender that inform athlete citizenship.

Historical Diagnoses of "Not Fully Female" Athletes

The gender-verification practices that existed in sport prior to 1968 varied. In 1948, the British Women's Amateur Athletic Association required sex certificates that had to be completed by doctors, but some governing sport organizations also required the visual inspection of women's genitals because of suspicions that documents could be falsified. At the 1966 Commonwealth

Games, for example, a gynecologist conducted examinations of the external genitalia of all female entrants.[55] At the 1966 IAAF World Championships, officials visually inspected 243 female athletes, reporting no abnormalities.[56] These observations, later known as naked parades, also took place at 1967 European Cup final in Kiev and the Pan American Games in Canada.[57] In 1967, the members of the IOC Medical Commission began to consider how to standardize testing in a less intrusive way.

Although some international sport federations, like the IAAF, considered physical evaluations necessary, other governing sports bodies protested them. Writing to the IOC executive in 1967, Mr. Wlodzimierz Reczek, the president of the Polish Olympic Committee, expressed reservations about the "improper publicity, unnecessary discussions, and controversial opinions" prompted by tests: "Repeated gynecological examinations of the young girl athletes, even several times in the course of one year, make an unpleasant environment around those athletes and are a form of discrimination. Unfortunately it has happened also that facts were published openly, that should be protected by the discretion of the medical profession. That all fills one with indignation because it disaccords with elementary ethics. There are no generally accepted criteria of sex for woman athletes and the lightminded arbitrariness in the interpretation of the results of examinations may harm the examined persons."[58] Reczek suggested that Medical Commission members consult other doctors and sport specialists as it devised its gender-verification requirements. President Brundage's response, however, did not provide much assurance. He merely concurred: "[The subject] must be approached with great caution in order to avoid [an] unwarranted invasion of personal privacy. One examination should be enough and the arrangements must be very carefully made to prevent stigma on innocent persons."[59] In responding in such a way, Brundage again revealed his disdain of suspected gender frauds in women's events, implying that they were not innocent or worthy of protection from the stigma that could result from testing.

The members of the IOC Medical Commission did not necessarily share Brundage's beliefs. Jacques Thiébault, a member of the organizing committee for the 1968 Grenoble Games, viewed the task of gender verification as distinctly different from drug testing. He wrote, "Whereas doping implies an obvious attempt of fraud, sex controls merely are to establish a lapse of nature on creatures to be pitied, who will all their life remain inadapted, and who— through sports—probably tried to make a difficult entry into an often hostile and stupid society."[60] He addressed their dissimilarity as an issue of nature versus will. In other words, Thiébault recognized that biological sex as often being out of one's control, yet felt that one could choose to use drugs (although later testimony about systematic doping reveal his characterization was inaccurate). Contrasted to those later findings, Thiébault diagnosed the biology of these "hybrid" persons as a medicalized condition, a "lapse of nature," that transcended fair play. He went on, writing, "I believe that—above all other things, even the Olympic Games—we should place our duty as physicians and, should we come across such hybrid creatures, prescribe medical treatment if possible, or at least help them to accept their fate, as we try to do when we discover any other infirmity. . . . Our action will therefore never be intended to punish, but always to dissuade."[61] Note how Thiébault referred to these athletes as "hybrid creatures" as if they were an amalgamation of two distinctly different female and male sexes. As rendered, intersexuality was an unfortunate condition that required treatment. The Medical Commission framed the purpose of its gender-specific regulation as health related, despite the fact these athletes were healthy enough to excel at the demanding levels of international sport.

The Medical Commission, however, did not evenly apply this language of treatment. The committee agreed that "punishment" was too harsh a phraseology, as evidenced in meeting minutes and edits to policy documents.[62] Despite changes to official language, not allowing these athletes to participate in the Olympic Games rendered "treatment" as similar to "punishment" or "penalties" in practice, at least in a sport context. Although Thiébault indicated some sympathy for "hybrid" athletes, he expressed a more pressing concerns for "fully" female athletes, writing that "so-called women" were the record holders. "Sooner or later," he wrote, "the true representatives of the weak sex will feel cheated and claim the feminine records for themselves."[63] Accordingly, gender verification and anti-doping regulation were to safeguard "true" female competitors from unfair competition. The paternalistic desire to protect the weaker sex operated at the core of the commission's work. The ostracism of certain women resulted not necessarily from unabashed acts of discrimination,[64] but from the ingrained belief in two distinct sexes and that male or intersex bodies would contaminate the purity of women's sport. In this case, purity was not merely the notion of a level playing field, but a first-world feminine ideal.

The practice of testing thus perpetuated two evident myths: first, that being a natural athlete was a necessary requirement to compete in the Olympics; and second, that science could serve as a gatekeeper by identifying those who were artificial. Science also veiled the political dimensions of these claims, even though tests would target bodies for the most part that represented Eastern Bloc countries.

In terms of the actual tests used to verify the sex of female Olympians, the Medical Commission initially proposed to conduct a sexual chromatin test on samples of mucus taken orally from the top three finishers in women's events.[65] The cytological analysis of buccal smears seemed "simpler, objective and more dignified," and the commission promised to ensure athlete confidentiality.[66] This evaluation was intended to detect the presence of the Barr body (the inactive X chromatin) as proof of female sex. Originally "sex control" was proposed as the terminology for the testing regime. But Thiébault argued that "sex control" sounded "like the police" and favored "femininity tests" (*recherches sur la féminité*), because it covered "the particular characteristics of women without crudely evoking anatomical details."[67] This development did not change the fact that the Medical Commission did seek to police participants, but it did more accurately reflect the motivations behind gender verification; that is, to monitor the femininity of competitors in women's events.

The IOC, as well as the international sports federations that followed suit (which was necessary to maintain Olympic status), later mandated that all female athletes undergo gender verification and receive identity cards if they passed the tests.[68] On its surface, looking at chromosomal makeup seemed an accurate and noninvasive method, but it was not without faults. The test barred any competitors who had chromosomal markers considered nonnormative for women, even those who did not have male characteristics. For example, scientists speculated that the first woman disqualified for failing the test, Polish sprinter Ewa Klobukowska, had genetic mosaicism, an abnormality where one's cells have a different genetic makeup, which can have varying effects on development.[69] Although she had satisfied visual inspections, Klobukowska failed the chromosomal test. Stripped of her medals and condemned publically (despite the guarantee of confidentiality), she distanced herself from sport, never to return to competition. Some reports stated that she fell into a state of depression and underwent hormone therapy and surgery.[70] Others indicated that she actually later gave birth to a child.[71] What we do know of her life after sport is thus speculative at best.

Using the Barr body analysis invited other problems. Female competitors with androgen insensitivity syndrome (AIS) failed the tests, because findings revealed XY sex chromosomes.[72] If one follows the logic that maleness is a natural performance enhancer, these women actually competed at a biological disadvantage because they cannot recruit testosterone as most women can.[73] If male athletes had been subject to this test, those with an extra X chromosome (as in the case of Klinefelter's syndrome) would have qualified as female.[74] Although more dignified than naked parades, tests still imprecisely determined sex and could result in the degrading treatment of female athletes. Despite these discrepancies, the Medical Commission did not reconsider this particular test, nor did it establish an appeals process for athletes disqualified as a result of abnormal findings. Instead, the presumption that maleness was a performance enhancement became transposed incorrectly onto women's biological makeup.

Beyond this discrepancy, Brundage reportedly expressed satisfaction about the progress made during the first four years of implementation, stating that female athletes appeared "more feminine."[75] Although this was a subjective statement, six female competitors did withdraw following the approval of systematic gender-verification testing. Among them were the highly successful Soviet track and field athletes, Irina and Tamara Press.[76] The Press sisters had already become the subject of Western criticism, often being referred to in the US media as the "Press Brothers."[77] These insults added to existing allegations by journalists that they and other (male) Eastern Bloc athletes bound their genitals in order to compete as women. In light of these rumors, the Press sisters denied that gender-verification protocols were the reason for their absence. The situation demonstrated that the legacies of the Nazi Olympics thirty years earlier informed the discourse around female athletes' bodies, especially those representing nations perceived as threats to Western values.

Speculations did not only target women's bodies; there were also speculations over the IOC's intentions. In addition to documented concerns from some international sports federation officials, such as Reczek, the IOC received some negative media attention. For example, IOC administrators expressed particular concern over a German cartoon (which was reproduced in other countries) that depicted female athletes unwittingly standing at the entrance of a bedroom where male IOC officials awaited (presumably naked) in bed to sexually conduct "sex control" procedures. Its caption read, "I think you will be in agreement, ladies. We have finally found an ideal solution to the problem of controlling the sexes."[78] Although this jest targeted the IOC by suggesting there was an underlying perversion to the examinations of competitors in women's events, the sexual objectification of female athletes remained central in narrating the criticism. It also dismissed women's apprehensions surrounding the tests. Depicting women's bodies as voyeuristic sites, it echoed the heteronormative logics that justified the use of tests in the first place. The male gaze that prompted the need for gender verification went unchallenged, discursively promoting the notion that female athletes were to be heterosexually desirable.

Changes to Gender-Verification Techniques

In an effort to more precisely detect so-called gender frauds in women's sports, the science behind gender verification changed over the years. In 1991, the IOC replaced the Barr body test with a polymerase chain reaction (PCR) test, which analyzes the aspects of DNA linked with testes growth.[79] This development marked a shift in evaluating scientific evidence of womanhood: the chromatin test had focused on evidence of female chromosomal patterns (XX), but the PCR focused on markers of maleness by testing for the genetic makeup of the Y chromosome. In essence, the change in rationale meant that female athletes no longer had to prove that they were women but that they were not—at least in part—male.[80] The introduction of newer methods suggested more accurate testing, but they did not result in greater effectiveness.

The events that would inform the change to the PCR test can be traced to controversial disqualifications based on failed gender-verification tests. The case of Spanish hurdler María Martínez-Patiño in 1985 was among the most notable disqualifications under the Barr body test. Despite looking like other competitors and having comparable strength, power, and speed, Martínez-Patiño tested as "not fully female" due to AIS. She would become the first disqualified athlete to regain her status as a woman, but it came at a price.[81] Recounting the aftermath, she wrote, "I was told to feign an injury and to withdraw from racing quietly, graciously, and permanently. I refused. When I crossed the line first in the 60 m hurdles, my story was leaked to the press. I was expelled from our athletes' residence, my sports scholarship was revoked, and my running times were erased from my country's athletics records. I felt ashamed and embarrassed. I lost friends, my fiancé, hope and energy. But I knew that I was a woman, and that my genetic difference gave me no unfair physical advantage. I could hardly pretend to be a man; I have breasts and a vagina. I never cheated."[82]

Martínez-Patiño's appeal—that she was just a normal woman without any masculine advantages or traits—proved compelling. She did not embody the transgressive muscularity associated with Eastern Bloc female athletes, yet tests determined that she was ineligible. Had she been subject to naked parades, this situation would not have arisen. This twist revealed, almost ironically, how certain forms of evidence were visible and knowable through one kind of test (e.g., visual inspection), but as the terms of new testing technologies became accepted (e.g., Barr body analysis), those earlier observations were no longer as visible; in a sense, they ceased to exist—at least as the formal grounds for disqualification. Scientific testing had essentially changed the terms of female athlete citizenship, catching those who did not appear to be gender frauds. The success of Martínez-Patiño's appeal, however, suggests that authorities recognized, at least to a certain extent, that science did not deliver the outcomes that regulators intended, prompting a need to change its testing measures.

Just as the IOC opted to use the PCR test, the IAAF revisited issues related to gender verification. After meetings in 1990 and 1992, the IAAF decided that athletes should be reinstated if it could be determined that they had no advantages stemming from their male attributes.[83] When eight women at the 1996 Olympics failed tests (seven due to AIS), follow-up evaluations concluded that they were resistant to the effects of androgens and could thus compete in accordance with the IAAF's rationalization.[84] In light of technical and ethical concerns stemming from these tests,[85] the IOC Executive Board accepted the Commission's recommendations and decided to end compulsory gender-verification testing at the 2000 Olympic Games in Sydney on a trial basis. Moving forward, IOC and IAAF authorities adopted a selective approach to gender verification, implementing it only when an athlete appeared suspect. This policy led to Indian runner Santhi Soundarajan's disqualification from women's sport in 2006, which also resulted in the loss of her Asian Games silver medal and in her public humiliation. Even though she was later diagnosed with AIS, her medal was not restored, and she did not return to competition.[86] Even though an exception had been made for Martínez-Patiño and other Olympic athletes, Soundarajan, a representative of the Global South, did not receive the same accommodation, or even an apology.

With these suspicion-based criteria still in place, aesthetic judgments of femininity remain important facets of gender verification. The failures of testing highlight the explicit desire—and inability—to preserve the divide between women and men through science. Like the Two Great Divides that Latour describes between science/culture and nature and between the so-called premodern and modern eras, science's attempt to police the unfounded partition between men and women is a symptom of modernity that carries problematic consequences.[87] In this context, science cannot find the pure marker of womanness that it seeks, because it is a nature-culture hybrid notion, not a natural boundary. The desire to protect this ideal in the name of nature retains a culturally inscribed impurity, as does the belief that intersex people are male-female hybrids. The ideal is an impurity embedded in athlete citizenship.

Policing the Gendered Divide in Sport Today

During recent meetings that led to the revisions in gender verification, medical doctors reportedly concurred that "athletes who identify themselves as female but have medical disorders that give them masculine characteristics should have their disorders diagnosed and treated."[88] Even though this policy significantly limits the number of women subjected to gender verification, its framing of certain intersexed conditions as biological disorders, not as biological advantages, is nonetheless similar to Thiébault's 1968 recommendations. Both suggest the need to treat women deemed to be abnormal. Although the current policy continues the history of gender verification, there is a notable qualifier. As past forms of sex testing have "discovered" more variability than originally anticipated, guidelines have come to reflect the recognition that sex is not reducible to the presence or absence of a Y chromosome (or an inactive X chromosome) as often erroneously believed. Relying upon a testosterone threshold appears to allow for more variability than chromosomal testing, but it still upholds a finite limit, a border. In seeking to find the a priori boundary between women and men, gender-verification testing has constructed and reconfigured the limits of who can be a competitor in women's events, not discovered them. Although preserving this binary, sport-specific policies have changed—and notably so. This section considers gender verification in relation to other regulatory practices aimed at fair play, highlighting how the gendered implications of athlete citizenship surpass gender-verification testing.

In the last decade, IOC doctors and scientists have adjusted rules to recognize transgendered individuals and allow for limited transsexual participation. These practices entail only qualified forms of inclusion, however. Gender verification draws attention to the fact that intersex athletes competing in women's events are ineligible in terms of Olympic participation without some kind of medical intervention and hormonal therapy—if they are suspected to be "too male." Similarly, the rules for transgendered athletes are narrowly circumscribed around medical and scientific conditions.[89] Transsexual athletes may participate in the Olympic Games if they meet the three conditions of the Stockholm Consensus:

- Surgical anatomical changes have been completed, including external genitalia changes and gonadectomy;
- legal recognition of their assigned sex has been conferred by the appropriate official authorities; and
- hormonal therapy appropriate for the assigned sex has been administered in a verifiable manner and for a sufficient length of time to minimize gender-related advantages in sport competitions[90]

As noted here, medical science can ensure that an athlete satisfies the two prongs, but not the issue of legal recognition, which can be problematic for athletes who face social or legal obstacles. Law is thus also a necessary barrier to consider, but it is also one that is increasingly complicated, especially as some countries, such as Nepal, Pakistan, and Germany, formally recognize more than two genders.[91]

Even though the Stockholm Consensus is written in a way that considers both sexes, it still upholds the advantage thesis described by Cavanagh and Sykes. As "gender-related advantages" that would undermine sports competition are often—but not exclusively—ascribed to biological maleness, Sarah Teetzel observes, the logic behind the Stockholm Consensus renders the chosen gender as presumably female.[92] Accordingly, it is not surprising that governing sports bodies such as the IAAF have implemented specific gender-verification policies that target athletes who have undergone male-to-female sex-reassignment surgery.

Under the Stockholm Consensus, a different dilemma can emerge for athletes born female who identify as male. To compete in men's sports, they must undergo sex-reassignment surgery, but if they compete in women's events, they must forego hormonal treatments and sex-reassignment surgery, as openly transgender American athlete Keelin Godsey did (although failing to qualify for the 2012 Olympics). Reflecting on these dynamics, Grodsey, a competitor in hammer, has stated, "I take a lot of pride in the fact that I have a good amount of muscle mass, and I've done it naturally," adding, "but in some ways, this is the last body I would ever want."[93] Beyond competition he lives as a man. "I'm a female when I compete," Godsey has explained in a *Sports Illustrated* interview. "Every day I have to sweat, stress, and freak out. How do I look? What is someone going to think of me? Is someone going to say something at a track meet?" Although Godsey made the choice not to undergo sex-reassignment surgery prior to the Olympics, he still faced everyday challenges and could not live in the body he chooses.

Beyond the rules explicitly aimed at transgendered participation or gender verification, anti-doping practices also police sex and gender, which the case of Andreas Krieger illustrates.[94] Drug-testing protocols require athletes to submit to a different kind of naked parade during the collection process, as officials observe athletes while they are urinating to ensure that they do not alter samples. Again, the underlying rationale is the protection of sport's integrity; however, precisely because this regulation is not explicitly earmarked as gender verification, it enables officials to visually observe athletes' genitals even if they are not considered suspect.[95] It is common knowledge among athletes that drug testing requires "being naked from the nipple down."[96] This kind of scrutiny allegedly substantiated the need to conduct the tests that led to Soundarajan's disqualification.[97] Further, anti-doping regulation circumscribes gender at the hormonal level. It states that if ratios between testosterone and epitestosterone fall outside the "normal" range (currently 4:1, lowered from 6:1), athletes are suspected to have doped. Current gender-verification guidelines add another qualification for women who are determined to be suspect, as their testosterone levels must also fall below a designated threshold.

These technocratic rules work alongside, and discursively promote, forms of "muscular management" that mediate tensions between maximizing one's physical capabilities and feminine conventions.[98] As analyses of women's body-building attest, aesthetic judgments of competitors straddle what Marcia Ian describes as "an (undefined) standard," and there is a tipping point at which too muscularity is a detriment.[99] The threat of this possibility encourages forms of feminine counterbalancing. Similarly, "female apologetic" behaviors in sport include corrective tactics to divert accusations of "manliness," lesbianism, and abnormality.[100]

Take, for example, former world record holder Florence Griffith-Joyner ("Flo Jo"), a highly successful African American sprinter known for her muscularity, athletic ability, and hyperfeminine accoutrements, including long acrylic nails, hair extensions, and bright makeup. Her death at the age of

FIGURE 4.3 Florence Griffith-Joyner after she won the final of the women's 100-meter race at the Seoul Olympics in 1988. Photo by Tony Duffy/Allsport/Getty Images.

thirty-eight added to speculation over her alleged steroid use; however, the autopsy report indicated that her death stemmed from an epileptic seizure. Taking place while she slept, it tragically resulted in Flo Jo being suffocated by her bedding.[101] In addition, there were no findings of banned substances in her system, only trace amounts of over-the-counter medications. Despite this fact, reports often provided a caveat, citing a statement by anti-doping expert Charles Yesalis that postmortem testing would likely not yield evidence of doping, as she had retired from sprinting nearly ten years prior to her death. Flo Jo remained suspect, even as grieving family members asked that speculation be put to rest.[102]

Conflicted accounts over Flo Jo's body and abilities often overshadow the circumstances of her death. According to three-time Olympian Pat Connolly, Flo Jo's body transformed "almost overnight. . . . Florence's face changed—hardened along with her muscles that now bulged. . . . It was difficult not to wonder if she had found herself an East German coach and was taking some kind of performance-enhancing drugs."[103] Even though performance-enhancing drugs have also been developed and used in the United States, this statement still ascribes their source to Eastern Bloc countries.[104] Not only are steroids rendered as a foreign contaminant to the body, but it is also a foreign contaminant to the nation. In contrast to this portrayal, other depictions of Flo Jo represent her as an "icon of exotic otherness" with "long, thick curly hair; lean arms and torso; thick, muscular legs; and dark skin" that, combined with her "physical transgressions"—her speed, power, and athletic prowess—made her "an object of desire."[105] Irrespective of doping suspicions, Flo Jo, like other African American sportswomen, was often cast as abnormal, even animal-like, versus her white counterparts.[106]

As in the case of East German women, albeit through a very different depiction, Flo Jo's alleged doping was marked by her violation of (white) gender normativity, even though it was masked by her apologetic appearance and never confirmed by testing. For CL Cole and Alex Mobley, post–Cold War speculation aimed at her and other black bodies is "a well-established rhetorical device" used "to stabilize America's ideal of itself and to establish the purity of U.S. national femininity."[107] The skepticism around Soundarajan in 2006 and Semenya in 2009 reinforce the point that racialized bodies have come to fill the vacancy left by East German and Soviet Bloc women, even though they were not caught doping. The intersectional contours of Soundarajan's and Semenya's cases rendered neither as a desirable other. Unlike Flo Jo, they never transitioned from being "natural" women to embodying a seemingly unnatural and suspect condition. Instead, their very nature came under scrutiny. Thus, even though these female athlete citizens of the Global South are permitted to compete in Olympic and international sport—unimaginable in Pierre de Courbertin's vision for the Olympics—they, like their Eastern Bloc predecessors, are still rendered inherently suspect in the eyes of authorities in the Global North.

Athlete citizenship has always been shaped in part by postcolonial politics, which often favor the values and preferences of the Global North. In the cases of Soundarajan and Semenya, their home nations came to their defense amid Western criticisms of their bodies and abilities, claiming them both as rightful and dutiful national citizens. Tamil Nadu government officials expressed sadness and insult at Soundarajan's disqualification and provided her with compensation.[108] By contrast, in levying charges of racism at the IAAF, South African leaders evoked a paternalistic defense of their "daughter." As Julius Malema explained, "As in any other country, parents look at new babies and can see straight away whether to raise them as a boy or a girl.... They are doubting the parents of this child and questioning the way they brought her up. God has his say on what people are.... A young girl has no input as she enters the world on what she will look like."[109] Despite Malema's statement, a photo spread in the South African magazine *You!* portrayed Semenya as a female apologetic, featuring her wearing a skirt and makeup with her hair styled. This display did not end public speculation from the Global North. Rather, the photo and story sustained it, as many Western media reports focused on how "abnormal" and "unnatural" she appeared in feminine dress.[110] South African media, however, did not—and had not—questioned her sex.[111]

Western scrutiny persisted as Semenya won her first three races when she returned to competition in 2010. When she went on to lose other races, conjectures emerged that hormonal therapies had effectively mediated her male characteristics, even though she never confirmed undergoing treatment. Even though Semenya won the silver medal in the 2012 London Olympics, she still occupied a bind: if she wins, she faces accusations that she has an unfair biological advantage; if she loses, spectators may presume that she undertook treatment to minimize her advantages, thereby seeming to prove accusations of her intersexuality and its unfair attributes.[112] The possibilities that she would win despite the influence of treatments or lose without treatments appear foreclosed.

Protecting Gendered Myths about Ability in Sport

The history of gender verification suggests that what distinguishes good from bad athletic performance is not what is or is not artificial but what appears seemingly unnatural to the gaze of overseeing authorities and the cultural conditions that color how they see their worlds. The treatment of athletes characterized as traversing the divide between women and men draws attention to the very real consequences of the imagined constructions of female purity as they have taken shape alongside historically contingent gendered and nationalistic formations. The technocratic tools intended to uphold rigid boundaries have only proven that a static articulation of binary sex is not founded. Despite evidence against steadfast binary sex, these gendered myths still grip sport, and regulatory doctrines targeting fair play constitutively preserve sex segregation in sport.

Even though the new age in gender verification continues the scientific veiling of myths around sex and gender, some, including Martínez-Patiño, have suggested that current guidelines may offer a more humane solution for female athletes who come under scrutiny.[113] While these proposals espouse advanced scientific testing, specialized medical treatment, and athlete confidentiality (something the IOC has promised in the past but failed to ensure), they still advocate that science should "fix" the lived mode of sex to better reflect its cultural mode. For example, between 2012 and 2013, at least three women from the Global South were investigated, found to have higher levels of testosterone, and then agreed to undergo irreversible and medically unnecessary surgeries in order to remain eligible to compete in sport.[114] The guidelines may have other consequences as well, including effects on rules around transgendered participation. As Claire Sullivan acknowledges, current rules could result in transsexual athletes not meeting some requirements or having to verify their gender more than once.[115] Accordingly, the IAAF, the first international sport federation to adopt the IOC guidelines, has abandoned its previous gender-verification policy altogether. Sullivan speculates that other governing sports bodies will follow this precedent, a prediction backed by historical precedent.

Stepping back from these details, we might ask whether testosterone is significantly different from the other physical advantages that many athletes— male and female—may have in their respective sports.[116] For many regulators, doctors, athletes, and spectators, indicators of maleness found in women are important to nullify, but why? Fair play is the common answer, but upon further review, it appears an artifice, one that contains interrelated paradoxes. Gender requirements prevail even though scientific gender-verifications practices reveal their own inaccuracies. The scientific practices undergirding fair play evade the very irrationality they expose: that the yearning for sex to reflect gender is a social, not natural, construct, a desired impurity.

In other areas of sport, however, scientific findings have prompted regulatory change, even a reversal in stance. Chapter 2's overview of the history of drug testing, for example, highlights how the prohibited list has changed to adapt to scientific findings. Substances have also been removed if scientific evidence or lobbying by stakeholders convincingly indicates that it does not to have a substantial impact. Another comparable example that marks these gendered distinctions is the speculation around Oscar Pistorius's petition to compete against able-bodied peers. Pistorius is widely characterized as the fastest man without legs.[117] An accomplished Paralympic and Olympic sprinter who runs using carbon-fiber prostheses that look like blades, his ability came under scrutiny when he petitioned to complete against able-bodied athletes. Questions arose around whether or not his prostheses gave him an unfair (unnatural) advantage over other (presumably natural) able-bodied athletes. The IAAF initially ruled that Pistorius did have an unfair advantage because scientific findings indicated that they enabled him to expend less energy than able-bodied athletes. Following his appeal, the Court of Arbitration in Sport questioned the validity of the science behind that argument, ruling that Pistorius's choice to compete against able-bodied peers did not undermine a level playing field.[118]

As such concerns were not expressed in relation to his Paralympic participation, Leslie Swartz and Brian Watermeyer argue that anxieties around Pistorius did not center around fair play but rather around his ability to "move from one discursive meaning system, where he may be seen to belong [the 'disabled'], to another . . . based on his personal prowess of a bodily nature"; this ability "serves to shake the very foundations of the attribution system which maintains the separation as meaningful."[119] His case illustrates how concerns about fair play relate to broader tensions around the boundaries between what constitutes a natural, human body and an artificial one.[120] Similar to the ruling on Pistorius's Olympic participation and anti-doping regulation, scientific findings of gender verification justify decisions regarding whether certain bodies comply with or transgress the terms of what we refer to as fair play. Fair play, however, appears to be a stand-in that justifies naturalized, not natural, difference. Moreover, many women who have so-called disorders of sexual development that violate current gender-verification guidelines do not necessarily know that they have a possible advantages over other women, whereas the individual use of performance-enhancing drugs—and even the use of modified prostheses—suggests an agentive act to achieve an advantage. Framing the issue of fair play in women's competition as an issue of ability and disability, it is clear that anxieties remain in relation to participants whose abilities surpass the abilities of so-called "normal" women.

Despite changes to gender-verification guidelines, there remains speculation over women's physiques. The scientifically backed delineation of the weaker sex only directly applies to those suspect women whose testosterone levels fall under the designated threshold. Moreover, while gender-verification practices have changed, they still mandate that athletes diagnosed as "too able" to be women in the context of sport alter their bodies in order to participate as female athletes. Visual judgments by onlookers from the Global North remain a key (and subjective) criterion used to determine who qualifies as a woman in sport. Further, naked parades still prevail under anti-doping rules, making regulation an enduring gatekeeper of the boundary between women and men.

Gender verification reinscribes the need for sex segregation under the guise that gendered divisions ensure fair play, even though skills, size, or other biochemical measures could serve as alternatives for organizing competition. Others who have provided similar analyses have rejected gender verification on the grounds that it is degrading to women.[121] Although this point is well taken, gender-verification testing—and the multiple regulatory formations that support these practices—do much more. They posit impurities about human bodies and their abilities, fabrications sustained by the myths about sex that continue to inform our understandings of fair play. Even though testing has provided scientific evidence of these impurities, authorities continue to make prescriptions that biological sex should align with these gendered myths.

These issues, in turn, reveal how the gendered terms of athlete citizenship renders non-Western bodies as suspect, making them more likely to be characterized as nonnormative outlaws who cannot obtain the status of athlete citizenship. Not only is there a history of transgression against women deemed transgressive in international sport, scientifically backed regulation buttresses powerful gendered ideologies that posit impurities about the relationships between sex and gender. Although the future under current gender-verification guidelines is not yet known, the history of medically treating intersex individuals beyond sport suggests that these more "humane" actions may not be as they portend.[122] Moreover, as the cases of particular outlawed female athletes reveal, international and national politics shape the conditions and narratives of these judgments, not scientific and legal mechanisms alone.

Thus, anti-doping regulation and gender verification, especially when read together as conjoined practices of gatekeeping fair play in sport, evidence how Olympic ideologies and their postcolonial underpinning continue to haunt how regulators continue to assess and determine which athletes are deemed to be transgressors. Like the racialized presumptions that aid in framing professional US athletes as inherently immoral discussed in chapter 3, racialized differences also surface in the speculative judgments of female athlete's bodies as well. While the intersectional conditions discussed here make the particular cases of individual women discussed in this chapter notably different, they occupy a common suspect status, one that is informed by Western skepticisms that their performances are unfairly enhanced. Similar to the characterizations of many male US professional athletes, the fact that their performances are exceptional and that their bodies do not appear normative to Eurocentric sensibilities makes them suspicious. In addition, these perceptions reveal that the essence of "pure" sport remains—and never was—"pure" in the sense that Coubertin and other advocates assert. Sport maintains and preserves inherent impurities, even as testing detects contaminates and natural advantages deemed to be unfair.

5

A Pure Playing
Field Nation

---●

The Curious Case of
New Zealand

Thus far in this book I have described how contradictions underpinning anti-doping regulation and athlete citizenship surface in embodied, national, and international ways by using examples from international sport. As sport contributes significantly to "meanings and symbols associated with national life," this chapter examines how the conditions of the anti-doping regime impact and mediate athlete citizenship at the national level.[1] As many athlete citizens compete in international competitions their respective nations have a vested interest in regulating their bodies. If athletes fail to live up to regulatory expectations of their own volition, national anti-doping systems can punish them or help to them comply with regulatory requirements. New Zealand, one of the first countries to become a signatory of the UNESCO Convention against Doping in Sport, offers a clear example of a jurisdiction that actively pursues its mandate to help athletes comply with the World Anti-Doping Code. In doing so, it demonstrates how international anti-doping rules become *vernacularized*, or "adapted by local institutions and meanings,"[2] as well as how nationalistic factors come to inform the implementation process. As a result, dilemmas of national citizenship coalesce and merge with the aforementioned concerns of athlete citizenship.

As a site, New Zealand offers a unique case study for the following reasons: it has a well-established national anti-doping system, including one of the few national sports tribunals in the world. New Zealand is also noted for its diversity, which includes persons of indigenous (Māori), European, Pacific, and Asian heritage, and the national recognition of cultural difference. I thus wanted to understand whether and how these national dynamics affected the delivery of sport-specific programming, particularly anti-doping regulation. After spending months in New Zealand, it became clear that helping athletes achieve compliance emerged as a more pressing concern than ensuring that anti-doping messages resonated in culturally meaningful ways. Regulation linked anti-doping values with the national agendas of purity, doing so in a way that held athletes accountable to Western values of individuality and self-discipline.

In keeping with international requirements, punishments for anti-doping rule violations were also often more punitive than those levied by the national justice system, even for the same offense, reinforcing distinctions between athlete citizens and the rest of the population. Moreover, instead of instances of athletes cheating, the majority of anti-doping rule violations stemmed from the recreational use of illicit drugs, namely marijuana. In short, the bodies condemned for doping make up a population that includes many more than those considered cheaters. This chapter analyzes how the surveillance and punishment of athletes demonstrate how the anti-doping system values a particular kind of responsible athlete citizen, a process that underscores how stratified biomedicalization comes to reflect other national, socio-economic, and racialized inequalities.

A Pure Playing Field Nation

In 2008, a press release about the Pure Playing Field Nation (PPFN) campaign caught my eye. Sponsored by Drug Free Sport New Zealand (DFSNZ), the Crown entity that oversees national anti-doping activities, the campaign sought to rally athletes to take a stand against doping in sport. It did so by having them sign the "PPFN Wall," a portable fence taken across the country to garner support. The press release quoted DFSNZ chief executive Graeme Steel as saying,

> We've deliberately chosen something that looks like your average Kiwi[3] backyard fence, because we wanted to stress that clean sport is one of our country's key values. We expect that huge numbers of Kiwis will agree with us and will want to add their names to the wall. . . . We need to buffer the next generation against these pressures [to dope] and provide them with tools to resist. One of our strengths is that our athletes tend to be firmly aligned with their communities

and clubs. That makes them part of a culture that largely objects to drugs. Pure Playing Field Nation is a way of strengthening that culture.[4]

The effort evoked nationalism to promote a message of bodily purity, and the message's appeal to "everyday" Kiwi values—or what regulators presupposed those values to be—served as a tactic to discourage drug use. Being a pure athlete—that is, one who does not use drugs—was part of being a dutiful athlete, citizen, and community member. In contrast, doping emerged as a shortcut that disregards civic values.

As the PPFN campaign suggests, athletes are to reflect the strength of the country's values and its commitment against drugs. Athletes are to be uncontaminated by physical or moral traces of cheating. In this way, Kiwi nationalism and purity emerge as compatible values; however, accompanying them are assimilatory messages. For example, the symbolism of the white picket fence as an ordinary object was striking to me as an outsider. As I read the press release, I found myself asking: to whom does this backyard fence appeal? All New Zealanders? And, what kinds of communal values do all Kiwis share? Although a small island nation of a little over four million people, New Zealand is not simply a place of rolling hills, peaceful sheep, and hardworking farmers. During my travels from Auckland, New Zealand's largest metropolis, to its South Island, I had seen distinct differences across both physical and cultural landscapes.

There was a notable absence of these kinds of white picket fences in Auckland, a central hub where many immigrants to New Zealand reside, especially migrants from Asia and neighboring Pacific Island nations.[5] In fact, some of these areas, particularly South Auckland where many Pacific Islander and Māori residents live, receive significant levels of negative attention, as popular culture and news reports often cast them as synonymous with the "hard" aspects of urban life—that is, higher rates of crime, poverty, and a foreboding sense of nihilism. During my initial visit to New Zealand, one (rather accomplished) athlete, Rubin, denounced these negative depictions. He explained that Auckland should be a source of national pride because it revealed the promise of multiculturalism. He characterized the city as home to "people coming from all over. People come here to try to make a better life for themselves, just like my family."[6] For him, New Zealand was, or at least should be, a country that embraces its diversity. "You see," he said, "a lot of people who grew up in New Zealand all their lives just don't get it. [They don't understand how] a lot of people struggle just to get here and stay here for their families. If they did, they wouldn't be so critical of different people from other places."

Rubin's allusion to a popular disdain of (non-white) ethnic difference would become a reoccurring theme throughout my research in New Zealand. These observations often crystallized around the treatment of Pacific Islander athletes, an increasingly visible population in high-level sport in New Zealand.[7] These intolerant expressions did not always emerge as explicit forms of discrimination. In fact, they often surface while celebrating ethnic and cultural diversity. In relation to the PPFN campaign, for example, the image of a white picket fence as emblematic of normal Kiwi values tacitly dismisses the norms and realities of many immigrants and urban dwellers, while also prescribing value judgments of what *should* be normal for New Zealanders. Like the PPFN representation, many other messages attempting to dissuade doping disregard ethnic and cultural difference discursively. Anti-doping regulation thus communicates not only the Western values embedded in the World Anti-Doping Agency's requirements, but also those that percolate from national legacies.

New Zealand's history is fraught with anxieties around its immigrating populations. According to Nan Seuffert's analysis of its colonial history, "national identity is both creative and dangerous" because "colonial tropes reshape and return like kaleidoscopic reconfigurations, recognizable repetitions of patterns, differentially figured, shaped and colored."[8] There are, for instance, ongoing efforts to reorient New Zealand's monocultural nationalism, which reflected Anglo-European (*pākehā*[9]) interests, toward a more inclusive "Aotearoa New Zealand" that values indigenous, or Māori[10], cultural beliefs equally. Such gestures may assert Māori and pākehā values as equal, but they do not remove or remedy colonial legacies. Further, as the PPFN example attests, pākehā values still strongly inform the expectation of what it is to be Kiwi.[11]

Despite its shortcomings, this national stance is notable in the sense that it responds formally to the country's historical legacies of deception and disavowal. The Treaty of Waitangi (Tiriti o Waitangi in Māori), signed in 1840, is a significant example. In many narrations of national history, the treaty marks the moment in which Māori people ceded sovereignty. While the English version of the treaty suggests such is the case, analyses of the signed Māori versions acknowledge that the British would maintain self-governance while upholding a doctrine of Māori self-determination (*te rangatiratanga*). In 1975, a permanent commission of inquiry, the Waitangi Tribunal, received its charge to investigate these claims, recognizing the Crown's legal authority and Māori power over resources.[12] Changing bureaucratic relations and public discourse have rendered Māori people in a "unique ethnic space" as the "indigenous people that the postcolonial state has failed."[13] The New Zealand government is now responsible for protecting Māori culture and language. While it is a significant step, critics argue that the focus on these efforts veils other ways through which the government encourages Māori conformity to Anglo-European norms.[14] These criticisms carry weight, especially when considering how New Zealand's government went about encouraging Māori inclusion. Neoliberal economic policies and incentives for Māori entrepreneurship have anchored the methods used to encourage indigenous economic and social mobility. Thus, in practice, reforms have upheld Anglo-European values through the promotion of capitalistic developmental models rooted in Calvinist ethics of individuality, free will, and economic liberalism.[15] Moreover, policies have not succeeded in leveling the economic playing field.[16]

This "focus on the bicultural context of New Zealand," argues Roannie Ng Shiu, often overshadows "the representational rights of Pacific communities and other minorities" by locating them "in an ambiguous position in New Zealand."[17] Forms of marginalization include overt acts. For example, immigration law has ostracized some of these populations, particularly Samoan residents (including those who are legally present), by declaring them "overstayers."[18] New Zealand's longstanding occupation of Samoa had extended many benefits of citizenship for Samoans, including the ability to work and reside in New Zealand; however the recession of the 1970s prompted the New Zealand government to alter its position. The propagated rhetoric of "immigrants taking jobs from 'real' New Zealanders" took on racial contours in which the "immigrant was conflated with the Pacific Islander."[19] The government, using these dynamics as political capital, mandated stricter immigration policies. Although aimed at all illegal immigrants (including white Europeans), the rhetoric reinforced the image of the overstayer as a Pacific Islander, even though the government acknowledgment that of the nearly ten thousand illegal immigrants in New Zealand, less than a third was of Pacific descent.[20] The stricter policies also left many Samoan immigrants and their extended families in a position of displacement after years of residing in New Zealand and establishing communities. Facing legal challenges to these policies, the government pushed through the Citizenship Act of 1982, which sought to ensure that Samoan people would not receive full citizenship rights. Further discrimination ensued with dawn raids where immigration officers would target the homes of immigrants for removal.

The negative overstayer stereotype still lingers in the New Zealand imagination. Pacific Islanders are sometimes characterized as taking jobs that should go to "proper" citizens or are stigmatized as reliant upon the state-provided forms of charity or welfare,[21] all of which implies that they undeservedly take from other citizens who provide. Nancy Fraser and Linda Gordon have argued that such rhetoric "posits an ideal, independent personality in contrast to which those considered dependent are deviant."[22] Through the condemnation of a Pacific Islander outsider, the normative ideals of "true" citizenship surface as pākehā values. This racial logic plays out almost ironically: Although Pacific Islander residents are often depicted as overstayers, British residents were the first overstayers on the lands that later became New Zealand.

Sport, a visible aspect of popular culture, is another arena that articulates national anxieties and expresses a postcolonial sensibility, a "replication of *home*" that "bespeaks comfort" to the colonizer, even when recognizing ethnic difference.[23] As Radhika Mohanram explains, "Home and nation must be evoked. New Zealand must function as Britain . . . as a tabula rasa—a blank page—for her people in diasporas to inscribe their lives upon."[24] In this chapter, I reflect on how popular expressions of Kiwi nationalism portray New Zealand as tolerant and encouraging of ethnic difference, while attending to embedded contradictions that emerge. I then consider how anti-doping regulation, by carrying out the terms of international guidelines imbued with Western values, reward and instill pākehā values, even as they claim to celebrate the ethnic and cultural differences that make up Aotearoa New Zealand.

New Zealand as an Active Sporting Nation

New Zealand's sporting heritage reflects the aforementioned shifting dynamics around race, representation, and nation, but in doing so, it also takes on explicitly gendered dimensions through the privileging of male bodies.[25] Consider rugby union, a national passion often portrayed as a site of ethnic inclusion in New Zealand. New Zealand is a perennial force with its men's team, the All Blacks, and its women's team, the Black Ferns, routinely considered the best in the world. While there are separate New Zealand Māori representative teams,[26] the most visible display of Māori recognition circulated globally, even beyond rugby, is the All Blacks' pre-game *haka*,[27] which is a ceremonial dance performed by players before every test match. Often mistaken as merely a war dance, the haka is recognizable in part because of advertisements launched by Adidas, the All Blacks' corporate sponsor.[28]

Ty P. Kāwika Tengan and Jesse Makani Markham explain that the "colonization of the haka as a 'national' symbol" is deeply problematic.[29] It erases "the histories of oppression in which Māori, though not passive, were far from equal participants in the structuring of colonial society," and the presence of many "Māori and non-Māori Pacific Islanders in the team" also contributes to "the appearance of equality."[30] Specifically, they argue, the visibility of these men "in many ways works to mask the underlying tensions still extant as Polynesian men compete on and off the field."[31] The All Blacks, instead, present as an image of reconciliation that serves as a source of national pride, and their athletic performances emerge as superior in part because of ethnic blending enabled by the country's embrace of diversity. Similarly, Brendan Hokowhitu has described sport in New Zealand as a site of "positive racism," particularly in the ways it depicts and rewards Māori men (*tāne*).[32] This "positive racism," he argues, reinforces negative stereotypes: whereas stereotypes of Māori aggression and physicality often portray these men as violent, sport embraces these tendencies in a positive light. Although framed as beneficial attributes for sport, these characterizations nonetheless reinforce truth-claims about their innate physical prowess. In being encouraged to pursue sport and other physically laborious careers, Māori men also can become discouraged from education, revealing a contemporary class divide that retains elements of the divisions between working-class participants and educated elites that Pierre de Coubertin and others of his era embraced. Distinct here, however, are the evident racial undertones and their linkages to colonial history.

The growing numbers of professional and national representative rugby athletes of Pacific heritage bring new dimensions to these issues.[33] In New Zealand and beyond, the professionalization of rugby union has made it a form of lucrative employment. Of these shifting dynamics Andy Grainger writes, "the athlete is reduced to a body, the body to a commodity; and, as such, the athlete becomes dehumanized, quantifiable, absorbed into the world of markets of productive exchange."[34] Specifically, he contends, sport-specific labor is a visible instance that reinscribes "positive racism" in the ways Hokowhitu describes. Similar to the stereotypes of tāne, depictions of Pacific Islander men as "natural" athletes retain strong linkages to racist ideologies, reifying beliefs that their strengths are limited to the realm of physicality. The perception of their abilities can, in turn, augment misdirected arguments that these men succeed in sport through less work than other racial groups. Their visibility in sport therefore does not necessarily debunk the racial stereotypes, but can actually contribute to them.

Despite these discursive formations of racism, national platforms express multicultural recognition as a core Kiwi value. Take the New Zealand Olympic Committee (NZOC) for example. Its headquarters in Wellington showcases an impressive collection of uniquely Kiwi exhibits that mark the nation's century-long Olympic history. Its museum reflects a sport-specific microcosm of the nation, with a quirky collection of artifacts, including one of triple Olympic gold medalist Peter Snell's running shoes from the 1960s and an autographed book that once belonged to Stan Lay, an athlete who represented New Zealand in the 1928 Olympics. Its centerpiece, though, is Te Māhutonga, the cloak (kākahu) designed for the New Zealand flag bearer to wear during the opening ceremonies of each Olympic Games. Originally presented by (now deceased) Te Arikinui Dame Te Ātairangikaahu, Queen of the Kīngitanga, in 2004, the handmade cloak boasts ornate details, including an engraved jade medallion framed by an overlay of kiwi feathers.[35] Its presentation is stunning, but the museum display provides only superficial information about its meanings. Distinguishing the kākahu as an objet d'art is, in part, a symbolic gesture that marks Māori recognition and inclusion, but the display is only a limited impression of Te Māhutonga's significance. According to the museum's information, it serves as a quasi-sacred safeguard that draws strength from the standing and integrity of the athlete chosen to serve as the nation's flag bearer during the Olympic opening ceremony, a very narrow explanation of the significance and recognition of *mana*.[36]

While the splendor of Te Māhutonga is eye-catching, so too are overwhelming number of pākehā bodies celebrated as New Zealand's athlete representatives. The few non-white athletes featured, such as Māori softball athlete Kiri Shaw, who represented New Zealand in the 2000 Sydney Games, often reiterate national interests. The display's caption, written in first-person narrative, reads, "I'm of Ngati Kahangunu and Ngati Porou descent. My mother's family is from Wairoa, and my dad is from Tokomaru Bay on the East Coast of the North Island and I have immense pride in being Māori." It continues as if she had written it, outlining her three "biggest achievements" as the birth of her children, participating in the Olympics, and "playing for the New Zealand Māori Women's softball team." All three items fall under the bolded header, "Cultural Identity/Pride in Identity," even though the exhibit offers little insight into her experiences as a Māori woman in contemporary New Zealand. Instead, the display includes a personalized message to youth observers:

> There are a lot of talented kids of all ethnic groups but because I have had more contact with Māori kids, I have found that they are reluctant to move out of their comfort zones and they prefer to cruise rather than extend themselves. It is frustrating, as I have experienced the opportunities that are available to athletes out there—worldwide. I pushed myself, I trained hard, set goals, listened and learned, got knocked down but got straight back up again and tried to do better. This attitude was due to my upbringing and the support of my mum and my whanau [family] and friends. Most importantly, it was a reflection of me as an individual and of the dreams I had. . . . If you push yourself and want it bad, then you are more successful than someone reluctant to take on the "challenge" and who will always be left wondering—what would have happened to me if I had given it my best shot?

Framed as a positive reinforcement of sport, the take-home point is not so much about Shaw's journey, or even her accomplishments, as it is about encouraging, even teaching, readers the value of hard work in order to excel. It reinforces an ethic of individualistic discipline, not values of ethnic difference or the unique challenges they can present. Instead, her observation that Māori kids "are reluctant to move out of their comfort zones and they prefer to cruise rather than extend themselves" is not contextualized or examined to see what structural inequalities or cultural influences might contribute to this "reluctance." Rather, it implicitly authenticates negative stereotypes of Māori peoples and celebrates Shaw as the exception.

The display also does not convey or provide insights into Shaw's specific struggles as a Māori woman, her cultural beliefs, or her local community beyond a few words in Māori language and brief references to how small her home of Naenae in the town of Lower Hutt is. It leaves viewers to their own cultural allusions in envisioning them. Without such details, the meanings of her identity, particularly as she makes sense of them, go unaddressed despite the fact that the museum narrative makes visible the ethnic difference she embodies. This representation, while enabling visitors to discern that Shaw is a female Māori athlete citizen, reinforces the point that she—like the many male pākehā bodies on display in museum—represented her community and nation through individual hard work and discipline. Thus, as a venue, the New Zealand Olympic Museum provides a digestible tale of sport and nationalism that promotes a discursive assimilatory logic. Such exhibitions, writes Lara Deeb, are "technologies of governmentality" that aid in "the construction of national identities and disciplining citizens."[37] The NZOC's celebration of sport provides an imagined depiction of New Zealand that simultaneously recognizes and dismisses cultural difference in one discursive move. It memorializes select Māori athletes and artifacts in order to tell a national fable about their achievement (and seeming progress) through sport.

NZOC officials reiterated this narrative, explaining how New Zealand has progressed from a British value system to an increasingly multicultural one. According to one representative, sport in New Zealand enables, to use his words, everyone to "galvanize around the nation." This is especially important, he stated, as New Zealand is still "figuring out its identity." Interestingly, as he explained his own enthusiasm for the Olympic Games, another reason emerged as to why he feels that the Olympic Games are so important: they offer an international stage on which a national identity can be performed and celebrated. Nation, as presented, appeared as a unifying narrative, even though citizens understand and feel the effects of nationalism in divergent ways in everyday life and in sport.

Government-supported actions also encourage national unity through physical activity and sport promotion. A clear set of goals imagined for New Zealand sport emerged out of the 2001 report, *Getting Set: For an Active Nation*, which responded to a trend of poor performances in the international arena, namely the 2000 Olympics held in Sydney, rugby union, and women's netball. The fact that the government endorsed the report speaks to the power of sport as a productive form of social control that supports nation-building aspirations. Better known as the Graham Report after its chair, John Graham (who was chancellor of the University of Auckland, a former All Black, and manager of the New Zealand Cricket team), it identified areas for improvement, developing a vision for a more inclusive and competitive sport.

In addition to Graham, six other members, all from sport, academic, and legal backgrounds, composed the ministerial task force that produced the report. Together, they developed a twenty-five-year vision for sport and leisure in New Zealand, which stated, "That all New Zealanders will have recognized and valued their fundamental right to an active lifestyle. The expression of *being a New Zealander* will include the positive experience of organized, or spontaneous, physical activity. This will lead to a healthier and more active nation, with social benefits for all, where individuals can realize their full potential."[38] Recognizing the importance of sport in the pursuit of national health and identity, the task force drew attention to a list of goals, including: "access for all, an education system that places value and emphasis on positive health, physical activity and physical education, a health system that places value and emphasis on wellness rather than illness, support by local and central government, the development and maintenance of appropriate resources, individual choice, a belief in the holistic development of active New Zealanders."[39] Essentially, it promoted a national project in which sport and physical activity would serve as important modes of encouraging health, joining together the constructive attributes of competition, wellness, and nationalism.

Following national agendas of ethnic recognition, the report outlines historical parallels and distinctions between European games and Māori arts of pleasure (*nga mahi a te rehia*), arguing that both qualify as valued forms of sport. It documents their historical points of intersection and departure as well as the role of physical culture in military readiness and economic development.[40] The report also attends to modern capitalist practices and the emergence of professional sport. Because of globalized commercial growth, sport, the report acknowledges, has "become justified less on grounds of social and moral values than as the domain of fitness, commercial imperatives and branding," thereby yielding "shifts in societal attitudes, the impact of international media, sport organizations with variable management capabilities, and variable numbers of volunteer participation."[41] Despite these changes, it maintains that physical fitness is, to a certain extent, reflective of moral fitness. Akin to the neoliberal policies used to encourage Māori economic inclusion, the recommendations promote individual discipline as a mode of productive and valued citizenship. It, however, only touches on how elite and professional competition can undermine the positive aspects of sport by incentivizing winning at all costs mentalities.

Government and sport agencies have central roles in promoting sport and recreation as outlined by the report. The task force's hope was that the next quarter century would be "imbued with a sense of moving from a Getting Set position to one of 'Go' that encourages all New Zealanders to be active in physical pursuits."[42] Suggesting that governmental intervention is necessary to make citizens better subjects through physical activity, it makes specific proposals for government efforts: 1) legislative targets; 2) a new Crown entity; 3) an outline of estimated costs for specific projects; and 4) strategies to encourage fitness for marginalized groups that were culturally specific. With regard to Māori communities, the report makes specific recommendations for targeted grassroots approaches to make these "inactive" populations more active through culturally tailored programs.[43]

Although health-promotion programs are well intended, their attempts to teach citizens how to become healthier and better subjects can carry negative repercussions. For example, anti-obesity campaigns in New Zealand, argues Lisette Burrows, pathologize certain "unhealthy" foods, many of which are staples of Māori and Pacific Islander households because they are traditional or affordable. Instead, they emphasize neoliberal ethics of self-discipline, self-responsibility and free choice in relation to bodily self-care.[44] Further, Māori and Pacific Islanders become visible targets for "reform" in part due to their documented higher rates of obesity and their larger families. This not only reinforces the public discourse around them as "lazy," dependent subjects, negating the labor intensive activities required to take care of extended families and meet other cultural obligations. Burrows says that these depictions in turn render their parenting suspect, even irresponsible, thereby reinforcing racist stereotypes. Rather than ensuring inclusion, such programs run the risk of perpetuating the belief that these groups are in need of disciplining or paternalistic forms of guidance.[45] In considering Burrows's insights, the remainder of this chapter examines how anti-doping practices come to imbue these and other historically ingrained Western ideologies, often to the detriment of working-class athletes and persons of color.

Tackling Doping in New Zealand

The New Zealand anti-doping system depends primarily on three governmental actors: Sport and Recreation New Zealand (SPARC), which is now known as Sport NZ;[46] DFSNZ; and the Sports Tribunal of New Zealand, which is a national arbitration court that hears and judges various sports disputes, including anti-doping rule violations.[47] SPARC was established to get "New Zealanders moving . . . from supporting elite athletes to getting out into local communities and encouraging people to get active."[48] In relation to anti-doping efforts, the agency contributes primarily by aiding in the facilitation of sports-dispute resolution. In 2003, the board of SPARC established the Sports Tribunal (as the Sports Disputes Tribunal of New Zealand), making it the enforcement branch of national anti-doping efforts. The Graham Report proposed a tribunal of this kind, but outlined no rules, leaving its inaugural members to determine how it would proceed in its work. In the resulting system, SPARC provided leadership in the overall governance of sport and recreation in New Zealand, while DFSNZ managed anti-doping efforts and the tribunal handled any resulting disputes.

DFSNZ, originally established by the 1994 New Zealand Sports Drug Agency Act, has expanded powers under the 2006 Sports Anti-Doping Act, giving it the ability to "take all the steps necessary to comply with and implement the rules," including the requirements of the WADA Code.[49] With this statutory language, the burden of complying with the UNESCO International Convention against Doping in Sport rests on DFSNZ's policies, a duty also recognized by the NZOC.[50] In terms of managing anti-doping violation procedures, the DFSNZ files the application for Anti-Doping Rule Violation Proceedings upon the discovery of an adverse finding. The Sports Tribunal only comes into play when evaluating the circumstances around an athlete's positive test for banned substances. The tribunal is composed of nine members with extensive sport or legal experience of which a panel of three members hears each case brought before it. The tribunal's registrar, whose role is primarily as a legal clerk, manages day-to-day operations and provides legal research, while also serving as a liaison to athletes and parties involved in proceedings so that they are aware of the steps leading up to a hearing, stating that it is important for them to understand the specific procedures followed and to be prepared for the possible outcomes.[51]

The processing of an anti-doping rule violation typically proceeds in the following manner: After testing reveals a sample contains a banned substance and DFSNZ files the necessary paperwork, the athlete has time to present a case. He or she can hire a lawyer (which is, for the most part, rare) or seek pro bono help. Tribunal members, however, understand that many athletes lack a comprehensive understanding of the rules and the repercussions of testing positive for a banned substance; this was especially true early on in the establishment of the tribunal. As one former tribunal member stated, "Most [athletes] just ignore the notices [of an anti-doping violation] and hope it goes away."[52] In these situations, the liaison role of the registrar can be particularly helpful in the athlete gaining a better understanding of the consequences and procedures. Tribunal proceedings then begin, following a general, yet flexible, format: a preconference meeting takes place with three tribunal members present, at least two of whom are lawyers and one a sports layperson (though this person may also have legal training). At this stage, the tribunal members can decide whether or not it is necessary or appropriate to hear the case or request more information from the parties involved. After this stage, a conference or a series of conferences can occur, either in person or over the phone with the athlete and his or her representative. The duration of proceedings largely depends upon the nature of the rule violation, the circumstances involved, and the extent to which the athlete appeals the finding.

Reflecting on the early efforts of the Tribunal, a former member of the Tribunal admitted that the original members felt compelled to speed up the process to ensure efficiency. When it became apparent that procedural

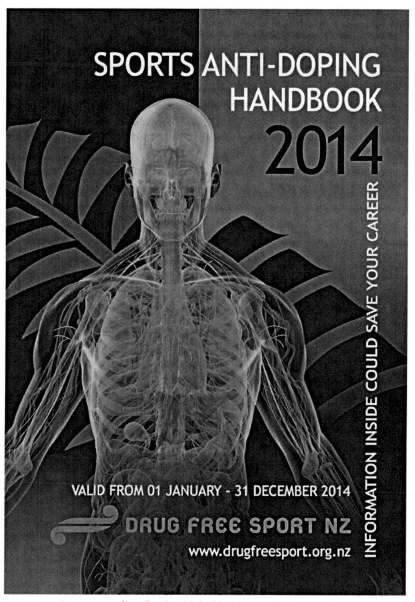

FIGURE 5.1 Cover image of handbook published by New Zealand's National Sports Anti-Doping Organization.

mishaps could result in appeals (and thus overturned rulings) heard before the Court for Arbitration in Sport, the global entity that hears sports disputes, the New Zealand–based tribunal made sure that necessary procedures were in place to maintain its credibility.[53] These subsequent changes, according to another member, included a deepened commitment to procedural efficiency and affordability by providing a pro bono legal assistance scheme for athletes appealing their violations in a manner that "was not too formal or threatening."[54] The primary advantage of the tribunal, according to members and the registrar, is that it provides an alternative to costly and lengthy court proceedings; however, it also imparts additional expectations of athletes. While the court is a resource, they must familiarize themselves with another form of legality in order to use it. These adjoining requirements, which are bound to those of international anti-doping regulation, are not those of the New Zealand justice system. In essence, for the tribunal to be of benefit, athletes must proactively engage with it.

Although the Sports Tribunal has developed its own procedures, international guidelines, such as the strict-liability standard and WADA's recommended sanctions, are still important. The tribunal is the venue for delivering internationally mandated sanctions, but these procedures have a certain level of elasticity in practice. For example, on an individual level, tribunal members and DFSNZ officials expressed divergent perspectives on how they negotiate the issue of intent, even though they collectively recognized the importance of the strict-liability standard, the standard that suggests use only proves intent. One administrator acknowledged that

> doctors have been prescribing prohibited substances for legitimate medical conditions, but not following the rules in terms of TUE [therapeutic use exemption], and the athletes, in at least two or three cases, are not adequately understanding their responsibility. So, we [DFSNZ] designed a program to directly address that. . . . Athletes should all be carrying a card, so whenever they are treated by anybody—which could be the dentist or whatever—the intent is that they put the card on the table and say, "Please understand I am an athlete who could be subject to testing, and you make sure to use the references that they can use on the back [of the card]."[55]

Focusing on prevention, not prosecution, DFSNZ uses this approach alongside other strategies to instill athletes with an awareness of the additional burdens they bear as an elite sport participant. DFSNZ also suggests the use of a smart phone application to check substances and provides a text messaging service to inquire about specific substances.

The card reiterates that athletes are responsible for these matters, as they are ultimately the only ones held liable for an offense, even if a doctor seems to be at fault. As one DFSNZ official explained, "The reverse of [the medical card program] is a series of posters we send out to sports medicine practices, for example, which hopefully reminds the athletes to do that. But, also, I guess, it's designed to show them the system is trying to support them. You know, that we're not just chucking them out there and letting them swim. They should be alerting those people in those practices or reminding them constantly that 'Hang on, we can't just be here. I need to be on top of it.'"[56] The card provides the doctor with necessary information about prohibited substances, including that the athlete is subject to testing. The image on the card (as well as other DFSNZ materials), which shows the internal organs, circulatory system, and skeleton of a human body, reinforces that the individual is held accountable for what is *inside* his or her body, which is not necessarily visible. The logic behind carrying the card, according to one regulator, is to remind the athlete of his or her obligations and to make compliance as easy as possible. What it also does, however, is suggest that athletes either cannot speak for themselves or do not know what to say. The card provides a substitute, thus speaking *for* them in a standardized language. A distinct biomedicalized form, the card reinforces the risks of being an athlete, but mediates them.

By instilling an awareness of and obedience to the rules, DFSNZ employees hope to prevent situations in which athletes do not understand the conditions of the strict-liability standard or try to divert responsibility onto a doctor without following proper procedures. In so doing, the reliance on the card encourages a unique kind of responsibilization whereby individuals are held accountable for what would otherwise be a duty of another entity, be it a governmental agency or an expert such as doctor. This tactic, like the recommendations in the *Getting Set* report that encourage physical activity as part of productive citizenship, reflects the growth not only in encouraging citizens to be individually responsible for their health, but also in devices that can aid in holding them accountable in taking on these responsibilities and duties in the pursuit of becoming (or remaining) healthy, dutiful citizens.[57] The specific techniques employed in the regulation of athlete citizens may be unique, but they are part of a broader trend affecting the general population.

There are other ways that DFSNZ instills such responsibilized citizenship. The agency provides educational and outreach seminars for athletes about what substances constitute doping and has support staff dedicated to making sure athletes meet specific monitoring requirements. One of the most time-consuming tasks, at least in terms of tracking down and ensuring athletes keep their information up to date, is the Whereabouts System, which requires athletes to provide information regarding where they are in or out of competition. Knowing athletes' whereabouts is to ensure that they are available for sample collection. Failure to abide by the system's requirements results in an anti-doping violation. As a result, DFSNZ assists in providing the necessary and correct information, which requires checking in and maintaining (primarily through electronic correspondence) regular contact with athletes so as to help them avoid an accidental anti-doping violation. In other words, DFSNZ not only is responsible for contracting the agents who conduct the tests, but also ensuring that athletes are available for random out-of-competition testing.

Because athletes provide information about their location, characterizing this testing as random is a bit of a misnomer: even though athletes do not know exactly when they will be tested, the process is an effort largely coordinated by DFSNZ. At the very least, if literacy is not achieved to the extent that they independently comply without hands-on assistance, they can at least navigate the terms of regulation. The agency's employees help athletes obtain the required literacy, thereby explicitly promoting cultural adaptations alongside and in response to the technocratic changes mandated by the international anti-doping regime.

With only seven full-time members on DFSNZ's staff at the time of my research, it was clear that they all desired more resources in order to comply with the increasing requirements of the international regime. Three staff who focused on the Whereabouts System oversaw 280 athletes when I visited DFSNZ offices in the spring of 2010, yet they all expressed great pride in their hands-on approach. Overall, they felt that their work enabled them see what they described as the "whole picture" of what athletes experience, attributing this approach to the "athlete-centered" vision instilled by Executive Director Steele. They also cited their own experiences as athletes as advantageous in terms of connecting with the people they monitor, expressing a desire to make a "positive impact" on athletes. This "positive impact" was not necessarily preventing doping, but, rather, it was achieving compliance. In other words, they aimed to prevent athletes who did not intend to cheat from violating the regulations as a result of their inability to navigate or follow complex international requirements. In essence, the embedded logics of suspicion and risk were so high that regulators had to actually help athletes *not* to get caught. Arguably, DFSNZ's biggest success was not saving athletes from themselves, as anti-doping rhetoric posits, but saving them from the terms of international regime itself.

SPARC has supported efforts to help athletes who do not intend to cheat. Recognizing that the WADA Code "focuses on the responsibility of the athlete," one representative explained that the "lax regulation of food means that temptation is there to use traditional supplements. There are two regulatory regimes in New Zealand, one for food and one for medicines, and the distinction lies when something claims a therapeutic purpose, so nutritional supplements are generally treated and regulated as food, which means ... they are not regulated as closely as medicines or tested for adulteration or contents, say, or quality, so things can slip by."[58] Thus, athletes face the risk of taking contaminated substances, which can be sold over the counter in grocery or health-food stores. Recognizing a space where governmental intervention would benefit consumers, especially given the fact that many supplements are imported into New Zealand, SPARC officials explained the importance of "working with Australia to set-up a joint approach to the regulation of therapeutic products that would bring supplements under medicine and be treated more strictly."[59] As this agreement had not yet materialized, contamination remained a possible reason for anti-doping violations. Athletes often use it to explain instances of unintentionally doping, even though it is not an acceptable alibi under anti-doping rules.

According to one regulator, a particularly tragic case that demonstrated the need for transnational partnerships and more rigorous food regulation was that of an athlete who tested positive for a banned substance after purchasing a supplement in the United States. It was the same product and brand that he usually used; the only difference was that he bought it in the United States, not New Zealand, and then tested positive for a banned substance. The DFSNZ staff member reciting the story claimed to trust the athlete's assertion that he did not know it was contaminated, because the athlete was very proactive in asking about which supplements were safe to use and forthright about using them. If anything, he was a model and proactive athlete citizen who consulted DFSNZ regularly. Regardless of this fact, the athlete received a suspension from sport in accordance with international requirements. Despite being a dutiful, athlete-subject, his body betrayed him. Responsibilization was not enough to prevent sanctions.

While the issue of contamination is considerable, it is not necessarily the most prevalent concern. Cannabis, a substance that is banned during competition, is a notable issue. According to the United Nations Office of Drug Control's figures, New Zealand has the second-highest annual prevalence rate for cannabis use among Western democracies overall, a rate higher than that of the United States, Australia, or any country in Europe.[60] As cannabis metabolites can remain in an athlete's system for weeks, out-of-competition use can result in an anti-doping rule violation. As of June 2009, thirty-three of the fifty-two anti-doping cases decided by the tribunal were for marijuana use, and at the time I met with the registrar in June 2010, 59 percent of anti-doping cases are for cannabis-related offenses. In the lead-up to the 2012 Olympics, the number of number of marijuana-related cases had begun to decline, but they still made up more than half of the over eighty cases.[61] As a result, the combined efforts of DFSNZ's policing and the Sports Tribunal's sanctions often served as an arm of the state in illicit drug prosecution.

Given the high domestic rates of marijuana use, it is perhaps not surprising that many athletes are caught for using it; however, it is worth noting that most recreational users go unpunished by the New Zealand justice system.[62] According to the 2010 New Zealand Law Commission Report, *Controlling and Regulating Drugs*, less than 1 percent of all users in 2006 received a cannabis-related punishment.[63] In most cases, marijuana is considered a class C substance, which is the lowest classification of harm for illicit drugs.[64] The Law Commission suggests that a less punitive attitude toward marijuana would mitigate the existing inequalities in the few cases in which the police take action against users. Although this number of cases prosecuted is statistically low, there remains a "significant proportion of criminal justice resource spent enforcing possession and use offences," and research suggests that Māori men, particularly those with at least one previous non-cannabis related conviction, are disproportionately arrested and convicted for a marijuana-related reason.[65] As athletes consent to the terms of the anti-doping regime, they are bound to it and are subject to higher levels of surveillance and punishment when compared to other citizens. Conversations with athletes, however, suggest that they are resistant to being held to these terms, even when they think regulation is warranted in this space.

Athletes' Perceptions of Compliance

Many athletes expressed resentment toward being monitored with few acknowledging that DFSNZ's extensive efforts to help them avoid inadvertent anti-doping violations. On more than one occasion, athletes would ask me if authorities wanted access to what they told me, expressing that the regulators wanted to know everything else about them. One athlete even jokingly asked if I was the new officer on the block (in reference to "doping control officers" who administer tests). Regulators were well aware of these sentiments, prompting one to say that New Zealand athletes do not realize how good they have it (compared to other countries) until they go overseas.

When I broached the subject with Tai, an international athlete who I kept in regular contact with throughout and after my fieldwork in New Zealand, she exclaimed, "They're just *always* around! I mean, I feel like they need to know everything I do, even stuff I try to keep from my parents!"[66] Tai's primary complaint about DFSNZ was the intrusiveness of the Whereabouts Program, an internationally mandated program. It was particularly difficult for her to cope with feeling that she could not travel to Australia to visit her boyfriend as often as she wanted to or on short notice. Already feeling some pressure in her relationship for seemingly prioritizing sport over her partner, she tried to travel to see him as often as she could afford. With proper notification and communication with DFSNZ, she could, but she said her aversion to "dealing" with them often prevented her from making such arrangements.

Resentment toward anti-doping surveillance was common among elite athletes and even some younger athletes, particularly rugby league players, the majority of which were young Māori and Pacific Islander men in their late teens and early twenties. Unlike Tai, normalization accompanied their statements of resentment, sometimes saying that it "wasn't a big deal" or that it was "normal" for them to feel watched by authorities. In fact, many male Māori athletes expressed that they were already viewed as suspect for being "black."[67]

Tonu, a player of Samoan heritage, said that he expected harsher levels of scrutiny: "I expect it. I should expect it, because they're always looking out anyways. You know, it's like this, they know I'm going to be good, because I am good at what I do [sport]. And, I got to watch my back because of it. . . . I got it, though."[68] Rather than admitting to any frustration, he iterated how he could handle it—just like a lot of other challenges he said he faced as an immigrant to New Zealand. He explained that he had an obligation to his family and community to do so. Tonu had accepted the additional levels of responsibility as an athlete, but was not necessarily proactive in complying with the rules as national anti-doping regulations encouraged. Thus, although an active citizen who understood that there were additional responsibilities as an athlete, Tonu nonetheless had not embraced the responsibilized duties instilled by anti-doping regulation.

Instead, Tonu seemed to tolerate the surveillance as he pursued his goals. He and many other male Pacific Islander athletes expressed a strong admiration for others like them who were able to keep their faith in their goals (and God) and were well-aware of the normative structures that "keep down" people of color. Accompanying this awareness was a level of identification with popular African American athletes. Being an American from Los Angeles, I often found myself fielding questions about black professional athletes in the United States and listening to stories of how the messages of hip-hop, particularly those around resistance and maintaining strength when faced with adversity, resonated with them. For example, when I asked Tonu about how he felt about negotiating the sport-specific surveillance, he spoke directly to how he felt racial difference played out in New Zealand.

> TONU: I bet it's not that different for black people back where you come from. We hear a lot about what goes on in LA [Los Angeles] and Oakland, so we have an idea of what goes on in America. We are just getting by the best we can. . . . It's like Kobe [Bryant of the Los Angeles Lakers].[69] He just did his thing, and people don't like that sometimes, so they make trouble for you. Same here. Everyone knows Samoans are athletes, strong, fast, hard. Good at sports they all love. They just don't always like us for being better at them. [laughs]
>
> ME: I think I see what you mean. So, do you think this affects how others view you? You know, as an athlete, and a better one at that?
>
> TONU: They don't know what it's like to be like us. Of course, I think *palagi* [white people] think it's easier for me, because we are just better. [laughs] You know, [they say] we are just faster and stronger because our people are just that way. I mean, *when we work hard.*

He emphasized this last phrase in a defiant, even sarcastic tone, referencing the stereotypical belief that Pacific Islander people are either lazy or not as diligent as their Anglo counterparts. Despite his joking tone, Tonu was openly indignant about what he considered an unfair judgment. He explained how he and many others felt that this belief kept many of his friends, including his older brothers, from playing in decision-making positions as they progressed to higher levels of sport. Instead, in part because of their larger size and athleticism, they found themselves in more physically demanding or more regimented roles, although Tonu said that he felt this trend was changing. In fact, he said he chose to play rugby league (instead of rugby union), because all of his teammates were Pacific Islanders, making it a more comfortable space that he felt gave him more opportunities to excel.

Like Tonu, many young male Māori and Pacific Islander athletes took sport seriously. Sione, a rugby union athlete of Tongan heritage, admitted that he did so at a cost: by not prioritizing school. Sione explained that he never felt right in school and acknowledged that he was anxious about "failing" in sport. He indicated that he would not rely on "the dole" (the common reference to welfare) because it was not enough to support his family. Instead, he explained, because his parents had taken on risks to immigrate to New Zealand for a better life, he wanted to ensure that he could reciprocate. He expressed that his faith in God and community would help him persevere. While Sione was more open about his anxiety than the other male participants with whom I spoke, his reflection revealed a common thread that many aspiring male athletes shared: Sport was, for them, a sphere in which they could—and would—excel, a place where they could receive public praise, gain status, and receive financial benefits.

Despite many participants asserting that they "did not care about what other people think," positive personal reinforcement through sport was a reoccurring theme that emerged as important. This sentiment was consistent with a desire to express oneself, which many felt they could do through sport but not necessarily in other spheres of their life. Against this backdrop, antidoping regulation was more of an additional burden to navigate, not a concern or fear. No Pacific athletes stated that they felt compelled to use performance-enhancing substances in part because of their strong beliefs in God and in part because many did not question their ability to succeed in sport. Some participants were instead more concerned about broader forms of marginalization holding them back, and anti-doping regulation was understood as part of that structural milieu. Their suspect status was thus something to overcome.

Male and female Māori and Pacific athletes often alluded to concerns that anti-doping regulation was a monitoring system in place to "catch," not help, them. They reflected on its significance very differently, though, depending on the importance that they placed on sport in their lives. For example, Antonina, a netball player, conjectured that men endured more pressure to excel not so much because of family obligations (which she, too, felt were important), but in part because their coaches and teammates treat young men more harshly. To this, she added, "I mean, all of us have coaches who rip into us. Guess that's the same for boys as much as girls, eh? I just think boys sometimes get it more than us girls, because they have more riding on [how they do in sport]."[70] Antonina did not see sport as her only pathway for success, as she prioritized her studies as well. Although cognizant of her own unique challenges, she, like her male counterparts, embraced them as milestones overcome in her pursuits.

Placing a high value on her education, she framed her background as a primary reason why she had to work hard to achieve. Although saying she valued her family, community, and church, she admitted that her upbringing had not prepared her for the challenges of school or sport in New Zealand. An honor student from a middle-class family, she reiterated the fact that she was among the worst in her advanced classes and one of only a few "brown faces." This, she stated, made socialization at first a difficult task, but one to which she became accustomed. Further, Antonina revealed a sense of isolation in the fact she knew few people—Samoan or palagi—who would understand her feelings. Admitting that sport was no longer really enjoyable for her, she said that she liked the busy and ritualized schedule. In fact, when we discussed the prospect of additional anti-doping monitoring, she merely said that it was "just another thing to add to the to-do list!" She dismissed the surveillance as a burden; rather, it mapped onto other obligations she already navigated. If anything, her primary concerns about sport stemmed from the fact that they conflicted with some familial and church duties.

Pākehā or pākehā-identified[71] athletes, male or female, did not make gendered or racial comparisons similar to those that Māori and Pacific Islander athletes had, even when I directly inquired about them. Instead, pākehā interviewees focused on their own individual hard work and struggle to achieve, suggesting that they subscribed to the disciplinary ethics instilled by anti-doping regulation. One athlete, David, explained, "I will do anything I need to do to get to the next level. I have always had to work to get where I'm at . . . harder than everyone else. Rugby, school, anything. It's just the way I am. I am proud of it. It's what makes me better than other people. I know I am going to work harder than anyone else."[72] Like David, many pākehā athletes expressed similar levels of pride and commitment to individual hard work and perseverance. They also acknowledged that they had to be "smart" about how they went about pursuing performance enhancement, something no Māori or Pacific Islander athlete stated. That is, most pākehā were well aware of supplementation and took calculated risks using products that they thought were safe, both in terms of health and in relation to the rules. While pākehā athletes discussed these choices in strategic terms, the vast majority of Pacific Islander athletes framed their athletic careers as "following what God intended."

Many Pākehā athletes reflected on how anti-doping regulation changed the way they viewed their individual bodies and what they consumed, evidence that they had internalized both the values of suspicion and responsibilization embedded in anti-doping regulation. While Pacific athletes did not talk about altering their food choices to comply with the rules (but did mention making healthier choices for sport), many pākehā athletes discussed concerns over certain supplements they consumed. Their anxieties about surveillance were not so much about external monitoring by authorities, as Tai and Tonu had described, but about their shifting perceptions of their own bodies and fears of contamination. In other words, many Pākehā actually self-surveilled themselves, an embrace of the prospective risks reinforced by anti-doping surveillance. For example, another athlete, Angela stated, "I get worried sometimes about it. I mean I never used to think about what I ate being bad or if I'd test positive for something. Now I look at my body differently. When I look at stuff [supplements] on the shelf and after I take something, I am always worried about it—even when they tell me it's okay to use. I just don't *really* know."[73] Like Angela, other athletes, irrespective of race or gender, rarely addressed a fear of others cheating. Instead, the anti-doping system had often turned their gaze onto themselves, and their narratives prioritized their fears and anxieties about regulation—either as policing them, as is the case for many Māori and Pacific Islander athletes, or making them self-conscious about what they consumed, as is the case for many pākehā athletes. In essence, risk was everywhere, but it did take on distinct forms that were shaped in part by cultural understandings and social difference. Regardless of the particular distinctions, managing additional concerns of risk was a key tenet of athlete citizenship.

When the Natural and Pure Diverge

As mentioned earlier, recreational drug use constituted the majority of anti-doping violations. Many athletes were aware that cannabis use could result in a violation. Their feelings about it varied. Some expressed it as just "another hoop to jump through," while others were frustrated that testing only caught young and naïve athletes with potential, not the adults facilitating environments that encouraged illicit drug use. For example, a former professional rugby league player, Piri, who is of Māori heritage, explained that cannabis use at the club level is "part of the culture." He said,

> It's not fair for those kids. It's all they know. Then, if they got some talent and get spotted when they are young, they don't know better. They just know that's what everyone does. If they [anti-doping authorities] want to punish anyone, they should punish those *men* that don't amount to anything but smoking that stuff and giving it to those kids. That's who. It's just wrong, mate, to take away an

opportunity from someone who doesn't even know. . . . Now I am not making excuses for blacks [Māori people[74]], but I heard that they are even banning first-grade players. First-grade players! Now, that's what first grade is for—just having some fun and playing.[75]

More generally, Piri felt it was unfair for any athlete, not just first-grade club players, to receive an anti-doping rule violation for using a common recreational drug like marijuana. He was also not the only one to address the issue of culture as something authorities did not understand or were not willing to engage. Other participants explained that such policies undermined the goal of ensuring wider high-level participation among New Zealand's best "natural" athletes, that is, Māori and Pacific Islander people.

One interviewee, Ese, a wife and mother who emigrated from Samoa to New Zealand as a child, explained that she did not understand why authorities punished athletes for using marijuana. A former netball player and partner of a recently retired high-level athlete in another sport, she expressed a sense of relief that her husband no longer had to travel as much or manage the time-consuming commitments of competitive sport. She preferred not having to travel, and while she thought her partner could have made more money in sport, she was relieved that they no longer had to worry over whether or not his contract would be renewed. Although she did not care to talk about sport more generally, she became more animated when the issue of marijuana arose: "It's fucken natural. No harm there, except for the smoke in your lungs. It's a just a bush. All you do is smoke it! I mean it's a plant. God put it here. And, we should smoke it!"

Ese laughed out loud as she explained, continuing in a lighthearted tone until she ended our conversation with a more solemn point: "Better for them [men] to be smoking than that stuff you see those boys doing—driving while drinking on weekends."[76] She went on to state that cannabis users never start fights when going out or beat their wives while using marijuana. Unsolicited, Ese explained that she had friends and acquaintances who would agree with her on the basis of their own violent experiences. She was happy that she or her children did not have that kind of firsthand experience. Ese also felt it important to clarify that the problems of substance abuse were not unique to her community, explicitly stating that her friends who had negative experiences with alcohol and violence were not just "dumb coconuts" (a derogatory slang term used to refer to Pacific Islanders). She pointed out that such repercussions can affect any community and that she would therefore prefer to have marijuana use encouraged as a safer alternative to alcohol. The New Zealand Law Commission's Report on drug control concurs with her point, indicating that a "less restrictive" regulatory approach might encourage its use as a safer alternative to other drugs.[77]

Most anti-doping regulators and Sports Tribunal members, nearly all pākehā, did not entertain or even consider this viewpoint as relevant to their goals. The Sports Tribunal's 2007–2008 annual report instead reflects on the continued trend of anti-doping violations stemming from recreational marijuana use.[78] As a result, rather than rely upon the standardized protocols that suggest a two-year ban as the default suspension, the tribunal suggested the use of harsher sanctions, hoping to deter these kinds of violations. The discursive message of their reasoning was that athletes were to be ethically stronger—by not using illicit drugs—than other citizens who used them.

Many tribunal members, although agreeing with the statement in the annual report, disagreed with marijuana being on the international prohibited list. Their hope was that harsher punishments would have a deterrent effect. On more than one occasion, DFSNZ and tribunal representatives expressed frustration with regulating marijuana use, pointing out that the focus on cannabis misdirected their regulatory gaze away from performance-enhancing drugs. Although some felt more strongly than others, one regulator, in expressing his personal indifference toward marijuana as a substance, acknowledged that not using it was a small price to pay for signing onto the anti-doping regime. In essence, he disagreed with its inclusion on the list, but he felt that any regulation had its shortcomings. He said, "It is worth toeing the line for the greater good."[79] This sentiment came in stark contrast to another regulator's opinion that the tribunal was not punishing cheaters, just "people being silly." She thus felt regulation often led to too many instances where athletes were unfairly humiliated.

Though presenting divergent perspectives, both tribunal members felt the target of anti-doping regulation should be "real" anti-doping violations; that is, for the deliberate use of performance-enhancing substances. Perhaps unconsciously, many participants distinguished cases involving the intentional use of performance-enhancing substances as "real" violations as distinct from the more common cases of supplement contamination or recreational drug use. One notable instance of a "real" case was that of an athlete who tested positive for a substance after coming back from an injury to qualify for the Olympics. This athlete had struggled to regain her form in the aftermath of an accident. A positive test for a performance-enhancing drug dashed her hopes. The case prompted one tribunal member, herself having been an international athlete, to express sincere sympathy. She stated that she had never been in the position, but understood why the athlete chose to dope: "I doubt I would go to that extreme," but would be heartbroken. "It would be massive. I think I'd suffer from depression after all that hard work and blood, sweat, and tears. Yeah, I don't know about that. It's hard to imagine."[80] She did not express the same level of understanding for marijuana use. If someone is a committed athlete, she said, it made no sense for someone to use it, especially knowing the consequences. In the case of the "real" anti-doping violation, she at least understood the athlete's motivation, even though she did not condone it.

There was a widespread acknowledgment that offenses for marijuana use primarily occurred in sports popular among working-class and Māori athletes. In response, DFSNZ increased its educational outreach to affected sports, primarily rugby league and touch rugby (a non-contact sport common in Australasia, but not North America). Relying on grassroots efforts and communications with other anti-doping groups to develop programming, the number of actual violations remained their only indicator of effectiveness. The DFSNZ staff member spearheading these efforts explained that he tried to "weave the [anti-doping] message through life" so that it would acknowledge athletes' demanding schedules.[81] As he discussed the advantages of this "more understanding approach," he expressed personal disappointment regarding his inability to make an impact, at least as evidenced by the continued trend of anti-doping violations. Specifically, he stated that he hoped that rugby league athletes would come to understand the importance of their actions and be more "proactive" in complying with regulation so as to avoid an inadvertent anti-doping rule violation. Although genuinely concerned for them, he admitted some pessimism in their ability or willingness—he openly stated that he was unsure which it was—to adhere to the rules. In contrast, the athletes who had undergone outreach programming often explained such seminars were a "waste of time" because they "don't use steroids." Others, while polite in expressing an appreciation for the time taken in outreach, felt that it took away from their training time and did not provide helpful information.

Ethnic and cultural differences also informed regulators' explanations of noncompliance. When discussing the case of Vince Whare, a Māori rugby league player banned from sport for ten years, including playing, coaching, or working in any formal capacity, after his third cannabis offense, many took a very critical stance toward him. For them, his last offense and the conferences focusing on his marijuana habit provided sufficient evidence for them to conclude he was an irresponsible athlete-subject. Rather than attribute this situation to the inappropriate inclusion of marijuana as a banned substance, members and onlookers alike condemned his "lack of intelligence" and "stubborn stupidity" for his continued use of the substance. One regulator even expressed how much he liked Whare, even how he would have made a good coach (had he not been banned for ten years), but then said, "It's just sad that he chose to continually use marijuana despite repeated warnings and accommodations provided to him."[82] This statement reiterated the belief that Whare's seemingly chronic use was merely a choice on his part to not accept the responsibilities instilled by anti-doping regulation, thus portraying his ban as a deserved consequence.

The tribunal's formal account concurred with the characterization, stating that members found Whare to be "a social user of cannabis who deliberately took the risk that he would not get drug tested and get caught."[83] Accordingly, his offense required a minimum suspension of eight years. Accounting for the "difference in assessing fault between a third time 'drug cheat' who has deliberately taken performance enhancing drugs and who will receive a mandatory lifetime ban and that of an athlete who has deliberately breached the rules for a third time by taking drugs like cannabis for social recreational reasons," the tribunal report rendered Whare's sentence appropriate and reflective of his recklessness and seeming disregard for the rules.[84] Punishment, the report suggested, was necessary because it presumed Whare continually chose to break them, even though it went against his self-interests.

This assessment, however, neglects that fact that Whare fit the profile of a "cannabis dependent user," which, as described by the New Zealand Law Commission, is most likely to a Māori man with "symptoms including an increased tolerance to a drug, withdrawal symptoms, more prolonged and intense use of a drug and unsuccessful attempts to control use."[85] According to the tribunal report and my interviews with the members involved in the case, there was no consideration of whether or not Whare could exercise a high level of choice in his use. In essence, the presumption of choice, something systemically imbued in international anti-doping regulation's attempt to counteract performance-enhancing drugs, became transposed onto this case of repeated illicit drug use. Rather than bringing these considerations to light, two members of the tribunal stated that they allow athletes to participate in a drug-education program and educational outreach in exchange for a suspended ban.[86] Even though this is likely a healthier alternative, their recommendation reveals two dimensions of athlete citizenship: first, that bodily scrutiny and surveillance is justifiable no matter what the offense is, and, second, that athletes who take on additional individual responsibilities to work toward self-improvement would be rewarded. They cited a case where an athlete used his story to contribute positively to counteracting doping in sport, thereby reifying the importance and value of active citizenship. Whare, however, received no such option.

In accordance with its members' stern consternation about cannabis, the tribunal changed its guidelines (in accordance with more flexible terms afforded by the revised WADA Code), particularly in relation to those who have committed a second anti-doping violation: "Previously an athlete who committed a second violation involving cannabis faced a mandatory two-year suspension. Now the new law gives the Tribunal discretion to impose a suspension ranging from a minimum of one year to a maximum of four years."[87] The following example of a New Zealand representative player who was a second-time violator illustrated how the tribunal would act on these matters:

The Tribunal accepted he had not taken cannabis to enhance sports performance but did not find any mitigating circumstances. The athlete claimed he had taken it to help with sleep and pain relief for an injury but that could not be classified as a mitigating factor. There were severe consequences for the player from even a minimum suspension of one year, such as missing a world cup tournament and losing an overseas playing contract. However, the player was an international player, who was expected to set an example for others, and who took cannabis just days before a national final, despite a strong warning from the Tribunal of the consequence of further cannabis offending at the time of his first cannabis violation three years ago. A minimum sanction was not appropriate in these circumstances and the Tribunal suspended him for 18 months.[88]

Though not as punitive as it could be, the tribunal's reasoning highlights two issues. On the one hand, it reveals the rationalization that as an international athlete, he should be a role model for other citizens. On the other hand, its dismissal of his reasons for using marijuana—as a form of intent—demonstrates an adherence to the strict-liability standard. Although one could interpret his explanation of treatment as a plausible justification for using marijuana, this athlete still endured fairly severe repercussions, including the loss of representing his country and a financial contract, for his unwillingness to submit to these conditions. The tribunal's ruling thus suggests its narrow construction of what constitutes a mitigating fact, which is usually considered to be something beyond the athlete's control, not one that is an intended act, as this case highlights.

The main issue in the case orients around the responsibilities and expectations of his status as a representative athlete citizen. Because his actions do not reflect the social roles and expectations of purity ascribed to New Zealand's international athletes, the tribunal made the final determination that he is, indeed, ineligible to represent his county as an athlete representative. This example, when juxtaposed with the one in which the athlete underwent drug education and helped anti-doping efforts, highlights how an athlete can regain his or her status as an athlete citizen. Fallen heroes, according to Lawrence Wenner, are not always afforded redemption, and their stories are informative about broader cultural norms and expectations of athletes' morality.[89] In this context, if the athlete takes on additional duties in the service of anti-doping education, he or she can avoid certain levels of punishment, reflecting the system's valuing of responsibilized citizenship. Because of these arrangements, many regulators characterized these opportunities for redemption as fair, for they enabled athletes to prove that they were better than their violation suggested or that they had helped reform people—neither of which have to do with their athletic abilities or the fact that they had not they cheated in the first place.

Responsibilizing Athlete Citizens versus Protecting Fair Play

DFSNZ's attempts to educate athletes have not overcome the socio-economic and ethnic disparities underpinning sport agendas. In fact, at the time of this writing, anti-doping regulation actually levies a *more* punitive response to some forms of recreational drug use (e.g., cannabis) than the national justice system. The resulting tensions are significant. For many working-class athletes who look to sport for their livelihoods (either through playing or coaching), sanctions essentially prevent them from employment opportunities in which they have expertise. Regulators expressed little sympathy because, they felt, that they had provided athletes with the opportunities and tools to comply. In this way, the anti-doping regime serves as a gatekeeper by ensuring that only certain kinds of responsible subjects serve as representatives, a duty many regulators think is appropriate; however, it comes at a cost. As sport, particularly rugby union, offers New Zealand an opportunity to receive global recognition, the loss of potential representative athlete citizens is also the nation's loss.

The New Zealand anti-doping system also does not escape the postcolonial tropes of nation, as only a particular kind of disciplined subject can excel. Coincidentally, testing often detects dope in the bodies characterized as overstayer (Pacific Islanders) or unruly Māori men, even though not for performance-enhancing drugs. Their crime is a failure to submit to the terms of the regime and of the disciplinary tactics of a uniquely proactive national anti-doping authority. They are denied the entitlements of athlete citizenship because they are merely gifted athletically, not pure according to the conditions of anti-doping regulation. Presuming the purity of a natural athlete while construing something natural (like cannabis) as impure may at first appear a contradiction; however, purity, in this case, is not natural, but a social construct attributed to bodies that actively comply with the rules in order to achieve representative status. This is not a paradox, but a prophecy of nation and its assimilatory practices. Transgressing athletes' inability to overcome their circumstances and inappropriate desires recasts them from a suspect subject to failed athlete citizen. Further, as in Whare's case, regulators often presume their acts to be an agentive form of refusal.

Although there are a relatively few athletes (under one hundred at the time of this research) who have been punished under anti-doping rules in New Zealand, their symbolism is nonetheless significant. Their punishment can confirm the expectations of some onlookers and undermine the hopes of others, revealing that these punished bodies have a pedagogical function. For many citizens, these athletes may be easily condemnable subjects for being unruly or unwise, but for others, such as the aspiring Māori and Pacific athletes with whom I spoke, such bodies may symbolize enduring forms of unfair marginalization. Regardless of interpretation, their condemnation speaks to how the national anti-doping system does not escape the postcolonial dynamics of nation through its hands-on approach. In fact, pursuant to complying with the terms of the international regime, DFSNZ instills ethics that embrace Anglo-European monoculturalism by favoring individual discipline at the cost of failing to recognize and tailor programming for other perspectives. DFSNZ's tactics are thus not a maneuver to protect fair play; instead, they are technologies imbued with cultural preferences. What becomes valued is not those bodies believed to be natural athletes, but those who actively work to meet the conditions of purity or those who have the resources to navigate technocratic requirements.

In sum, DFSNZ does protect the everyday values of a Pure Playing Field Nation; however, they are decidedly reflective of pākehā values. The agency's efforts demonstrate how biomedicalized and legalized terms of regulation disavow ethnic and cultural difference in ways that enable disproportionate punishment without overt acts of discrimination. The fact that local authorities understand the complexities of international requirements and take a hands-on approach to achieving compliance highlights not only that risk is a structural feature of the regime, but also that it still holds bodies accountable to WADA's ingrained Western values. Thus, the assimilatory processes of athlete citizenship are instantiated not simply through the punishment of so-called tainted athletes' bodies on the global stage, but also through the localized anti-doping practices that promote responsibilized citizenship. As such, anti-doping regulation subscribes to and enforces the terms of purity as not simply being drug-free but pure in accordance with nationalized values of active citizenship.

6

Conclusion

I began the research for this book with the hopes of gleaning insight into hybrid governance arrangements by understanding anti-doping regulation. It was a response to John MacAloon's invitation to study sport:

> the exploration of cultural conceptions will reveal connections to other institutions and contexts that may be quite surprising or unexpected, that is, concealed or suppressed by cultural commonsense, everyday speech, disciplinary, and professional boundaries. In this way inquiry into sport can broaden toward the very general social morphologies that cultural studies researchers are most interested in, not by theoretical reduction but by demonstrated relationships among widening circles of actors and contexts.[1]

As MacAloon's words foreshadowed, pursuing this line of inquiry revealed a much more complicated picture of sport and its social entanglements than I initially expected.

Anti-doping regulation is not merely an effort to "clean up" sport or to protect athletes from doping; it is a transnational regime in which legality conjoins with biomedicalization to synergistically reinforce ideals of fair play that are embedded in sport, terms to which athletes' bodies are held accountable. Anti-doping regulation emerges at the nexus of historical, ideological, legalistic, and biomedicalized factors, all of which constitutively inform the boundaries in and around a transnational group of citizen subjects. Emerging as an effort to protect ideological tropes of amateurism, the logic of regulation has shifted from an arms-race mentality to one more characteristic of a risk society.

The study of anti-doping regulation provides insight not simply into a transnational legal order, but into the broader context of globalization and the rise of biomedicalization. In this book, I have endeavored to describe how various technologies and forms of social control interact to communicate powerful messages about human ability and difference. The regime posits three inter-related myths about the body: that athletes can attain a form of bodily purity, that regulation can protect a kind of naturalness, and that science can provide evidence that proves these myths are truths. These messages, buttressed by law and science, both naturalize and refigure the racialized, gendered, and classed power relations that informed the original impetus for regulation.

The research for this book was a personal pursuit whereby I came to better understand the meanings that circulate in and through anti-doping regulation, as well as in relation to the numerous practices of performance enhancement in which I and many others partook. The cultural implications became clear to me after I left New Zealand and returned to the United States in late 2010. This study required me to negotiate various emic narrations of sport—that is, descriptions of others' cultural understandings and values from their perspective—and to adopt etic stances—that is, my synthesis of these behaviors and practices—in recounting them. My research in turn, actually shifted my perspective of sport and regulation more generally, making it difficult to transition back to life as only an athlete. My position as an athlete-researcher remains part of the athlete and the academic I am today.

The encounters that enabled me to write this text would also help me to make sense of how anti-doping discourse enters into my everyday encounters, especially those with other athletes. One conversation with a friend, Mathew, a former resident athlete at the US Olympic Training Center, was particularly illuminating in relation to my changing positionality and thus the ideas found in this book. We had been reflecting on how one's athletic career can change when one least expects it. Even with diligent training and preparation, a personal breakthrough can happen just as easily as an unexpected injury; the most life-changing developments are sometimes the shortest. He knew this from first-hand experience: once one of the fastest collegiate sprinters in the United States, he found himself too slow to make the Olympics in part due to a lingering injury and in part due to the fact that the US competition in that sport is among the toughest in the world. He recalled how his blind commitment to the pursuit of elite sport left him with regrets about some of his decisions. The "what if" aspects of his career bothered him, not so much those that he felt he could not control (e.g., his injury), but what aspects he felt he could have controlled.

I had heard his story many times before, but I had not reflected on how performance-enhancing drugs factored into those "what if" considerations. He never had never taken anabolic steroids or other banned substances (at least to his knowledge). Instead of taking pride in being a so-called "clean" or "pure" athlete (neither of which he ever used to refer to himself), he explained that he was only moderately successful in part because he was "dumb" and "naïve." More specifically, he regretted *not* taking performance-enhancing drugs, admitting that he probably would have if they were more readily accessible. He stated, "I probably would have done it if I had had more opportunities to do so. And, I don't think it really would have been about winning. Maybe that was my motivation at the time. . . . I still just want to know just how fast I *could've* been. So many of those guys I competed against went on to the next level. They were Olympians, and almost all of them were on something." He paused and went on: "Well, at least that's what everyone says. I guess I really don't know if they were, but I am pretty sure they were!" He laughed. "Look, I know that I didn't reach my goals, and I still don't know how fast I could've been."[2] This candid disclosure made it clear that Mathew's pursuit of representing the United States was not a patriotic endeavor or even an effort to be among the best natural or morally upstanding athletes.

Olympic medalist Kate Schmidt's comments on elite athletes came to mind as Mathew recounted his regrets. Athletes, she explains, are "normal in every way except for being born with a singular skill with which they become obsessed, chasing its allure until age and injury stop them."[3] The structures of sport further encourage their obsession, particularly when prestige, social status, and even financial benefits may accompany athletic success. Mathew's narrative revealed more than an obsession, though; it revealed how he internalized anti-doping messages that cast fellow competitors as suspect bodies. He presumed that the most successful had used performance-enhancing drugs, even though he admitted to relying on mostly anecdotal evidence. There is some evidence, however, to support his beliefs. Recent survey findings indicate that an estimated 29 percent of track-and-field athletes who competed at the 2011 World Championships and 45 percent of those who competed at the 2011 Pan-Arab Games admitted (anonymously) that they had doped within the last twelve months.[4] Those research findings were actually withheld by WADA, one of the funders of the research, as only 2 percent of drug tests analyzed yielded positive results. The study suggests that banned performance-enhancement practices may in fact be widespread, not simply an activity undertaken by a deviant minority of athletes who threaten the integrity of sport. Thus, the way anti-doping advocates characterize athletes, particularly those in chapter 3 of this book, is not only misleading, but it would also seem that doping is an outgrowth of the corporatized sport arrangements that have enabled anti-doping regulation to expand.

Mathew's narrative about the trials and tribulations of being an athlete in sport with widespread doping was not the first I had heard over the course of my research. Nearly all of those who had expressed such sentiments had competed at the elite level in track and field or road cycling. In fact, another US athlete, Gina, who I had previously spoken with, came to mind as I reflected on Mathew's words. Gina had felt so strongly about the pervasiveness of doping in her sport that she competed for another country. (She had been born in the other country and was therefore eligible to do so.[5]) Identifying as an American, she presented her decision not to represent the United States in ethical terms, as a choice not to participate in what she considered to be a contaminated sport. As we spoke, however, it became clear that her intentions were rooted in experiences not unlike those upon which Mathew reflected. The direct impetus for representing another country was her failure to qualify for the United States. Although humble in her demeanor, Gina expressed that she felt she was among the best, admitting that she did not believe others were that much better than her without cheating. Her evidence? Beyond other competitors' improved performances? Gina stated, "Well, I could tell just by looking at them. It just didn't look right, you know?"[6] For her, seemingly unnatural female muscularity served as evidence of doping, an assumption that has rendered women suspect in relation to their biology and to performance enhancement. Again, her competition emerged as suspect, and her observations of their physical improvements and aesthetics served as evidence. Interestingly, when I saw a picture taken of her during her competitive career, I could not help but notice her own evident muscularity and female apologetic displays of feminine accessorizing, which, at least to me as an outsider, did not look dissimilar to images of her competitors. Athletes, in both cases, projected suspicion outward, not inward.

Both of their narratives reveal that athlete citizenship entails high levels of suspicion and risk, compelling themes that came out of my research. For Mathew and Gina, their internalized suspicion of others and their risk aversion (compared to other competitors who they suspected of doping) is an outgrowth of the regulatory logics documented here. In this case, two athletes, both from the United States, revealed how they had accepted foundational messages about embodiment communicated by anti-doping regulation to the extent that it shaped their perceptions of others, as well as their own subjectivity.

Despite their successes, Mathew and Gina conveyed a clear sense of longing, having ended their athletic careers dissatisfied, even heartbroken, both feeling cheated in different ways. Doping factored into their feelings of loss, assuaging, or at least explaining, the pain of not achieving what they felt they could have or should have. In juxtaposing their perspectives on doping, I wondered if such feelings were enough to justify current regulation, as many of anti-doping advocates argued. Or, were their feelings an outgrowth of regulation and the climate of competitive sport? Perhaps both. Regardless, doping provided a scapegoat for both athletes, enabling them to channel the sense of sorrow that they felt when they were unable to excel at the levels for which they strove. Anti-doping regulation did not end that sense of loss. Instead, it helped them to explain their failures. Despite admitting knowledge gaps in terms of what they knew about who had been doping or what substances they presumably took, both athletes rendered their competitors as suspicious, even as they recounted the number of times that they and others had endured testing. During that same discussion, however, Gina also mentioned that she had variety of resources—by being a US citizen—that others in the country she would go on to represent likely did not. A hard-working and proud athlete, she showed no inclination that other athletes could have construed her advantage as unfair. She did not see her privilege as suspect, but, instead, channeled the accepted messages that doping is the cornerstone violation of fair play in sport.

The bitterness expressed by both retired athletes resonated in a tone similar to what I heard on television when competitors in the 2009 800-meter World Championship condemned Caster Semenya, the South African runner accused of being too masculine and unfairly competing in women's sport, even though she was as natural and uncontaminated as any other athlete against which she raced. The narratives of those competitors revealed that the perceived impossibility of winning came to be read as unfair, especially for someone who did not present, at least to the more vocal competitors, as normatively gendered. Even though Semenya has always has asserted that she is a women, not intersex, speculation persisted. Regulation aimed at protecting fair play gave athletes a language to express and justify the feelings of injustice when up against these exceptional—seemingly unnatural—competitors. It also perpetuates a cycle of suspicion, even reminding spectators to be suspicious of the bodies that may look "normal."

Far from the "comrades in arms" ideal originally promoted by Pierre de Coubertin as the foundation of the Olympics, other athletes instead appeared as threats. Even though anti-doping advocates at the 2007 World Conference on Doping in Sport expressed a desire for contemporary sport to reflect traditional Olympic values, regulation has failed to deliver such outcomes. Instead, athletes are held to elements of amateurism, namely the subscription that bodies should be natural and unadulterated, through a host of technocratic and scientific surveillance mechanisms. Accompanying the expansion in surveillance has come an increase in individual risks and anxieties of contamination endured by athletes, ranging from doubts about the substances one ingests to perceptions of fellow competitors. With more athletes held accountable through surveillance, regulation does then deliver aspects of the sport envisioned by Coubertin, for it is still laden with inequalities in terms of who can participate.

Here, by way of conclusion, I reflect on broader implications of anti-doping regulation as they surface around two issues: first, the practical shortcomings of the anti-doping regime's efforts to police an (inherently contaminated) ideal of fair play, which demonstrates the second, how athlete citizenship both relies upon and sustains a kind of law-like power ascertained through the regime's legalized and biomedicalized architecture. Despite its limitations and failures, the regime retains its status as a necessary regulation in sport to which there are only limited forms of resistance. This is in part because the cultural and binding forms of social control that it leverages.

Consequences of Anti-Doping Regulation

Complexities are inherent in any global regime. Anti-doping regulation upholds a vast array of problems despite what appear on the surface as well-intended goals. From a historical vantage point, Rob Beamish and Ian Richie argue that WADA's preoccupation with testing and surveillance actually encourages the use of potentially hazardous "designer" steroids available in black markets.[7] Water-based anabolic androgenic steroids became more desirable because they could be quickly absorbed and discharged after injection; however, they are also arguably more toxic than oil-based formulas, especially with regard to their impact on kidney and liver health. Today, findings from recent sports scandals in professional cycling as well as in some professional Australian sports reveal that there are still instances where athletes are encouraged to experimentally and systematically use substances not approved for human intake. The result is unfortunate: in attempting to eliminate doping, WADA's guidelines provide incentives to use such drugs and methods, subsequently fueling the growth of underground economies. WADA's actions exacerbate the very crisis that the agency seeks to attack, exemplifying critiques of drug-prohibition regimes that convincingly argue that such approaches are ineffective and can make matters much worse.[8]

The escalating number of resources committed to counteracting doping highlight that anti-doping regulation is situated in and interacts with other markets, which can be both illicit and legal in nature. As John Braithwaite notes, there are markets of vice, and there are markets for virtue.[9] They are often intertwined. Given the limited focus of anti-doping interventions, regulation does little to alter, or "flip" to use Braithwaite's language, the markets that encourage doping as a vice. Instead, regulation exacerbates the risks posed by these markets, doing so in ways that disproportionately affect working-class athletes and athletes of color, those groups that protectors of the amateur ideal once deemed as "lower orders" not deserving or capable of enjoying sport and its privileges. Markets do not escape the inequalities engrained from the past; rather, they evidence them through different modes. In this case, the exclusion of such bodies in sport emerges through individual punishments—and not always for using banned performance-enhancing methods—rather than through a formal ban on their inclusion. The nature of their inclusion reflects neoliberal shifts.

In the current global regulatory environment, athletes, particularly those who pursue sport as a professional outlet, are a captive group with few alternatives. Kate Schmidt describes elite and aspiring elite athletes as having a relentless desire for individual excellence, a disposition that not only binds them to the terms of the current anti-doping regime in order to participate but also incentivizes doping. She writes, "Fans have created such high expectations for athletes that success seems to require steroid use for any sport requiring speed, power, or a combination of the two. . . . Athletes always will be a step ahead of the testing labs in concealing substances because of the multibillion-dollar industries that have been built on their sweat and their obsession. They will seek out the next great 'thing'—a vitamin, a nutritional supplement, a training technique, a piece of training equipment, a new shoe, a drug."[10] Her argument alludes to a broader observation: anti-doping regulation does little to alter incentives for doping, and it does not challenge the various markets of performance enhancement fueled by the corporatization of global sport. This is in part because those markets also help to sustain anti-doping regulation. For instance, WADA leverages corporate incentives to obtain compliance with the UNESCO Convention and the WADA Code by including IOC-backed sanctions for non-signatory countries, such as the inability to host sporting events. WADA also maintains formal agreements with pharmaceutical groups, such as Amgen, F. Hoffmann-La Roche Ltd., GlaxoSmithKline, and the International Federation of Pharmaceutical Manufacturers Association, in order to obtain information about and ban potentially performance-enhancing substances under development in their labs in anticipation that athletes might obtain and use them for doping. By adopting a future-oriented plan of action, the leveraging of such partnerships reinscribes and creates individual risk as more detection tools are developed.

The debate around doping appears both etched by and circulated though regulatory capitalism, risk, and coercion. Anti-doping regulation's embrace of such modes yields cyclical consequences in practice. Because anti-doping regulation is preoccupied with individual behaviors, not broader organizational or corporate influences, athletes shoulder much of the risk. These risks, according to Deborah Lupton's analysis of health and the regulated body, become part of responsibilized subjects who internalize the gaze focused onto bodies.[11] While Lupton's observation applies across health regulation, the particularities of the risks shouldered by athletes distinguish them from other citizen subjects. For example, taking dietary supplements, which many average citizens perceive as responsible self-care, is an area of risk and risk management for aspiring elite athletes.[12] As many state-sanctioned regulations do not ensure that supplements and alternative medicines are free of banned substances, the burden falls primarily on the athlete. Any formal assistance in navigating these risks usually comes from the anti-doping agencies, which are part of the regime that make taking such substances more risky in the first place. These agencies are also often tasked with enforcement, further dissuading athletes from seeking assistance or guidance about supplement use. In fact, most agencies, including Drug Free Sport New Zealand, actively discourage athletes from using any food supplements at all. The prohibition stance, which is reiterated at various levels of regulation, forecloses the discussion of what risks might be less harmful to athletes' heath and well-being or the introduction of legal reforms that could help mediate such dangers.

Instead, markets offer athletes some ways of negotiating risk, but they come at a cost. For example, supplement companies certify products as "safe" for athletes to take, two of the most notable being Informed Choice and the Banned Substances Control Group in the United States. Both companies affix their labels onto products that they have tested and certified as not containing contaminants. This certification is embedded in the product's price and carries over to the athlete. That extra fee can be thought of as a kind of insurance, one that is not necessarily guaranteed. Although these companies provide lists of the batches they have tested, including expiration dates of those clearances, they also maintain a disclaimer about their work. This form of certification is one of the few legal options, though, in an otherwise largely unregulated market. It emerges as another technology to aid athlete development, but it still circumscribes both risk and responsibility onto the athlete. It is essentially an opportunity to invest in risk reduction if one can afford and access them. Despite claiming to preserve fair play for all, anti-doping regulation has actually contributed to the growth of an industry that serves a more affluent clientele.

There are also accusations that doping in professional sport intersects with and actually fuels illicit markets, claims that featured prominently in an Australian report made public in February 2013. According to the report by the Australian Crime Commission (ACC), an agency with special coercive investigative powers that was established to help provide intelligence for investigations into serious and organized crime, findings from the year-long Project Aperio investigation suggest that doping in professional sport was "widespread," had filtered down to the sub-elite levels of competition, and created opportunities for criminal groups to exploit, including forms of fraud such as match fixing, which is the pre-determination of a match's outcome before it is played.[13] This finding diverges from the few criminological studies of other jurisdictions, and many critics contend this is a misuse of resources that diverts from the ACC's intended purpose.[14] Further, and despite public accusations by authorities that they would go after "drug cheats," the ACC could not release evidence and encouraged the Australian Sports Anti-Doping

Authority (ASADA) to further investigate professional sports clubs, prompting critics to characterize the announcement as a "political stunt."[15] At the time of this writing, ASADA had investigated six clubs with professional sides in the National Rugby League (NRL) competition and two Australian Football League (AFL) teams over the course of more than a year. These efforts yielded one clear instance of an athlete suspension for an anti-doping rule violation and agreements that led to the temporary suspensions of a few coaches until ASADA offered a plea agreement to other athletes: if they admitted guilt, athletes would receive a backdated suspension, which limited the actual time away from competition to only weeks, enabling them to avoid drawn-out legal proceedings.[16] In response, Olympic athletes complained that ASADA was upholding "double standards," which held Olympic athletes to much higher—and harsher—standards.[17] Proceedings continue in the AFL case, despite the league threatening significant sanctions on grounds that their actions had brought "the game into disrepute," even though there was not a clear anti-doping rule violation.[18] Overall, though, despite a great deal of media speculation and controversy, few so-called criminals were caught; rather, many players were searched under the presumption of criminal activity. These developments, combined with a number of cyclists (some of whom are Australian) admitting to doping after seven-time Tour de France winning cyclist Lance Armstrong was sanctioned, made doping a popular headline throughout 2013 in Australasia and beyond. Moreover, they highlight the differential treatment of athletes, even between those within the same national jurisdiction.

Amid investigations and accusations, the Australian Parliament expanded ASADA's investigative powers. The bill, entitled the Australian Sports Anti-Doping Authority Amendment Bill, brings athletes, "support personnel, and athletes' family members under its disciplinary gaze," giving the agency unprecedented scope.[19] In essence, law extended the bounds of who can be surveilled and brought under the umbrella of risk. Specifically, it enables the agency to compel individuals to produce materials pertaining to an anti-doping investigation or face a substantial civil penalty (currently 5,100 Australian dollars per day of noncompliance).[20] This instance of national law adopted the regulatory logics of governing through crime analyzed at the international level in this book. It, according to some observers,[21] marked a move closer toward criminalization, which some scholars have cautioned against, based on experiences in other jurisdictions.[22] That is, when authorities could not catch athletes suspected of doping, the government expanded the agency's capacity to monitor and surveil citizen subjects so that it could catch them. Again, the demonization of professional athletes perpetrated these events, and again, regulatory tactics still focused on individuals, casting them as deviant.

The legal developments that pertain to the anti-doping regime are not simply those of expansion, however. The regime has faced some legal challenges as well as some resistance from athletes and stakeholders. Although the Court of Arbitration for Sport (CAS) has endorsed WADA's anti-doping rules and jurisdiction, a ruling by the US Court of Appeals for the Eighth Circuit has rejected the rationale behind the strict-liability standard, upholding a 2009 district court decision.[23] Although the Court's decision was later overturned after years of case review, it nonetheless points to a tension within the law. The ruling emerges from a case that involved two Minnesota-based athletes who tested positive for a diuretic banned by the NFL Policy on Anabolic Steroids and Related Substances. Specifically, they had tested positive for bumetanide, a substance found in the once common weight-loss supplement StarCaps, which can also mask steroid use. Arguing that arbitration offered no remedy, the athletes filed a legal complaint, breaking from the terms of the Collective Bargaining Agreement. The US courts concurred that the policy violated the Minnesota Drug and Alcohol Testing in the Workplace Act, which prevents the termination of employment on the basis of a drug test alone. This ruling is important in two ways: first, it considered athletes' intent, acknowledging that the NFL failed to inform players that StarCaps contained bumetanide and that the accused unknowingly ingested the banned substance; and second, it rejected every attempt by the NFL to evade state laws in order to uphold the terms of the Collective Bargaining Agreement and its internal policies.[24] In short, the Court of Appeals resisted perpetuating the cycle of elevating individual risks; however, after years of case review that eventually found in the NFL's favor, the athletes opted for a reduced suspension rather than continue with the lengthy appeals process.

Such conflicts may only scratch the surface of the extent to which WADA's expanded practices may be incompatible with certain legal principles, especially if considered across jurisdictions. Practicing lawyers and academics alike recognize that future disputes may confront longstanding concerns regarding athletes' rights in relation to methods of sample collection and testing.[25] Legal challenges take direct issue with the WADA's methods of surveillance, namely its Whereabouts Program. Among them is a complaint filed in Belgian courts alleging that the system violates article 8 of the European Convention on Human Rights (which addresses privacy).[26] The case, as one regulator during my fieldwork speculated, poses the question of whether or not CAS can actually provide athletes a fair trial. If the courts were to find that CAS cannot do so and that accused athletes deserve legal procedures and protections, CAS, sometimes referred to as the "Supreme Court of World Sport," would be weakened. This possibility, he explained, could occur even though the Swiss Federal Court has held previously that CAS is an independent and "true arbitration court" in response to an earlier appeal that contended it was too closely aligned with the IOC and potentially biased.[27] More recently, in early 2014, a decision by a German Regional Court in Munich undermined decisions by

CAS and the Swiss Federal Tribunal (*Pechstein v. German and International Skating Unions*), holding that the rulings were invalid because athletes were compelled to enter them, not doing so voluntarily.[28]

Taken together, these legal issues point to an embedded feature of the anti-doping regime. Under WADA's rules, athletes are required to consent to certain non-negotiable terms, such as submitting to arbitration. For many, this is a tradeoff for choosing to participate in sport. But, is it a choice? Considering the regime's hybrid character and how it has fashioned its agreements with incentives and binding repercussions, it seems logical to ask whether and to what extent athletes' consent is coerced. The incentives of sport may entice athletes not only to dope, but also to compel them to comply with fundamentally unfair aspects of the regime. Increased legal interventions expose a notable tension: although advocates argue that increased governmental involvement will lead to a stronger, more efficient anti-doping system, there are broader inconsistencies among anti-doping rules, democratic social values, and notions of procedural justice. As some argue that the anti-doping regime undermines athletes' rights,[29] the checks and balances of law could also erode or hinder the regime's accepted tactics. Just as likely, as surveillance becomes more routinized across populations, law may become complicit with the practices, especially as anti-doping monitoring is not considered a humans-rights violation.

The legal possibilities present an inconsistent picture of enforcement. In the United States, while a number of MLB players accused of using performance-enhancing drugs have managed to evade formal punishment (or at least lengthy punishments), attempts by the United States Anti-Doping Agency (USADA) to prove that Lance Armstrong committed acts of doping were eventually successful, even despite notable resistance and criticism from the media and fans. After the Department of Justice ended its two-year investigation of Armstrong in 2012, anti-doping authorities, without physical evidence of doping, obtained testimonies from other athletes attesting that he had. In some cases, they obtained these statements by striking plea bargains for reduced anti-doping rule-violation sanctions. Calling it a vendetta against him, Armstrong filed for a restraining order against USADA, even going so far as to say that the agency broke its own rules to pursue him.[30] The presiding judge, the Honorable Sam Sparks, unceremoniously dismissed the filing in just hours, describing it as "eighty mostly unnecessary pages" and "a lengthy and bitter polemic against the named defendants."[31] After Armstrong's lawyers revised their submission, Sparks expressed strong reservations about having legal courts intervene when arbitration is well established, even as he questioned the fairness and clarity of USADA's allegations.[32] Although authorities had not yet caught Armstrong, the law did not come to his aid.

Armstrong's success and personality may have made him a suspect athlete who would ultimately become a fallen hero; however, they also contributed to his ability to command resources that made it more difficult to punish him formally.[33] Even with access to many resources, Armstrong was eventually caught, and despite evidence of systematic doping, there were no sanctions or reforms seriously considered for the sport of cycling and its management.[34] Initially, there were, however, calls made by some members of the anti-doping community, including former WADA chief, Dick Pound, to remove cycling from the Olympics, a proposal that did not materialize.[35]

Although Armstrong has been vilified by many and endured significant financial losses, his story has also emerged as a cautionary tale of celebrity and indulgence, a forgiving narrative that is notably absent around the Marion Jones case. His is a distinctly different polluted body than that of Jones. The fact that Armstrong overcame cancer to retain his international icon status (a shift from a sick and disabled body to a strong and super-abled body), combined with his masculine whiteness, has prompted many to cast him as a "lesson" from which to learn.[36] Even when condemned for a similar anti-doping rule violation, other athletes are treated in ways that reflect the significance of gendered and racial difference. With a growing number of suspect athletes, who are the subject of surveillance even after they retire, more names are likely to join the category of "offender." Not only are testing and surveillance broader and more intrusive in nature, they can also be applied retroactively for up to eight years after a sample has been collected. As Armstrong's case highlights, authorities can mobilize other kinds of evidence, such as testimony, against athletes as well. If science or regulators cannot catch someone doping during their athletic career, they may be able to in the future.

Another overlooked dimension of how athletes are treated under the regime is the impact on children, the innocents often upheld as being in need of protection. According to Sarah Teetzel and Marcus Mazzucco, current rules allow anti-doping organizations to test athletes regardless of age, and even though minors cannot provide informed consent, they can be subject to sanctions comparable to those of their adult counterparts.[37] Young athletes who are selected for high-level sport are not always subject to WADA-compliant testing procedures, but they are still subject to the normative messages of the regime and receive instruction about the requirements of anti-doping surveillance. For instance, as an interview with an Australian-based coach revealed, minors selected for elite development pathways in some sports are "taught" when they are adolescents that they need to be compliant with drug testing. His particular example was an instance where athletes were sent home after practice with "piss cups" in hand after "their coach told them to bring the cups to the next practice with them full [of urine]."[38] Although not the concern of formal testing that Teetzel and Mazzucco address, the practice of requiring minors to bring samples back socializes them, even at a young age, to comply with the terms of the anti-doping regime if they are to progress to higher levels of competition. Although not a drug test where athletes are required to urinate in the presence of a doping control officer, the task was nonetheless presented as a requirement for athletes participating in the program, not as a choice from which they could refrain.

Although regulation continues to expand and is seemingly stacked against athletes, it is important to note that citizenship is not simply a formation where authorities exercise power. It is also a space where subjects can, at least to some extent, negotiate or push back. While there are notably few instances of this occurring in anti-doping regulation, they do exist. Lance Armstrong was perhaps the most notable until he was sanctioned. Revisiting the developments in Australia reveals some clear instances. NRL star Jonathan Thurston verbally attacked anti-doping authorities via news interviews and social media for "bashing down the front door" in the early morning hours, unnecessarily intruding into his home and waking up his newborn daughter.[39] Even though the NRL reiterated that it supported ASADA's efforts and that Thurston was not exempt from the rules, the athlete remained defiant even as he complied with the request, and many fans expressed support for him. During ASADA's investigations into NRL clubs, players from one club initially refused a plea bargain that would require them to admit guilt for doping in exchange for a reduced penalty, in part because the proposal emerged in the absence of formal anti-doping rule violation charges.[40] Moreover, a survey administered during the early investigations revealed overwhelming support from fans, indicating they felt athletes and clubs had been treated unfairly by authorities, in turn, suggesting a disregard of authorities and claims that doping ruins the essence of sport.[41] Although a group of rugby league players did eventually accept a plea bargain, public discourse rendered their choice a practical one, akin to accepting a "speeding fine" as an alternative to pursuing their innocence through drawn-out legal action.[42]

Such developments, combined with the other narratives highlighted in this book, demonstrate that the current terms of athlete citizenship are vastly different than those expressed by Coubertin in relation to his notion of the *race sportive*. Although elite sport now includes athletes who were not permitted to compete within Coubertin's vision of the Olympics, such as women and many non-European peoples, the gatekeeping mechanisms employed under the banner of "cleaning up" sport reflect that higher risks and consequences retain elements of the enduring inequalities underpinning Coubertin's visions. As changes to athlete citizenship reveal the impacts of broader globalized changes, what then can sport tell us about citizenship and legality more generally?

Lessons from Sport about Citizenship
and Legality in a Globalized World

The practical side effects of anti-doping regulation point to the inevitable shortcomings, conundrums, and inequalities manifest in formations of citizenship. Here, I have sought to unearth how anti-doping tactics take on contextually contingent meanings in localized contexts. In doing so, this analysis highlights how the power of ideals (such as fair play) at the global level reflect gendered, racialized, and classed dimensions, the trappings of which can have varied consequences in practice. Even though the technocratic tools (such as law and science) in this field assert an objective veneer that seems preoccupied with protecting natural bodies, this genealogical analysis of the regime suggests that these tools more often than not police boundaries of naturalized difference.

Against the backdrops of history and nation analyzed here, what prevails is not safer or more egalitarian practices of sport, but rather the protection of an ideal, a foundation myth of who an athlete citizen should be: a disciplined body that is as ethically pure as it is biologically. Although the justification for regulation is to protect fair play, with scientific measures providing proof of athletes' transgressions, there remain clear political, gendered, and postcolonial implications in relation to punishment and who emerges as visibly suspect. This attests to the invariable pluralism of what appears to be a clearly defined goal: the elimination of doping in sport. Distinctly different from the narratives highlighted in this book, public rhetoric around doping in sport continues to suggest that the notion of a level playing field is a tangible entity that regulation can protect in a globalized world. Regulatory technologies render the ideals of athlete citizenship as enforceable expectations, translating ideologies of the past into truth-claims of the present. In attempting to preserve an ethic of purity, anti-doping regulation relies on ideas that emerged during a time when boundaries between citizens and subjects—and between men and women—seemed easier to define through visibly gendered and colonial lenses. Early Olympic legacies still inform how we perceive sport and the regulation of athletes, but not necessarily in clear or deterministic ways. Law, regulation, and science may interact in complicated and constitutive ways, yet they still tend to catch bodies that were originally ostracized from sport.

The anti-doping regime's hybridized features help to sustain the crisis rhetoric surrounding doping in sport. Through the routine and systematic bodily surveillance of athletes, regulation sustains anxieties around concerns deemed threats (doping) to values once thought of as the cornerstones of Olympism (amateurism). In doing so, individuals athletes, not the broader structure of corporatized sport, are held to account. In fact, as chapter 5 describes, the regulatory gaze directed at athletes has manufactured risk to the extent that some anti-doping agencies' primary duties are often to help athletes remain compliant with the terms of the regime. Consequently, a race sportive persists in the sense that elite athletes are expected to be morally and physically upstanding by being held to significant bodily scrutiny. This group of athletes is still expected to transcend the expectations of mere mortal men. Stronger than other humans, they are not to succumb to the influences others would. Previously, this was assumed under their status as amateurs. Today, it is actually policed.

In attempting to ensure that elite athlete bodies live up to these traditional expectations, the anti-doping regime seeks to prove athlete citizens' superhumanness by asserting they be fully human yet not partake in human vices in or outside of competition. The anti-doping mission and the beliefs upon which it hinges, however, are more than unrealistic; they are fallacies now backed by Western technoscience. As Donna Haraway reminds us, bodies are already always contaminated, and the determination of being 100 percent human is restricted to the limitations of the scientific instruments used to make evaluations.[43] The anti-doping regime can only provide proof of purity through the detection of certain artificial substances that it deems unethical and the condemnation of bodies that it deems to be impure. As a result, whether an athlete dopes is not always a choice, but instead often a calculation of risk and risk management. In fact, many so-called "clean" athletes negotiate this inherently contaminated position in their everyday activities by selecting supplements that they think can take to avoid an anti-doping rule violation and by utilizing approved technologies of performance enhancement. Such balancing is a consequence of not being able to be pure bodies.

Another telltale sign of the international regime's power emerges around the bodies characterized as polluted or inherently suspect. Much of this book focuses its attention on these bodies in order to illuminate the contradictions around how and why they are classified as drug cheats. Even though there are relatively few athletes caught doping, this analysis attests that there remains skepticism around (black) professional US athletes and women of color who do not fit (Western) gender norms. In raising these issues, I am pointing to a broader concern related to public discourse: why are there relatively few questions about the depictions of these bodies, the nature of the punishment, and which substances are considered doping? With the tacit acceptance of doping as a condemnable offense (enforced by a specific regime), the modes of pursuing compliance in this domain often go overlooked or underscrutinized. In order to preserve a particular ideology of purity, regulation has shifted and expanded to take on hybridized contours, giving it rationalized aesthetics. Backed by science and law, the regime presents as if it can know and explain that which nonexpert onlookers may presume but cannot prove. The everyday gaze of spectators is only conditioned to see abnormalities to naturalized orders, not scientific evidence of their transgression. This exemplifies a regulatory "god-trick," to use Haraway's words; that is, the belief that law and regulation are uniquely attuned to and able to find impurities that laypersons cannot.[44] Upon further review, the regime's work emerges as an "illusion of even, unmediated, and rational vision" that is aimed at a social ill, one that veils the more complicated interplay between risk, surveillance, and postcolonial inequalities.[45]

Stepping back from the rhetoric, we might ask how significant a social ill is doping in sport in the first place and how rational are the terms of the regime that targets it? Doping in the form of performance-enhancing drugs and methods receives substantial media attention and appears to undermine fair competition, but are the popularized cases representative of a broader suspect class that has not yet been caught, or are there relatively few athletes doping? If it is widespread, does it constitute an act of deviance? Or, is doping in sport merely a form of occupational performance enhancement similar to other forms of workplace performance enhancement that are not scrutinized?

The New Zealand case study provides preliminary answers to these questions. It provides chilling implications about what the protection of fair play actually yields in practice, even within an athlete-centered agency. As chapter 5 suggests, DFSNZ's findings evidence that few anti-doping rule violations occur. While this may be a testament to its hands-on approach, it may also suggest that those athletes with resources elude detection. More importantly, we see that DFSNZ's practical objectives are not so much to prevent doping, but to protect athletes who do not intend to dope from getting caught by the terms of the system. Meeting requirements of compliance, themselves a disciplinary apparatus, is the primarily preoccupation, not the broader regulatory claims of catching drug cheats. In doing so, the detection of marijuana and other illicit drug use emerges as a mode of discerning what subjects are unworthy of being athlete citizens.

While this project appears to deviate from what the international anti-doping regime asserts as its goals, that is, eliminating doping in sport, it accords with the original goals of amateurism and its alternative motives in protecting bodily purity: to prevent groups deemed to be "lower orders" from participating. Racial, gendered, and classed differences are still significant, even as regulation has refashioned their colonial justifications as objective, technocratic terms. As chapters 3 through 5 indicate, working-class bodies of color remain suspect, not because they actively seek to cheat, but because their visibility renders them more at risk, especially when their behaviors do not actively embrace the cultures of biomedicalization and risk.

By rethinking how the plurality of anti-doping regulations can posit values seemingly external to its stated objectives, this analysis of athlete citizenship draws attention to the importance of embodiment, as athletes' bodies, irrespective of whether they are considered "clean" or deemed to be contaminated, serve as symbolic markers of authoritative claims, be they governmental, nongovernmental, or hybrid in nature. By querying the regulation of athletes' bodies, this book has described how the movements to protect fair play in sport inform the boundaries in and around who may and may not become an athlete citizen. But, that is not the only objective of this book. Through the analysis of sport, a site where we can empirically observe the explicit policing of athletes' bodies, I have sought to draw attention to the impurities inherent within legalized spaces more generally. While anti-doping regulation is in some ways an exception to traditional forms of law, it is also in many ways the norm in that it is symptomatic of modern desires and surveillance. The basis of anti-doping campaigns draws attention to the desire to delineate the boundaries between the natural and the artificial, which are a manifestation of the presumed binary between nature and culture/society. This perpetuates a modern myth, a Great Divide to use Bruno Latour's language,[46] which is not so much about protecting the natural body, but about regulating the degree to which athlete citizens can transgress normative orders naturalized, vis-à-vis the gendered and postcolonial frames. The regulation of athletes' bodies is a kind of insurance that ensures the Olympic brand remains a "pure" (and arguably marketable) spectacle, directing spectators' attentions away from the foundations myths upon which this brand is built.

Sport highlights the degree to which the false dichotomy between nature and society/culture becomes so pervasive that we, even as scholars, rarely question it. While the limitations of science in diagnosing and preserving the natural body are significant, there is a deep concern underpinning them; that is, how this mythical binary conjoins with technoscience and legality to fortify and uphold value systems. Whereas anti-doping regulation enables us to query these relationships, a number of classic texts that shape foundational ideas about law and society reaffirm this binary. For instance, Thomas Hobbes's *Leviathan* justifies the social contract and the laws of society as a necessary intervention to protect men from themselves, their violent tendencies, and the "solitary, poor, nasty, brutish, and short" lives in the state of nature.[47] Extending Hobbes's presumption, property, in a Lockean sense, is dependent upon the labor invested into nature, thus making labor important and reaffirming it in terms of economic *and* ethical value. Anti-doping regulation reflects a commitment to both of these tenets, discursively promoting them in a mediated format: on the one hand, the justification of anti-doping regulation's intervention is to protect athletes from themselves, and on the other hand, regulation condemns doping as unethical on the grounds that it undermines the value of work that athlete citizens are to embody. Sport emphasizes these values around labor in ways that support capitalist objectives and responsibilized behaviors. Accordingly, athletes are to embody and symbolize those ethics.

This book sheds light on how legality and biomedicalization operate to preserve values ascribed to athletes' labor and bodies and to misdirect attention from broader neoliberal dynamics at work. Anti-doping regulation is not simply about how athletes achieve results (unfairly or not), but also about which bodies actually do the work and conform to the ideologies ascribed to their capacities. Impurities underpinning regulation become evident in the spaces where punishments diverge from their stated goals of preserving bodily purity, the places where bodies are sanctioned for transgressions that do not fit within WADA's stated mission. The history of gender verification illustrates this contradiction clearly; however, it also emerges in lesser-known anti-doping cases, such as those discussed in chapter 5. Suspect and punished athletes highlight the boundary work of athlete citizenship, particularly how the promotion of a global sport community committed to ideals of fair play overshadows the cultures of risk and suspicion enabled by the surveillance activities that uphold this rhetoric. The condemnation of outlawed subjects is important to the regime's delineation of subjects and contributes to maintaining the status quo in global sport. Apparatuses of social control, including sample collection and testing, subsidiary anti-doping agencies such as DFSNZ, and public scrutiny of athletes' bodies, fortify the presumed connections between fair play and bodily purity through a calculated and empirical language of technology and law. They also veil the unfair playing field where sport markets continue to profit from the performances of athletes who are subject to notably high levels of bodily intrusion and scrutiny.

The ideologies that justify the anti-doping regime's purpose attest to the embedded politics of regulation. These politics, while seemingly about globalization and corporate relations, are also postcolonial. As scientific apparatuses have changed alongside technocratic, medical, and legalistic practices to more accurately and effectively catch cheaters, postcolonial articulations of difference enter "through the backdoor" in much the same way that Troy Duster has argued that racism informs biomedical explanations.[48] In this case, science does not subversively promote genetic answers to problems associated with certain ethnic groups, as is Duster's argument. Rather, in seeking to empirically justify fair play and ideals about bodies and their abilities, racialized and gendered logics creep into the anti-doping regime's rhetorical strategies and regulatory practices. This, the colonial excess acknowledged by Nan Seuffert, is inherent within the regime and its claims to be a transnational community-building project.[49] Regulation, as Alison Young suggests, inherits such "excess as the logical precondition of the community, tradition, the home, the nation." Its embrace of legalistic and scientific tools marks not only a disavowal of how other forms of inequality directly inform fair play in sport, but also a failure to grapple with this excess—and the contradictions its condemnation reveals—in meaningful ways.

Considering anti-doping regulation in relation to its protection of fabricated binaries and its denial of difference renders it a transnational extension of what Jane Collier, Bill Maurer and Liliana Suárez-Navaz described as "bourgeois law." Although a hybrid regulatory regime, its rules "by requiring the equal treatment of all subjects" through standardized protocols and procedures, "appears to ignore differences that exist before or outside law;" however, it "*demands* difference even as it disclaims it."[50] Regulation, by "treating those who share an identity as equals, casts as unequal those who do not share that identity."[51] While policing difference, anti-doping regulation creates it, albeit in refashioned form. The athlete citizen that regulation aims to protect, an enlightened body in which science serves to enhance but not taint, relies on the categorical dismissal of Other bodies banned from participating in sport. Over the years, these Othered bodies have included a range of subjects: Native peoples deemed "savages," professional athletes, intersex individuals, women diagnosed as biologically abnormal, and bodies characterized as doped, regardless of whether or not they intentionally used performance-enhancing drugs.[52] Today, these practices continue and expand through practices rationalized by science and law.

The treatment of athletes' bodies under anti-doping regulation is thus more telling of legality than it would at first seem. It shows us that law and regulation can clandestinely draw upon and mobilize extralegal discourses in its differential treatment of subjects, something the language of its rules does not—and arguably cannot—acknowledge formally. This, a fundamental issue of legality, demonstrates the ways that law can posit ideals as realities and mask their contradictions. Lisa Hajjar describes this as the "disjuncture between [law's] promises and people's lived realities."[53] In relation to anti-doping regulation, the promises of international law posit a series of utopian ideals from the Global North: those of fair play, a level playing field of equal participants, and even a harmonized vision that government can partner with other stakeholders to deliver these outcomes. Cumulatively, they assert visions from which experience inevitably deviates just as athletes' bodies and behaviors inevitably diverge from imagined notions of what "clean" athletes should be.

Anti-doping regulation perpetuates both the myth and reality of the athlete citizen. It promises to protect the ideal as if it is achievable, confounding the space between that which regulation asserts as real and its pursuit of this goal. Science too works in the service of the regime's aims by perpetuating the myth of purity as a natural condition, suggesting that subjects are on equal footing. But, as the bodies of outlawed athlete-subjects remind us, this stance is a false pretense, one that fortifies contemporary imaginaries of what athlete citizens *should* be. In doing so, the regime has arguably become the impetus for what anti-doping regulation is intended to protect against: a body so committed to winning at all costs that it zealously leverages technologies of performance enhancement, some proven and some experimental, in ways that have disrupted the playing fields of sport.

Although pursuing a mission that advocates bodily purity and ethics, the policing of athlete citizenship reveals that regulation has not assuaged technological fears of modern sport. If anything, they have become institutionalized. Colonial and exclusionary legacies persist, even though there is no longer an amateur ideal, and women—at least most women—can now compete in sport. Instead of the Olympic mantras of "sport for all" and "fair play," anti-doping regulation contributes to a contested field where only idealized bodies are valued as pure and most elite athletes are rendered suspect. Further, amid growing calls to criminalize doping among athletes, the practices of the regime and its corporate partnerships are largely ignored. Few question whether doping actually constitutes an act of deviance for elite athletes who are subject to pressures to continually improve athletic performances. These outcomes appear decidedly different than in the rhetoric employed by regulators to promote a moral crusade that protects sport's integrity and the rights of "clean" athletes because those pure athletes are imaginary. Rather than fostering a space where athletes do not feel the pressure to commit acts of doping, anti-doping regulation entails a system where athletes endure multiple requirements and risks to prove that they are clean enough to be athlete citizens.

Developing Anti-Doping Alternatives in a Globalized World

Although the goal of this book is not to provide a comprehensive evaluation of WADA's regulatory performance, I recognize that it provides a significant critique of the anti-doping regime. As this and preceding chapters shed light on its regulatory shortcomings, readers might be left with questions regarding what alternative frameworks could better serve the interests of fair competition and athletes' health. Rather attempt to fully describe and develop those alternatives here, I leave readers with questions and concerns that, as this book attests, are necessary to attend to if this regulatory space is to ever become more equitable. Taking seriously the narratives and experiences of suspect and outlawed athletes presented here, how might we develop a more humanistic approach to sport—even in its current technocratic, biomedialized, and capitalistic form—one that demonstrates a deeper respect for the complexities of human difference? How might we reconsider even basic functions of regulation so as to help athletes make informed choices about their bodies without further escalating the cycles of risk and risk management that they navigate?

Given the inequalities and inequities inherent to modern sport, discussions of reform must attend to racialized, classed, gendered, and nationalistic legacies undergirding regulation and how they have carried over into the criminalization of particular bodies. While sport likely cannot escape these conditions, developing more democratic ways of engaging athletes so as to better understand how these issues materialize in local jurisdictions is important. A more feasible approach in the short term would consider athletes' distinct environmental, workplace, and health needs. Simple steps, like offering athletes an information service about prospective doping behaviors or supplements without the fear of punishment or coercion, could make meaningful impacts on the everyday lives of elite athletes, especially for those without resources to elude the current system of surveillance and detection. Do the consequences, both formal and discursive, of current regulations undermine athletes' health and welfare? If so, what are the first steps that could be taken towards changing them? Largely unexplored are possible reforms that would hold professional sports management accountable for not supporting athlete health and welfare more generally. Overall, if we can take the time to better assess whether doping is widespread and risky in sport (as well as other workplaces), we can also gain a better understanding of what those practices are. Doing so, however, first requires instilling trust between athletes and authorities, an environment that is antithetical to the current conditions promoted by the regime.

It is also perhaps timely to ask broader questions beyond the scope of law and regulation in this space. What do we want from sport in the twenty-first century, and what does that entail in a globalized, largely capitalistic world? What kinds of safeguards can be put in place for athletes who do not enjoy the protections that other more privileged citizen subjects enjoy? What established regulatory models and reforms might we draw upon to make these practices in sport safer for participants?

How could alternative regulatory methods communicate values around health and well-being without perpetuating a (largely) ineffective cycle of risk and surveillance? Such questions are mere starting points, but if they bear in mind the injustices endured by athletes who did not intend to cheat, but were nonetheless subjected to or caught by this regulatory machinery, there is but hope for some level of reform.

Appendix

Research Methods

On Secrets and
Multi-Sited Storytelling

At the end of *The Common Place of Law*, Patricia Ewick and Susan Silbey reflect on the appendix found at the end of Diane Vaughan's book, *Uncoupling*. In her appendix, Vaughan discusses participants' willingness to disclose secrets, an observation that Ewick and Silbey extend to their relationship with the audience of their book. Instead of interviewees sharing secrets with a stranger (the researcher), they (the researchers) explain the secrets to the reader (a stranger).[1]

Here, as an acknowledgment of both appendices and the value of sharing such secrets, I offer a reflection that attends to the cyclical relationships between participants, researchers, and readers that *Uncoupling* and *The Common Place of Law* address. Like those works, this book, informed by qualitative research, brought me in contact with a variety of persons, texts, and social things, many of which shared and withheld information selectively. Because this is a multi-sited study of the lived experiences of socio-legal myths and relies on interviews, participant observation, archival research, and ongoing discussions with interlocutors to inform its narrative, my appendix features a commentary on secrets that diverges from those written by Vaughan and Ewick and Silbey. This appendix traces the intimate issues of not only the research topic at hand—that is, doping in sport and the regulation of bodies—but also the intimate encounters that transpire through research. In particular, I discuss two kinds of secrets: first, the issue of studying behaviors often thought of as secretive in nature and, second, the disclosure of how I obtained the forms of knowledge that underscore the pages of this book.[2]

"A Hook on Which to Hang Your Narrative"

The research for this book began in 2007 when I was observing the establishment of the California State Athletic Commission's anti-doping program. The California State Athletic Commission is the administrative agency that oversees the licensing and regulation of amateur and professional combat sports in the state, which includes boxing, kickboxing, and mixed martial arts.[3] The goal of that research was to understand how anti-doping regulation had been *vernacularized*—that is, as Sally Merry explains, "adapted by local institutions and meanings"[4]—and its effects on professional and aspiring fighters, most of whom are working-class male athletes with few other professional opportunities. I soon realized that getting answers to my questions about vernacularization required a much larger multi-sited study of the global regime. This in turn became my primary preoccupation and the focal point of this book.

Three objectives made up that broader research agenda: first, to describe the transnational development and deployment of anti-doping regulation in a way that attended to the politics and ideologies that informed its genesis; second, to identify the influential actors—be they persons, technologies, ideas, rituals, or events—that impacted developments in the field; and, third, to document the trends and variations in the ways people came to understand and negotiate regulation as well as the interpersonal and social effects of those encounters. In pursuing these lines of inquiry, the resulting analysis could have followed many different angles; however, as Tom Boellstorff cautioned at the onset of this project, I needed a "hook" on which to hang my narrative. I was fortunate that my encounters throughout the research process, those with texts and with persons, helped me to understand that the regulation of sport was not simply about preserving the integrity of competition, but about protecting and instilling deeper meanings ascribed to sports competition and the bodies who partake in athletic events. Over the last six years, I have therefore pursued this embedded concern through the three aforementioned areas of focus.

Data Collection

This project set out to understand the emergence of the anti-doping regime and how regulation polices athletes' bodies in an effort to uphold a set of ideas about bodily fortitude. The resulting process yields a complicated interplay of belonging and exclusion (what I refer to as athlete citizenship). To do so, I employed a multi-sited approach as my method of studying the construction of this ethnographic object, an object I did not have a name for at the onset of this research. The concept of athlete citizenship was, at least to me as a researcher, a regulatory secret that I did not yet know. The research process was a means of discerning and unpacking the dimensions of this secret so as to share it through this text. With little ethnographic research experience, I embraced George Marcus's recommendation to study an object of inquiry through the "tracing and describing the connections and relationships among sites previously thought incommensurate" as a "way of making arguments and providing its own contexts of significance."[5] This "multi-sited imaginary," explains Marcus, does not follow accepted boundaries or defined spaces (sometimes characterized as cultures) but, instead, pursues the various connections forged, in this case, through the emergence of a regulatory regime.[6] This approach was particularly appealing in light of commentaries by sports-studies scholars. Michael Silk, David Andrews, and Daniel Mason, for instance, contend that interrogating sport in ways that make it "strange to us" facilitate "new descriptions of the world" that "can offer the possibility of improvement of the human condition."[7] Developing such descriptions was a key objective to this research.

In light of these goals, my approach required multiple methods. Research entailed participant observation (both passive and active), face-to-face interviews, and archival research. My aim was to extrapolate the narratives of these texts and put them in dialogue with broader discourses around fair play and doping in sport. Since 2007, I have conducted fieldwork in various sites, including Madrid, Spain; Montreal, Quebec; Lausanne, Switzerland; and a number of cities and towns in Australia, New Zealand, and the United States. Even though data obtained from all sites are not quoted directly in this book, they nonetheless inform the text.

Participant observations required both passive participation, primarily in conference settings and formal meetings, and active engagement, primarily with athletes, regulators, and other communities whose practices and beliefs I sought to better understand. Some of this was akin to more traditional notions of anthropological research through extended periods in one location, such as my time spent in New Zealand. Other aspects of participant observation were shorter, which, Michael Silk explains, are often required given the conditions of modern sport environments and organizational structures. These shorter observations, Silk contends, can still yield important information in the form of "micro-ethnographies," which provide in-depth accounts when combined with other methods of data collection.[8] Such observations usually took place during sporting competitions, sport and community social events, and administrative meetings and conferences with regulators. While conducting observations, I often received opportunities to ask participants open-ended and targeted questions. Whenever possible, I recorded these using my phone or an audio recorder, but most of these conversations required taking written notes and later transcribing them (within twenty-four hours), adding additional details from memory. The majority of data collected for this research took place through active participation.

In addition to actively engaging participants and maintaining contact with interlocutors whom I met during fieldwork, I conducted many more face-to-face interviews with athletes, administrators, coaches, academics, and some families of athletes (n = 113). Most interviews took place at a neutral site, usually their home or a restaurant during nonpeak hours. I had to conduct some interviews at the workplaces of many regulators or sport officials. Interviews focused on participants' substantive and subjective understandings of anti-doping rules and, when possible, their attitudes toward other authorities. I often sought to elicit examples of their experiences with doping and anti-doping regulation (e.g., drug taking, testing, education and outreach efforts, policymaking), and especially when speaking with athletes and their families, I asked targeted questions about their everyday routines and practices of performance enhancement.

Given the nature of my access and the topic at hand, I relied primarily upon snowball sampling and, whenever possible, purposive sampling (namely in relation to anti-doping administrators). Given the jurisdictions where I collected data, it is perhaps not surprising that most participants were of Anglo-European heritage; however, while in New Zealand, I endeavored to speak with as many Māori and Pacific Islander participants as possible, especially given authorities' expressed concerns that their outreach was largely ineffective in these communities. I was fortunate to have ties to some of those communities in Auckland, which strongly benefited and informed this research—as well as my understandings of the historical distrust that shapes many of those participants' attitudes toward pākehā.

Despite going to great lengths to develop a rapport with these and other participants, usually through introductions facilitated by close friends or respected members of their communities, individual levels of engagement varied. Most athletes and anti-doping administrators came across as surprisingly forthright, even enthusiastic; however, even with this open demeanor, I doubt many participants fully disclosed their most personal feelings or secrets, especially given the sensitive nature of the topics covered. For instance, whereas most female athletes discussed instances in which doping control officers failed to follow sample collection protocols (often to levels of embarrassing detail), male athletes and doping control officers rarely spoke of such encounters. In some situations, when I disclosed my own unintentional acts of doping as an athlete, many participants shared their own anxieties, if not in relation to themselves then in relation others who they knew (or claimed to know). During other interviews, many athletes first asked me questions about my knowledge of and interest in the rules—itself an important finding as it often indicated a distrust of sport administrators or anti-doping authorities—before they appeared comfortable enough to speak more openly with me.

As a result, interviews rarely followed a prescribed script; instead, they proceeded through a series of topics related to their beliefs and knowledge of sport, fair play, and sport-specific rules as well as their encounters with performance enhancement, anti-doping authorities, colleagues, and competitors. Interviews usually began with open-ended questions about their own sporting careers and background and included at least one opportunity for them to ask me questions. Because my aim was to ascertain as much information about them and their relationship to the rules, interviews ranged from one and one-half to twelve hours, but on average lasted for nearly three hours.

With regard to historiographic analysis, I analyzed historical accounts and archival records with the goal of relating these narratives back to a discourse analysis of the contemporary rhetoric around the regulation of fair play. The majority of the archival research for this project took place over the summer of 2009 when I visited the Olympic Studies Centre Archives housed in Lausanne (although I also accessed the Avery Brundage Collection and other documents made available through the LA84 Foundation website). Data collection and analysis were intended to do more than provide an account of the context in which the Medical Commission and anti-doping regulations came into being; they were to enable the examination of the context in which broader narratives of fair play took shape and changed.

Linguistic anthropologists have argued that context is not a determinant of environmental factors but the outgrowth of interactions between participants.[9] Their particular interest is metanarration, the "devices which comment upon the narrator, the narrating, and the narrative both as message and as code."[10] Keeping with their focus, I examined the construction of these text-objects, as they became entextualized through the letters and notes from formal meetings, as well as the ways in which metadiscursive practices linked these text-objects to specific historical developments and events. Analysis, therefore, focused on the intertextuality of these archived narratives to glean insight into "the ways in which recounted events and replayed performances can be made to appear within specific linguistic ideologies and historical contexts as timeless, ahistorical, and even universal phenomena."[11] This focus proved especially valuable when analyzing the ideological reasons cited for the development of anti-doping rules and descriptions of doping that emerged alongside Medical Commission platforms. These methods and analysis drew attention to the relationships between social practices and "intertextual gaps" that inevitably emerge between archival texts and their prior articulations via other semiotic forms such as speech-acts, corporeal expressions, and contemporary discourse that built upon these texts. According to Charles Briggs, such research can clarify and produce new meanings that have the capacity to bring about profound social and political effects,[12] a primary focus of this research.

With the experiences of those deemed to be tainted, abnormal, or unnatural largely written out of these texts, I looked to feminist studies for guidance on reassembling the multiplicity of the IOC Medical Commission's project not fully revealed by the texts available to me. Jennifer Terry, in her reading of the medicalization and pathologizing of homosexuality, suggests the need for a deviant historiography because it would offer a "method for mapping the complex, discursive and textual operations" at work in constructing deviant subject positions within and against these "medico-scientific discourses."[13] In following her prescription, I looked at the Medical Commission's implementation of gender-verification testing not as running alongside the development of anti-doping regulation, but as directly and discursively implicating the politics of the commission's work in the management of athletes' bodies. This approach directly informed the thesis of this book, as I began to put the texts documenting the past in conversation with the texts elicited during fieldwork that reflected on contemporary relationships.

Qualitative Analysis

Upon reviewing the materials obtained, I transcribed data for analysis. Some texts and recordings were destroyed early on to protect the confidentiality of some participants, especially in cases where the information provided did not pertain to the analysis at hand or revealed identifying information. Given the thousands of pages of data that this process yielded, I first reviewed field notes (all of which had been transcribed from handwritten notes) and listened to audio recordings of interviews to ascertain what warranted transcription and further analysis. As many details about interpersonal, familial, and communal relationships were often informative of participants' understandings of sport, rules, and doping, I transcribed most the data collected, combining these transcripts with any notes that I had taken during the interview. In addition, I saved a separate document that reflected my own thoughts and feelings during an interview or observations, noting what information I had divulged to participants and whether or not it promoted participants to be more open (which, in many, but not all cases, had prompted them to share more personal details).

This initial step helped to me to formulate major themes and topics that later guided my open and fine-grained coding. To assist data analysis, I organized transcripts by the participants' primary orientation to anti-doping rules at the time of our meeting (e.g., athlete, coach, anti-doping administrator, government official/policymaker), documenting the geographic location, gender, age, and whether or not they also had a sporting background and the duration of their highest level of participation. Where relevant, I noted whether or not participants had committed an anti-doping rule violation and whether it was detected or not. Given the sensitivity of many of these and the other issues discussed, I saved no identifying information. After documenting these characteristics, I re-read the transcripts, developing basic codes that applied to or captured reactions to anti-doping regulation. This process yielded over fifty codes, many of which were later collapsed into broader analytic themes upon further review. This is not to say that themes were homogenous. Rather, it suggests the opposite: the variety of circumstances and subjective responses to similar issues attested to the dynamic relationships that participants had toward the rules, performance enhancement, and ideas of fair play.

Beyond coding individual transcripts, I also wrote up synopses of interviews and observations, attaching a cover page for each document, in order to capture the general issues that emerged from the data and to preserve the contextual elements between and across the data. During and after the coding process, I also selected quotes from interviews that captured broad themes or particular nuances, adding them to the cover page that included the summary.

It was through this reiterative process that the notion of athlete citizenship began to crystallize, as it reflected the socio-legal dimensions overlooked by earlier analyses of bio-citizenship. Its most profound expressions came through in the ways that various participants explained who belonged or did not belong in elite sport and the ways they and others negotiated the requirements of being (or striving to become) elite athletes. It was thus imperative to preserve some of the seemingly extraneous information about them, which often did not relate to doping or anti-doping regulation, in order to get a better sense of them, their desires, and the influential actors, both human and nonhuman, in their lives. During analysis, I asked, What directly influences and motivates these persons? What role does sport play in their lives? How do they explain their feelings towards sport, performance enhancement, notions of fair play, and authority? Beyond verbal expressions, what do their body language, emotional responses, and moments of silence suggest about their feelings about these issues? What specific cues and forms of expression might I not grasp as significant and need assistance in better understanding? The answer to this last question often prompted me to discuss these details with participants or trusted interlocutors (without disclosing personal information).

In relation to archival texts, I asked, What directly influenced and motivated the authors of these texts? What are the ideological stances being communicated by the stances captured in these documents? What positions are neglected or dismissed in these official accounts? How did regulators' notions of doping (and sex) change over time, and what were the impetuses for these changes? How do these perceptions resonate with or diverge from other historical accounts? Answers to these questions directly shaped the narratives found in chapters 2 and 4.

A Final Note on Storytelling

In Ewick and Silbey's detailed appendix, they offer a final note on storytelling, discussing how they strove to preserve their participants' voices while also making some strategic editorial decisions. Acknowledging that voices can be meditated in many ways, they pose the question, "To what degree, and in what ways, do we tamper with them?"[14] Similar to their decision to "clean up" participants' language, I decided to edit the direct quotes only to the extent that they clarified the meanings being communicated. This also applied to documents, some of which are English translations of the original French texts. I also had to make decisions about the extent to which I would share the details of athletes' and regulators' stories, understanding that many specificities included quite personal information. Because my aim was to tell a story of how the terms of athlete citizenship have emerged to protect an ideal of fair play (and the various forms of social control that inform that process), I decided not to include many of the potentially embarrassing and even shocking details that athletes and regulators admitted to seeing or doing in sport and beyond. I chose not to prioritize the exceptions uncovered during the research process, but instead drew upon data that reflected broader trends in the narratives and texts I found, selecting quotes that best captured them.

In writing this acknowledgement, I wish to flag that these decisions mark the significance of the researcher's voice in framing, shaping, and even altering participants' voices—which are already mediated—for the purposes of storytelling. While we may strive to maintain the integrity of their voices and narrations, there exists a tension underpinning the ethnographic desire to provide a convincingly authoritarian and in-depth narration of others that fits within the parameters of "our" (that is, the researcher/narrator's) normative purview. Again taking a page from Marcus,[15] I have endeavored to question how regulation, from its origins as a moral crusade, constitutes and perpetuates its own cultural logics. In doing so, my goal has been to construct a story that is comprehensible to readers, one that is enabled, not hindered, by its interdisciplinarity.

It is worth noting, then, that my methods of representing the actors who make up this regime are inherently limited, not simply by my editorial choices in fashioning this narrative, but also by my interlocutors' secrets and my inability to fully access them. Such secrets are not always deliberate denials of knowledge; they can be the outcomes of self-protection, erasure, censorship, misunderstanding, and even misrecognition. Although there are methodological strategies to triangulate and mediate these knowledge gaps, the lives of participants—as well as the ways that they narrate their worlds—always exceed and elude the representational limits of ethnography.[16] This observation, I would find, speaks to a deeper socio-legal concern, which Justin Richland elaborates upon: law shares ethnography's shortcomings. Law, like ethnography, constitutes a narrative that, in making authoritative claims to sustain itself, denies its own inability to "write" the multi-faceted logics and "the temporal trajectories implicit" in human action.[17]

In an effort to recognize and address these limitations, my research and writing practices have sought to incorporate methods that shed light on how legality, as it is understood in the hybrid formations of the anti-doping regime, seeks to mask its own contradictions. This, an effort to construct a multi-sited imaginary, brings together critical anthropological methods with historriography. The story told here is an inquiry into how the socio-legal myths policed and enforced by this regulatory regime are constitutive of the social excesses that it denies on its surface through a technocratic veneer. In doing so, I have sought to navigate the power dynamics of my position as researcher and writer, while also acknowledging the power of my participants' secrets, withheld from me through both ethnography and law, which I cannot share, even if I so desired. This account is not, and cannot be, a full, or even thick, description of anti-doping regulation. Instead, it is a reading that seeks to undo the narratives posited by regulatory apparatuses, doing so through an account of the ways in which this transnational regime has sought to reshape the social lives of athletes and sport participants, even though it cannot. In sum, my goal has not been to tell the secrets of my participants but, rather, to articulate the secrets of legality as they are expressed in this context.

Notes

Preface

1. I recall this conversation mostly from memory, so these quotes are not recounted verbatim. They have been confirmed with the participant as reflective of statements made to me.

Chapter 1   Introduction

1. Richard Pound, opening remarks, World Conference on Doping in Sport, November, 15, 2007.
2. Address by Koïchiro Matsuura, director general of UNESCO, delivered by Marcio Barbosa, deputy director general of UNESCO, World Conference on Doping in Sport, November, 15, 2007.
3. Becker, *Outsiders*.
4. Gusfield, *Symbolic Crusade*; Reinarman, "Moral Entrepreneurs and Political Economy."
5. Mitten and Opie, "'Sports Law,'" 308.
6. Beck, *The Brave New World of Work*, 62.
7. Neilson Wire, "Beijing Olympics Drew Largest Ever Global TV Audience" (2008), accessed October 10, 2010, http://blog.nielsen.com/nielsenwire/media _entertainment/beijing-olympics-draw-largest-ever-global-tv-audience/.
8. Park, "Governing Doped Bodies," 177.
9. Birrell, "Sport as Ritual," 354.
10. Ibid., 177.
11. Coubertin, "Why I Revived the Olympic Games," 543.
12. Cited in MacAloon, "The Olympic Idea," 508.
13. Krüger, "The Origins of Pierre de Coubertin's *Religio Athletae*," 91.
14. Krüger, "The Origins of Pierre de Coubertin's *Religio Athletae*"; MacAloon, "The Olympic Idea."
15. Women were not formally allowed to compete in the first modern Olympic Games.

16. Schantz, "Pierre de Coubertin's Concepts of Race, Nation, and Civilization," 163–164.

17. For an illustration of how these bans were in place, yet often failed, see Brownell, *The 1904 Anthropology Days and Olympic Games.*

18. Other scholars acknowledge this trend, but there remains limited works on the regulatory issues at hand (e.g., Amos and Fridman, "Drugs in Sport"; David, *A Guide to the World Anti-Doping Code*; Mitten and Opie, "'Sports Law'"; and Ravjani, "The Court of Arbitration for Sport.") Backhouse and colleagues have also documented all publications on doping in sport through 2006 and are currently updating this list to include publications through 2013 (*Attitudes, Behaviours, Knowledge and Education*).

19. Sheridan, "Conceptualizing 'Fair Play,'" 3.

20. Ibid., 163.

21. UNESCO, "Physical Education and Sport," accessed August 1, 2013, http://portal.unesco.org/education/en/ev.php-URL_ID=2223&URL_DO=DO_TOPIC&URL_SECTION=201.html.

22. Morgan ("Fair Is Fair, Or Is It?") puts this concern in dialogue with other ethical and ideological considerations as a way of reflecting on anti-doping campaigns, their limitations, and alternative possibilities.

23. Loland, *Fair Play in Sport*; Mangan, *Athleticism in the Victorian and Edwardian Public School.*

24. Butcher and Schneider, "Fair Play as Respect for the Game," 119.

25. Guttmann, *The Olympics*, 12.

26. Mangan, *The Games Ethic and Imperialism.*

27. Hong, "Doping and Anti-Doping in Sport in China"; Tamburrini, "Are Doping Sanctions Justified?"; and Teetzel, "On Transgendered Athletes, Fairness, and Doping."

28. Scott, "Regulating in Global Regimes," 1.

29. Douglas, *Purity and Danger.*

30. Ibid., 12.

31. Ibid., 65.

32. World Anti-Doping Agency, *World Anti-Doping Code*, 32–33.

33. Ibid., 33.

34. Tamburrini, "Are Doping Sanctions Justified?"

35. Guttmann (*The Olympics*) offers a history of the modern Olympics that highlights the problematic nature of amateurism, also noting that Coubertin was never preoccupied with amateurism but did appeal to it in order to mobilize support for the modern Olympics.

36. Gleaves, "Doped Professionals and Clean Amateurs."

37. As cited in Beamish and Ritchie, "From Chivalrous 'Brothers-in-Arms' to the Eligible Athlete," 361.

38. Andrews and Ritzer, "The Grobal in the Sporting Glocal," 140.

39. Brown. "Neoliberalism and the End of Liberal Democracy"; Harvey. *A Brief History of Neoliberalism.*

40. Foundational texts include Beck, *Risk Society: Towards a New Modernity*; Giddens, *The Consequences of Modernity*; and Giddens, *Modernity and Self-Identity.*

41. Lupton, *The Imperative of Health*; Lupton, *Medicine as Culture.*

42. Ericson, Doyle, and Barry, *Insurance as Governance*; Ericson and Haggerty, *Policing the Risk Society.*

43. I elaborate upon these dynamics elsewhere (Henne, "WADA, the Promises of Law and the Landscapes"). Casini also describes the regime in more detail ("Global Hybrid Public-Private Bodies").

44. For more detailed coverage of the offenses, see CNN's Olympic coverage: "Nine Athletes Banned for Doping Offenses," accessed January 30, 2013, http://edition .cnn.com/2012/07/25/sport/olympics-iaaf-doping-tobias.

45. WADA. "About WADA" (2013), accessed January 30, 2013, http://www.wada-ama .org/en/About-WADA/; WADA. "Anti-Doping Community" (2011), accessed July 1, 2011, http://www.wada-ama.org/en/Anti-Doping-Community/.

46. Jacques Rogge, opening remarks, World Conference on Doping in Sport, November, 15, 2007.

47. Wenner (*Fallen Sports Heroes, Media, and Celebrity Culture*) discusses how a range of "fallen heroes" condemned for moral transgressions evidence these role model expectations.

48. Wenner, *Fallen Sports Heroes, Media, and Celebrity Culture*.

49. Ewick and Silbey, *The Common Place of Law*; Hirsch and Lazarus-Black, "Performance and Paradox"; Merry, "Legal Pluralism"; Merry, "Transnational Human Rights and Local Activism"; Philips, *Ideology in the Language of Judges*; and Sarat and Kearns, *Law in Everyday Life*.

50. Moore, *Law as Process*, 3.

51. Moore, *Law as Process*; Strathern, "Cutting the Network"; and Strathern, *Partial Connections*.

52. Halliday and Shaffer, *Transnational Legal Orders*.

53. McMichael, "Globalization," 50.

54. Dimeo, *A History of Drug Use in Sport 1876–1976*, 136.

55. Wrynn, "The Human Factor," 211.

56. For more detailed analyses, see, for example, Beamish and Ritchie, *Fastest, Highest, Strongest*; Dimeo, *A History of Drug Use in Sport 1876–1976*; Hoberman, *Mortal Engines*; Houlihan, *Dying to Win*; and Hunt, *Drug Games*.

57. Clarke et al., "Biomedicalization," 161.

58. Ibid.

59. Although doping for sexual enhancement may carry a social stigma in some contexts, it does not usually result in formal sanctions; however, there are anti-doping cases in sport where the violations are allegedly due to the use of such drugs.

60. Edwards, "Sport's Tragic Drug Connection," 1.

61. Dumit, *Drugs for Life*.

62. Ong, "Mutations in Citizenship," 505.

63. While there are many such examples, analyses relevant to this book include discussions and critiques of (trans)national citizenship and biological citizenship: Anderson, *Imagined Communities*; Ong, *Flexible Citizenship*; Petryna, "Biological Citizenship"; Rose and Novas, "Biological Citizenship"; and Taussig, *Ordinary Genomes*. For a broader discussion, see Turner, *Citizenship and Social Theory*.

64. Clarke et al., "Biomedicalization," 184.

65. Seuffert, *Jurisprudence of National Identity*, 133.

66. Althusser, "Ideology and Ideological State Apparatuses."

67. Specific discussions of the symbolic power of athletes in relation to the state include detailed accounts of their biopolitical dimensions, even when not using a Foucauldian framework (Brownell, *Training the Body for China*; Hargreaves, John,

"The Body, Sport and Power Relations"; and Pfister and Reese, "Gender, Body Culture, and Body Politics in National Socialism").

68. These concerns occupy the pages of various published texts and reflections by Foucault (e.g., "The Confession of the Flesh" and "Nietzsche, Genealogy, History").

69. Foucault, "Nietzsche, Genealogy, History," 93–95.

70. Cabot, "The Governance of Things"; Coutin, *Legalizing Moves*; Coutin and Yngvesson, "Backed by Papers"; Fassin and Rechtman, *The Empire of Trauma*; and Ong, *Flexible Citizenship*.

71. Rabinow and Rose, "Biopower Today," 200.

72. Wenner, *Sports, Media and Society*, 72.

73. Rowe and Lawrence, "Beyond National Sport"; Roche, "The Olympics and 'Global Citizenship.'"

74. Andersson, "The Relevance of the Black Atlantic" 76.

75. Keys, *Globalizing Sport*.

76. Anderson, *Imagined Communities*.

77. Mitchell, *Cultural Geography*, 269.

78. Foucault, *The History of Sexuality, Vol. 1*, 140.

79. Young, *Imagining Crime*.

80. Cole and Denny, "Visualizing Deviance in Post-Reagan America.

81. Young, *Imagining Crime*, 16.

82. Ewick and Silbey, *The Common Place of Law*, 22.

83. Feldman, *Formations of Violence*, 115, emphasis in original.

84. As many other scholars acknowledge, bodily surveillance increasingly targets particular groups as well as the general public (Gerlach et al., *Becoming Biosubjects*; Haggerty and Ericson, *The New Politics of Surveillance and Visibility*). Biological monitoring is also a condition of participation in medical treatment and research studies; individuals must comply with certain requirements in order to become a subject (Montoya, *Making the Mexican Diabetic*).

85. Lupton, *The Imperative of Health*, 9.

86. Foucault, *The History of Sexuality, Vol. 1*, 167.

87. Rose and Novas, "Biological Citizenship," 439.

88. Ibid., 440.

89. Halse, "Bio-Citizenship," 45–59; Halse, Honey, and Boughtwood, "The Paradox of Virtue," 219–235; and Rail, Holmes, and Murray, "The Politics of Evidence on 'Domestic Terrorists,'" 259–279.

90. Halse, Honey, and Boughtwood, "The Paradox of Virtue," 220.

91. Halse, "Bio-Citizenship," 48.

92. Harwood, "Theorizing Biopedagogies," 17.

93. Butryn and Masucci, "It's Not about the Book"; Cole, "Resisting the Canon"; Cole and Orlie, "Hybrid Athletes, Monstrous Addicts and Cyborg Natures"; Jönsson, "Sport Beyond Gender and the Emergence of Cyborg Athletes"; Miah, *Genetically Modified Athletes*; and Swartz and Watermeyer, "Cyborg Anxiety."

94. Haraway, *Simians, Cyborgs, and Women*, 149.

95. Latour, *We Have Never Been Modern*, 11–90.

96. Ibid.

97. Marcus, "Ethnography in/of the World System"; Holmes and Marcus, "Cultures of Expertise and the Management of Globalization."

98. Haraway, "Situated Knowledges," 575–599.

99. Brownell, *Training the Body for China*, 10.

100. Ibid.
101. There are extensive historical accounts of doping in sport, performance enhancement, and the development of anti-doping regulation (Beamish and Ritchie, *Fastest, Highest, Strongest*; Dimeo, *A History of Drug Use in Sport 1876–1976*; Hoberman, *Mortal Engines*; and Hunt, *Drug Games*).
102. Nader, "Up the Anthropologist."
103. The lack of women in international sport governance is a well-documented criticism (see, for example, Wrynn and Smith. "Women in the 2012 Olympic and Paralympic Winter Games."
104. "Aotearoa" is the Māori term for New Zealand, which is usually interpreted in English as "land of the long white cloud." Using "Aotearoa" recognizes Māori peoples and their claims to nation (Barclay, "Rethinking Inclusion and Biculturalism"; Greig, ed., *Immigration and National Identity in New Zealand*). Throughout this book, I use "New Zealand" to refer to the nation-state, as is common and reflective of the strong British influence on its governing structures.
105. Cole, "Testing for Sex or Drugs"; Lock, "The Doping Ban"; and Olsen-Acre, "The Use of Drug Testing to Police Sex and Gender."
106. Cited in Rabinow, *The Foucault Reader*, 83.

Chapter 2   Diagnosing Doping: The Institutionalization of the Moral Crusade

1. Dirix and Sturbois, *The First Thirty Years of the International Olympic Committee*; Gleaves and Llewellyn, "Sport, Drugs and Amateurism"; and Maraniss, *Rome 1960*.
2. Gleaves and Llewellyn, "Sport, Drugs and Amateurism," 5.
3. Ibid.
4. Hunt, *Drug Games*, ix.
5. Franklin, "Science as Culture, Cultures of Science," 179.
6. Fouché, "Cycling's 'Fix.'"
7. Park, "Governing Doped Bodies."
8. Goode, *Sport Doping as Deviance*; Henne, *The Origins of the International Olympic Committee Medical Commission*, 11; and Stokvis, *Moral Entrepreneurship and Doping Cultures in Sport*.
9. Becker, *Outsiders*, 147–148.
10. Gusfield, *Symbolic Crusade*; Reinarman, "Moral Entrepreneurs and Political Economy."
11. Hunt, *Drug Games*; Hunt, Dimeo, and Jedlicka, "The Historical Roots of Today's Problems."
12. There are noteworthy limitations to relying on these primary texts. There is a twenty-year embargo on IOC documents, which, given the time frame of this article, is not significant. There is, however, no guarantee that documents containing contentious, disconcerting, or humiliating information about the IOC or its members is available to researchers.
13. Fouché, "Cycling's 'Fix.'"
14. Becker, *Outsiders*, 147.
15. Dimeo, *A History of Drug Use in Sport 1876–1976*, 95.
16. Hunt, Dimeo, and Jedlicka, "The Historical Roots of Today's Problems," 55; Keys, *Globalizing Sport*; and Ritchie, "Pierre de Coubertin, Doped 'Amateurs' and the 'Spirit of Sport.'"
17. Ritchie, "Pierre de Coubertin, Doped 'Amateurs' and the 'Spirit of Sport.'"

18. Beamish and Ritchie, "From Chivalrous 'Brothers-in-Arms' to the Eligible Athlete"; Gleaves, "Doped Professionals and Clean Amateurs"; and Gleaves and Llewellyn, "Sport, Drugs and Amateurism."

19. Donnelly, "Prolympism," 246.

20. Beamish and Ritchie, "From Chivalrous 'Brothers-in-Arms' to the Eligible Athlete," 361–363.

21. Dimeo, *A History of Drug Use in Sport 1876–1976*, 94–95.

22. Haraway, "Situated Knowledges," 581.

23. Barnes, "Olympic Drug Testing," 23.

24. Ibid.

25. Specifically, according to Gleaves and Llewellyn, Brundage hand wrote a statement between 1937 and 1938 that the IOC doping subcommittee would later use as the basis for its formal condemnation of doping ("Sport, Drugs and Amateurism," 11).

26. Ritchie, "Pierre de Coubertin, Doped 'Amateurs' and the 'Spirit of Sport.'"

27. MacAloon, "The Olympic Idea," 559.

28. Edwards, "Sport within the Veil." For a broader discussion of these criticisms and their historical context, refer to Hartmann, *Race, Culture, and the Revolt of the Black Athlete* and Williams, "American Exported Black Nationalism."

29. Dirix and Sturbois, *The First Thirty Years of the International Olympic Committee*; IOC Minutes of the 56th General Session, 9, IOC Archives, Lausanne.

30. Cited in Hunt, *Drug Games*, 10.

31. Møller, "Knud Enemark Jensen's Death."

32. Dimeo, *A History of Drug Use in Sport 1876–1976*, 55.

33. Ibid, 11.

34. Dimeo, Hunt, and Bowers, "Saint or Sinner?"; Hunt, *Drug Games*.

35. For more information about Porritt's tenure, see Gleaves and Llewellyn, "Sport, Drugs and Amateurism" and Hunt, *Drug Games*, 12–23.

36. Porritt, "Doping."

37. Porritt, "Doping and the Use of Chemical Agents," 48.

38. Porritt. "Doping," 47–49.

39. Cited in Todd and Todd, "Significant Events in the History of Drug Testing," 68.

40. Beamish and Ritchie, "From Chivalrous 'Brothers-in-Arms' to the Eligible Athlete," 361.

41. Hunt, *Drug Games*, 14–15.

42. Henne, *The Origins of the International Olympic Committee Medical Commission*, 10.

43. Cited in Houlihan, *Dying to Win*, 151.

44. IOC, Press Release, September 27, 1967, 2.

45. Dimeo, *A History of Drug Use in Sport 1876–1976*.

46. La Cava, "The Use of Drugs in Competitive Sport," 53.

47. Prokop, "Drug Abuse in International Athletes," 86.

48. Dirix, "The Doping Problem at the Tokyo and Mexico City Olympic Games," 185.

49. IOC, Press Release, September 27, 1967.

50. Ibid.

51. Becker, *Outsiders*, 156.

52. See Hoberman, *Testosterone Dreams*. Dimeo, Hunt, and Bowers ("Saint or Sinner?") re-examine these characterizations of de Mérode by considering the circumstances and events surrounding his chairmanship, a nuanced reading that this study supports.

53. Medical Commission meeting minutes, December 20, 1967, 2. IOC Archives, Lausanne.
54. Ibid., 3.
55. Ibid., 2.
56. Epstein, *Impure Science*, 26.
57. Medical Commission meeting minutes, December 20, 1967, 3. IOC Archives, Lausanne.
58. Alexandre de Mérode, letter to Avery Brundage, September 6, 1968. IOC Archives, Lausanne.
59. Beamish and Ritchie ("From Chivalrous 'Brothers-in-Arms' to the Eligible Athlete") provide a closer reading of how these changes not only affected the rules around Olympic participation, but also reconfigured Olympic principles.
60. Avery Brundage, letter to Alexandre de Mérode (copied to international federations, NOCs, and IOC) (underline in original), September 14, 1968. IOC Archives, Lausanne.
61. If following these rules, this was not possible when collecting samples from female athletes at the time.
62. For identification purposes, fingerprinting had been ruled out as a result of a previous protest filed by a Soviet doctor in charge of the modern pentathlon. See "Report on the Tests for Detecting the Use of Stimulants by Athletes Participating in the III International Sports Competition, Mexico City," October 1967, 2–3 (original document in Olympic Studies Centre archives, Lausanne, Switzerland).
63. Medical Commission meeting minutes, December 20, 1967, 2. IOC Archives, Lausanne.
64. Medical Commission meeting minutes, July 13–14, 1968, 3. IOC Archives, Lausanne.
65. Thiébault, Report on the Medical Commission of the International Olympic Committee on the Grenoble Games, 1969, 12 (translation). IOC Archives, Lausanne.
66. Ibid., 1.
67. Medical Commission meeting minutes, July 13–14, 1968, 4. IOC Archives, Lausanne.
68. Letter from D. T. P. Pain to Alexandre de Mérode, October 1, 1968 (original document in Olympic Studies Centre archives, Lausanne, Switzerland).
69. Report on the Tests for Detecting the Use of Stimulants, 1 (cited by Dimeo, Hunt and Bowers, "Saint or Sinner?").
70. Dimeo, *A History of Drug Use in Sport 1876–1976*, 94.
71. Landry and Yerlès, *The International Olympic Committee One Hundred Years*, 259.
72. Barnes, "Olympic Drug Testing," 22.
73. Minutes of the IOC Executive Board, September 8, 1972, 46–47. IOC Archives, Lausanne.
74. Landry and Yerlès, *The International Olympic Committee One Hundred Years*, 167, 257.
75. Dimeo, Hunt, and Bowers, "Saint or Sinner?," 933.
76. Ibid.
77. Beckett, "The Future of the Olympic Movement."
78. Beamish and Ritchie, *Fastest, Highest, Strongest*.

79. Beamish and Ritchie, "From Chivalrous 'Brothers-in-Arms' to the Eligible Athlete," 362–363; Beamish and Ritchie, *Fastest, Highest, Strongest*; and Hoberman, *Mortal Engines*.

80. Woodland, *Dope*, 57.

81. Dimeo, *A History of Drug Use in Sport 1876–1976*, 79.

82. Hunt, Dimeo, and Jedilicka, "The Historical Roots of Today's Problems," 57.

83. NZ Olympic and British Commonwealth Games Association Inc., letter to Monique Berlioux, March 19, 1973. IOC Archives, Lausanne.

84. Report on the Medical Commission, Sex Testing and Doping, December 13,1974, 8. IOC Archives, Lausanne.

85. Walter Winterbottom, letter to International Federations, National Governing Bodies of Sport and other interested Organizations, October 30, 1973. IOC Archives, Lausanne.

86. Report on the Medical Commission, Sex Testing and Doping, December 13, 1974, 11. IOC Archives, Lausanne.

87. Dimeo, *A History of Drug Use in Sport 1876–1976*, 83–86.

88. Ibid., 85.

89. *Track and Field News*, February 1, 1973, enclosure sent by Monique Berlioux to Alexandre de Mérode, March 14, 1973. IOC Archives, Lausanne.

90. Winterbottom, letter to International Federations, National Governing Bodies of Sport and other interested Organizations, October 30, 1973. IOC Archives, Lausanne.

91. Roger Bannister, Letter to Lord Killanin, November 1, 1973. IOC Archives, Lausanne.

92. Ibid.

93. Historical analyses attest to Western fears focusing on hypermasculinized athletes in women's events (e.g., Beamish and Ritchie, "The Spectre of Steroids").

94. Cited in Landry and Yerlès, *The International Olympic Committee One Hundred Years*, 257.

95. Beamish and Ritchie, "From Chivalrous 'Brothers-in-Arms' to the Eligible Athlete," 365.

96. "Anabolic Steroids Used in Commonwealth Games," Press Release, May 8, 1974. IOC Archives, Lausanne.

97. Organizing Committee of the Games of the XXI Olympiad, Official Report, 454.

98. James Worrall, Letter to de Alexandre Mérode, January 3, 1975. IOC Archives, Lausanne.

99. Beckett. "Misuse of Drugs in Sports,"190.

100. Gottfried Schödl, Letter to Alexandre de Mérode, August 31, 1976. IOC Archives, Lausanne.

101. Ibid.

102. Medical Commission meeting minutes, October 14–15, 1976. IOC Archives, Lausanne, 1; Declaration of the Bulgarian Weightlifting Federation, enclosure sent by secretary general of Bulgarian NOC, Andonov, to the IOC Medical Commission, September 11, 1972. IOC Archives, Lausanne.

103. The cost of testing surpassed 2 million US dollars at the 1976 Montreal Games (Al-Habet, and Lee, "Uses and Abuses of Anabolic Steroids by Athletes," 221).

104. Dimeo, Hunt, and Bowers, "Saint or Sinner?," 934.

105. "Olympic Athletes Cleared," *Washington Post*, February 25, 1980.

106. IOC Medical Commission, "Doping Control at Games of the XXIInd Olympiad," February 1981.

107. Cited in Dimeo, Hunt, and Bowers, "Saint or Sinner?," 935.
108. Landry and Yerlès, *The International Olympic Committee One Hundred Years.*
109. Hunt, *Drug Games,* 93.
110. Landry and Yerlès, *The International Olympic Committee One Hundred Years.*
111. Ibid., 260.
112. MacAloon, "Steroids and the State," 42.
113. Ibid., 52–53.
114. Jackson, "Exorcizing the Ghost," 126.
115. Landry and Yerlès, *The International Olympic Committee One Hundred Years.*
116. Ibid., 261.
117. There are many documented references to questionable, arguably politically motivated dealings and cover-ups with regard to alleged positive tests under de Mérode's chairmanship of the IOC Medical Commission. For more about how these dynamics play out in the history of drug testing, see Hoberman, *Mortal Engines* and Hunt, *Drug Games.*
118. Dimeo, Hunt and Bowers, "Saint or Sinner?," 935–937.
119. This charge is well documented, the details of which have been explored by investigative journalists and academic researchers (e.g., Barney, Wenn, and Martyn, *Selling the Five Rings*; Jennings, *The New Lords of the Rings*; and Lenskyj, *Inside the Olympic Industry*).
120. Landry and Yerlès, *The International Olympic Committee One Hundred Years,* 261.
121. Ibid., 256.
122. Ibid., 267.
123. A specific doctrine related to this concern has since been adopted in article 3 of the Charter of Fundamental Rights of the European Union.
124. Amy Shipley. "Diana Taurasi, Alberto Contador Cases Highlight Questions Facing Anti-Doping Movement." *Washington Post,* February 27, 2011.
125. Messner, *Power at Play.*

Chapter 3   Codifying the Code: The Legalization of Anti-Doping Regulation

1. Pound, *Inside Dope,* 188.
2. Ibid., 29.
3. Ibid.
4. Levi-Faur, "The Global Diffusion of Regulatory Capitalism."
5. WADA maintains formal agreements with F. Hoffmann-La Roche Ltd., Glaxo-SmithKline, and the International Federation of Pharmaceutical Manufacturers Association. WADA also hosted the 2012 International Conference on the Pharmaceutical Industry and the Fight against Doping: New Partnerships for Clean Sport, which was held in Paris, France.
6. Calavita, *Invitation to Law and Society.*
7. International Olympic Committee, *The Olympic Charter,* 9.
8. "About WADA," accessed May 23, 2012, http://www.wada-ama.org/en/About-WADA/.
9. See WADA's website for an updated list of its partner organizations, which it refers to as the Anti-Doping Community: accessed May 23, 2012, http://www.wada-ama.org/en/Anti-Doping-Community/.
10. Trubek and Trubek, "Hard and Soft Law in the Construction of Social Europe," 344.

11. "International Convention against Doping in Sport 2005," UNESCO, http://portal.unesco.org/en/ev.php-URL_ID=31037&URL_DO=DO_TOPIC&URL_SECTION=201.html.

12. This number is based on the members that participated in the first Convention of State Parties, which included states that ratified the convention as of December 31, 2006. This list is updated and available at http://www.unesco.org/new/en/social-and-human-sciences/themes/anti-doping/international-convention-against-doping-in-sport/states-parties/.

13. World Anti-Doping Agency, World Anti-Doping Code, 114.

14. Ibid.

15. Transcript excerpts quoted in this chapter were obtained from recordings of the World Conference on Doping in Sport proceedings held in Madrid from November 15, 2007, to November 17, 2007. Because most of the conference proceedings were accessible via WADA's website and many presentations are available publicly, identifiers are used when quoting public figures who spoke during the first day of the conference. I therefore use names, not pseudonyms, of formal presenters; however, when drawing from interview data with conference participants, even those considered public figures, I do not use identifiers in order to ensure confidentiality.

16. The rules, as mentioned in the introduction, state that a banned substance must meet two of the following criteria: be performance enhancing, harm athletes' health, or violate the "spirit of sport" (World Anti-Doping Agency, *World Anti-Doping Code*, 32–33). Teetzel discusses these implications in practice ("On Transgendered Athletes, Fairness and Doping").

17. Ritchie, "Pierre de Coubertin, Doped 'Amateurs' and the 'Spirit of Sport.'"

18. To substantiate this point, less than 2 percent of athletes tested in the jurisdictions studied here (Australia, New Zealand, and the United States) tested positive for a banned substance.

19. Park, "Governing Doped Bodies."

20. Richard Ings, intervention, World Conference on Doping in Sport, Madrid, November 15, 2007.

21. Jaime Lissavetzky Diez, introductory remarks, World Conference on Doping in Sport, Madrid, November 15, 2007.

22. Beamish and Ritchie provide a detailed description of the events leading up to and following the scandal (*Fastest, Highest, Strongest*).

23. Operación Puerto resulted identified a network of athletes using blood doping methods, but fifteen athletes were acquitted by the time of the World Conference on Doping in Sport (Soule and Lestrelin, "The Puerto Affair"). According to WADA representatives, Operation Gear Grinder was a "significant advance in the closing down of a number of [drug-producing] laboratories in Mexico" (Henne, "WADA, the Promises of Law and the Landscapes," 315).

24. The full impact of naming these players had not yet been realized at the time of the World Conference. The Signature Pharmacy scandal and BALCO investigation fueled allegations about steroid and HGH use by professional players. This later became the subject of the Mitchell Commission Report, which was the impetus for congressional hearings on doping in professional baseball.

25. Viacheslav Fetisov, intervention, World Conference on Doping in Sport, Madrid, November 15, 2007.

26. Ibid.

27. David Howman, conference session, World Conference on Doping in Sport, Madrid, November 15, 2007.
28. Ibid.
29. Howman, conference session, World Conference on Doping in Sport, Madrid, November 15, 2007.
30. Goode, *Sports Doping as Deviance*. For more about the original concept, see Cohen, *Folk Devils and Moral Panics*.
31. Seddon, *A History of Drugs*.
32. WADA, "Intelligence Experts Emphasize the Importance of Legislation and Information Sharing," February 8, 2013 (e-mail correspondence).
33. Simon, *Governing through Crime*, 4.
34. Glassner, *The Culture of Fear*, 300.
35. Simon, *Governing through Crime*, 20.
36. This statement is based on formal presentations and discussions with participants (field notes by author, World Conference on Doping in Sport, Madrid, November 14–17, 2007).
37. Pound, *Inside Dope*, 92.
38. Henne, "WADA, the Promises of Law and the Landscapes," 312.
39. Lord Mayor Alberto Ruiz-Gallardón, opening remarks, World Conference on Doping in Sport, Madrid, November 15, 2007.
40. Simon, *Governing through Crime*.
41. Jacques Rogge, speech, World Conference on Doping in Sport, Madrid, November 15, 2007.
42. Mercedes Cabrera Calvo-Sotelo, welcome address, World Conference on Doping in Sport, Madrid, November 15, 2007, italics mine.
43. Rubin, "Thinking Sex."
44. Ibid., 151.
45. Richard Pound, introductory speech, World Conference on Doping in Sport, Madrid, November 15, 2007.
46. Interview by author, Madrid, World Conference on Doping in Sport, November 17, 2007.
47. Becker, *Outsiders*.
48. Dimeo, *A History of Drug Use in Sport 1876–1976*; Gleaves, "Doped Professionals and Clean Amateurs."
49. Henne, "WADA, the Promises of Law and the Landscapes," 310.
50. Howman, conference session, World Conference on Doping in Sport, Madrid, November 15, 2007.
51. There were also expressed concerns around cycling, one that pointed to another division: perceptions of northern and southern European riders.
52. Ibid.
53. Richard Pound, conference session, World Conference on Doping in Sport, Madrid, November 15, 2007.
54. Sekula, "Body and the Archive," 15.
55. Messner, *Taking the Field*.
56. Ibid., 29.
57. Enck-Wanzer, "All's Fair in Love and Sport," 3.
58. Cole and Mobley, "American Steroids," 6.
59. Ibid., 7.
60. This was likely because I was forthright about being an American athlete and researcher.

61. Interview by author, Madrid, World Conference on Doping in Sport, November 15, 2007.

62. Field notes by author, Madrid, World Conference on Doping in Sport, November 15–16, 2007.

63. Hoberman, *Testosterone Dreams*, 183.

64. Gleaves, "Doped Professionals and Clean Amateurs."

65. Interview by author, Canberra, Australia, November 22, 2011.

66. In the eyes of organizer James Sullivan, the co-founder of the Amateur Athletic Union, the Anthropology Games showcased the evolutionary superiority of the West over untrained nonwhite competitors. For others involved, like W. J. McGee, the founding president of the American Anthropological Association, it highlighted Native athletes' innate physical dexterity and athletic aptitude. Despite McGee's good intentions, record keeping served, at least according to Sullivan, as a way to measure the extent to which they proved inferior to white participants (Brownell, *The 1904 Anthropology Days and Olympic Games*).

67. These accounts are discussed by various authors in Brownell's edited collection, *The 1904 Anthropology Days and Olympic Games*.

68. DuBois, "The Prize Fighter," 181. This later became the title of the documentary film on Johnson's life directed by Ken Burns.

69. Edwards ("Sport within the Veil") further elaborates upon how black male athletes prioritize sport over education because of these cultural beliefs.

70. Curry, "Fraternal Bonding in the Locker Room"; Fine, *With the Boys*; and Smith and Hattery, "Hey Stud."

71. Interview by author, World Conference on Doping in Sport, Madrid, November 16, 2007.

72. Barney, Wenn, and Martyn, *Selling the Five Rings*.

73. Aganthangelou and Ling, "Desire Industries," 133.

74. Howman, conference session, World Conference on Doping in Sport, Madrid, November 16, 2007.

75. Ibid., italics mine.

76. Marcio Barbosa, opening remarks, World Conference on Doping in Sport, Madrid, November 15, 2007.

77. D. M. Stofile, intervention, World Conference on Doping in Sport, Madrid, November 16, 2007.

78. Ibid.

79. Address delivered by Paul Marriott-Lloyd at the European Conference, Education through Sport (2008), accessed January 10, 2010, www.education-through-sport.eu/en/files/lloyd-en.pdf.

80. Field notes, Conference on Crime and Sport, Canberra, Australia, March 23, 2012.

81. I use MD to reference "medical doctor" to maintain confidentiality.

82. Brownell, *The 1904 Anthropology Days and Olympic Games*.

83. Bale, "From Anthropology Days to Anthropological Olympics."

84. Ibid., 339.

85. Ibid., 340.

86. Ibid., 339.

87. There is an ESPN documentary film on the aftermath of her case, *Marion Jones: Press Pause*, directed by John Singleton. Jones resurrected her athletic career as a professional basketball player in the Women's National Basketball Association

(William C. Rhoden, "Marion Jones Aims for a Comeback, in Basketball." *New York Times*, December 1, 2009, B13).

88. ESPN has dedicated a comprehensive page to the verdict and reactions to it: accessed January 15, 2012, http://sports.espn.go.com/mlb/news/story?id= 6347014.

89. Hobsbawm, "Inventing Tradition."

90. Hanson, "The Making of the Maori," 891–902; Linnekin, "Cultural Invention and the Dilemma of Authenticity," 446–449.

91. Coubertin, "Olympia."

Chapter 4   Impossible Purities: The Gendered Science of Fair Play

1. Dietz, "Context Is All"; McClintock, *Imperial Leather*; Munday, "Gendered Citizenship"; and Walby, "Is Citizenship Gendered?"

2. McClintock, *Imperial Leather*, 359.

3. Hargreaves, Jennifer, *Heroines of Sport*.

4. Messner, "Sports and Male Domination."

5. Dworkin and Cooky, "Sport, Sex Segregation, and Sex Testing."

6. Heggie, "Testing Sex and Gender in Sports."

7. Wackwitz, "Verifying the Myth."

8. Birrell and Cole, "Double Fault," 18.

9. Phillips, "Australian Women and the Olympics,"189.

10. Ibid., 189, italics mine.

11. Birrell and Cole, *Women, Sport, and Culture*; Messner, *Taking the Field*.

12. Fausto-Sterling, *Sexing the Body*; Skirstad, "Gender Verification in Competitive Sport"; Vannini and Fornssler, "Girl, Interrupted"; and Wackwitz, "Verifying the Myth."

13. Fausto-Sterling, *Sexing the Body*, 3.

14. Jordan-Young and Karkazis, "Some of Their Parts." See also Karkazis, *Fixing Sex*.

15. The wording of the framework allows for exceptions in the event that the athlete has an androgen resistance. Such women cannot recruit as much testosterone as other women.

16. IOC, "IOC Addresses Eligibility of Female Athletes with Hyperandrogenism," April 5, 2011, accessed April 11, 2011, http://www.olympic.org/content/press -release/ioc-addresses-eligibility-of-female-athletes-with-hyperandrogenism/.

17. Karkazis et al., "Out of Bounds," 3.

18. Elsas, Hayes, and Muralidharan, "Gender Verification in the Centennial Olympic Games"; Fausto-Sterling, *Sexing the Body*; and Martínez-Patiño et al., "An Approach to the Biological, Historical and Psychological Repercussions."

19. Cavanagh and Sykes, "Transsexual Bodies at the Olympics," 77.

20. IOC Medical Commission. IOC Regulations on Female Hyperandrogenism, June 22, 2012, http://www.olympic.org/Documents/Commissions_PDFfiles/Medical _commission/2012-06-22-IOC-Regulations-on-Female-Hyperandrogenism-eng .pdf; Joanna Marchant. "Women with High Male Hormone Levels Face Sport Ban," *Nature* (2011), http://www.nature.com/news/2011/110414/full/news.2011.237.html.

21. Sánchez, Martínez-Patiño, and Vilain, "The New Policy on Hyperandrogenism."

22. IOC, "IOC Addresses Eligibility of Female Athletes with Hyperandrogenism."

23. Katrina Karkazis and Rebecca Jordan-Young, "The Problem with Too Much T," *New York Times*, April 10, 2014, http://www.nytimes.com/2014/04/11/opinion/ the-trouble-with-too-much-t.html?_r=0.

24. Viloria, "Gender Rules in Sport." See also Wahlert and Fiester, "Gender Transports."
25. Viloria, "Gender Rules in Sport—Leveling the Playing Field, Or Reversed Doping?"
26. Beamish and Ritchie, "The Spectre of Steroids"; Vannini and Fornssler, "Girl, Interrupted."
27. From the abstract of the unpublished manuscript, "Looks like a Duck, Quacks like a Duck: Transgression and Transgender in Olympic Sports Medicine."
28. Beamish and Ritchie, "The Spectre of Steroids"; Wiederkehr, "We Shall Never Know the Exact Number."
29. Fausto-Sterling, *Sexing the Body*, 3.
30. Coubertin, "Chronique du Mois," 109–110.
31. "Sport: Olympic Games," *Time*, August 10, 1936, accessed April 11, 2011, www.time .com/time/magazine/article/0,9171,762309,00.html.
32. Ritchie, Reynard, and Lewis, "Intersex and the Olympic Games."
33. As cited in Landry and Yerlès, *The International Olympic Committee One Hundred Years*, 257.
34. Vannini and Fornssler, "Girl, Interrupted."
35. Lock, "The Doping Ban," 404–405.
36. Ibid., 409.
37. Ariel Levy, "Either/Or: Sports, Sex and the Case of Caster Semenya." *New Yorker*, November 30, 2009, 46–68.
38. Ibid.
39. Ibid.
40. Munro, "Caster Semenya"; David Smith, "Caster Semenya Row: Who Are White People to Question the Makeup of an African Girl? It Is Racism." *Observer*, August 23, 2009, 20.
41. Levy, "Either/Or"; Munro, "Caster Semenya."
42. Levy, "Either/Or."
43. Multiple news sources cited this press release. The full text is available at http:// www.politicsweb.co.za/politicsweb/view/politicsweb/en/page71656?oid=143078 &sn=Detail&pid=71656.
44. Many accounts inappropriately refer to Saartjie as her real name, even though her birth name is unknown. The Dutch family she worked for referred to her as Saartjie (meaning little Sarah), which infantilized her as a subordinate (Qureshi, "Displaying Sara Baartman, the 'Hottentot Venus,'" 235).
45. Cited by Levy, "Either/Or."
46. Munro ("Caster Semenya") explicitly embraces such a reading; however, Magubane ("Spectacles and Scholarship") troubles it by offering a postcolonial analysis of how the category of intersex is itself racialized. White intersex bodies, she argues, received treatment to "normalize" their bodies in closer accordance with gender binaries, while black intersex bodies have not been historically treated. Thus, race has actually "overdetermined whether bodies in doubt needed to be resolved and whether that resolution would take place" (782).
47. Cooky, Dycus, and Dworkin, "'What Makes a Woman a Woman?'"
48. Munro, "Caster Semenya," 387.
49. Cited by Anna Kessel, "Caster Semenya May Return to Track after IAAF Clearance," *Guardian*, July 7, 2010, 10.
50. Beamish and Ritchie, "The Spectre of Steroids."

51. Andriy Tsaplienko, *Doping: Factory of Champions,* directed by Oleg Kamasyuk, Inter: 2008. An episode of the PBS series, *Secrets of the Dead* offers similar account by Krieger ("Doping for Gold," *Secrets of the Dead,* directed by Alison Rooper, New York: Firefly, 2008).

52. Jere Longman, "DRUG TESTING; East German Steroids' Toll: 'They Killed Heidi,'" *New York Times,* January 20, 2004, D1. Despite this acknowledgement, he has repeatedly asserted in interviews and court that because of doping, his body "had changed beyond all recognition. . . . It was as though they had killed Heidi. Becoming Andreas was the next logical step" (Matthew Syed, "How Blue Pills Turned Heidi Krieger into a Man," *Times Online,* July 5, 2008, http://www.timesonline.co.uk/tol/sport/more_sport/article4273050.ece.

53. Ungerleider, *Faust's Gold.*

54. Longman, "DRUG TESTING; East German Steroids' Toll: 'They Killed Heidi,'" *New York Times,* January 20, 2004, D1

55. Martínez-Patiño et al., "An Approach to the Biological, Historical and Psychological Repercussions."

56. Ritchie, Reynard, and Lewis, "Intersex and the Olympic Games," 396.

57. Martínez-Patiño et al., "An Approach to the Biological, Historical and Psychological Repercussions."

58. Correspondence from Wlodzimierz Reczek to Alexandre de Mérode, October 24, 1967 (original document in Olympic Studies Centre archives, Lausanne, Switzerland).

59. Correspondence from Avery Brundage to Wlodzimierz Reczek, November 4, 1967 (original document in Olympic Studies Centre archives, Lausanne, Switzerland).

60. Jacques Thiébault, "Final Report to the Medical Commission on the Grenoble Games" (1968), 1 (original document in Olympic Studies Centre archives, Lausanne, Switzerland).

61. Ibid., 1.

62. Draft of IOC Medical Commission sex and dope control policies (1967); IOC Medical Commission minutes of the meeting in Château de Vidy (1968), 4 (original documents in Olympic Studies Centre archives, Lausanne, Switzerland).

63. Final Report on the 1968 Grenoble Games, 1 (original document in Olympic Studies Centre archives, Lausanne, Switzerland).

64. Teetzel, "On Transgendered Athletes, Fairness and Doping," 230.

65. Memoranda from IOC general secretary J. W. Westerhoff, October 26, 1967; IOC, "Press Release," September 27, 1967 (original documents in Olympic Studies Centre archives, Lausanne, Switzerland).

66. Hay, "Sex Determination in Putative Female Athletes," 998.

67. Final Report on the 1968 Grenoble Games, 1 (original document in Olympic Studies Centre archives, Lausanne, Switzerland).

68. "IOC Medical Commission Minutes of the Meeting in Château de Vidy" (1968), 4 (original document in Olympic Studies Centre archives, Lausanne, Switzerland).

69. Ritchie, Reynard, and Lewis, "Intersex and the Olympic Games," 397.

70. Martínez-Patiño et al., "An Approach to the Biological, Historical and Psychological Repercussions."

71. Cavanagh and Sykes, "Transsexual Bodies at the Olympics"; Sullivan, "Gender Verification and Gender Policies in Elite Sport."

72. Ritchie, Reynard, and Lewis, "Intersex and the Olympic Games," 397.

73. Elsas, Hayes, and Muralidharan, "Gender Verification in the Centennial Olympic Games."

74. This scenario is unlikely in elite sport, as people with Klinefelter's syndrome often have motor impairments and less physical strength.

75. Wiederkehr, "We Shall Never Know the Exact Number," 560.

76. Martínez-Patiño et al., "An Approach to the Biological, Historical and Psychological Repercussions."

77. Beamish and Ritchie, "The Spectre of Steroids."

78. Correspondence from Monique Berlioux to Alexandre de Mérode, May 19, 1972 (original document in Olympic Studies Centre archives, Lausanne, Switzerland, Author's translation).

79. Fausto-Sterling, *Sexing the Body*, 3.

80. Sullivan, "Gender Verification and Gender Policies in Elite Sport," 406.

81. Martínez-Patiño et al., "An Approach to the Biological, Historical and Psychological Repercussions."

82. Martínez-Patiño, "A Woman Tried and Tested," S538.

83. Martínez-Patiño et al., "An Approach to the Biological, Historical and Psychological Repercussions."

84. Sullivan, "Gender Verification and Gender Policies in Elite Sport"; Sánchez, Martínez-Patiño, and Vilain, "The New Policy on Hyperandrogenism."

85. For example, the Norwegian government considered gender verification "illegal and unethical" and did not allow such testing at the 1994 Winter Olympics in Lillehammer (Martínez-Patiño et al., "An Approach to the Biological, Historical and Psychological Repercussions," 313).

86. BBC News, "Indian Athlete Fails Gender Test," December 18, 2006, accessed June 20, 2013, http://news.bbc.co.uk/2/hi/world/south_asia/6188775.stm; Nilanjana Bhowmick, and Jyoti Thottam. "Gender and Athletics: India's Own Caster Semenya," *Time World*, September 1, 2009.

87. Latour, *We Have Never Been Modern*.

88. Gina Kolata, "I.O.C. Panel Calls for Treatment of Sex Ambiguity Cases," *New York Times*, January 21, 2010, B3.

89. Sykes, "Transsexual and Transgender Policies in Sport."

90. IOC, "Statement of the Stockholm Consensus on Sex Reassignment in Sports," November 12, 2003, accessed April 11, 2011, http://www.olympic.org/ioc -commissions/documents-reports-studies-publications.

91. There are, of course, other countries that have historically conceived of gender beyond binary distinctions, including India, Thailand, and many Pacific Island nations. The three countries mentioned here legally recognize a third gender for transgendered or intersex citizens.

92. Teetzel, "On Transgendered Athletes, Fairness and Doping," 228.

93. Pablo S. Torre and David Epstein, "The Transgender Athlete," *Sports Illustrated*, May 28, 2012.

94. Olsen-Acre, "The Use of Drug Testing to Police Sex and Gender."

95. Cole, "Testing for Sex or Drugs," 331–333; Steel, "Anti-Doping in Sport—What Is WADA's Mandate?," 78–79.

96. Interview by author, Canberra, April 20, 2010. Since this interview, I have heard other Australian athletes and academics use the same language. The origins of this phrase are unknown, however.

97. Sullivan, "Gender Verification and Gender Policies in Elite Sport."

98. Cavanagh and Sykes, "Transsexual Bodies at the Olympics," 84.
99. Ian, "The Primitive Subject of Female Bodybuilding," 74.
100. Therberge, "A Critique of Critiques."
101. Jeff Gottlieb, "Seizure Led to FloJo's Death," *Los Angeles Times*, October 27, 1998, D2.
102. Ibid.
103. Cited by Cole and Mobley, "American Steroids," 7.
104. Dimeo, *A History of Drug Use in Sport 1876–1976*; Hunt, *Drug Games*.
105. Balsamo, *Technologies of the Gendered Body*, 46.
106. McKay and Johnson, "Pornographic Eroticism and Sexual Grotesquerie."
107. Cole and Mobley, "American Steroids," 6.
108. Nilanjana Bhowmick and Jyoti Thottam. "Gender and Athletics: India's Own Caster Semenya." *Time World*, September 1, 2009.
109. As cited in Smith, "Caster Semenya Row," 20.
110. Levy, "Either/Or."
111. Cooky, Dycus, and Dworkin, "'What Makes a Woman a Woman?'"
112. Vannini and Fornssler, "Girl, Interrupted," 254–255.
113. Martínez-Patiño et al., "An Approach to the Biological, Historical and Psychological Repercussions," 317–318.
114. Katrina Karkazis and Rebecca Jordan-Young, "The Problem with Too Much T." *New York Times*, April 10, 2014, http://www.nytimes.com/2014/04/11/opinion/the-trouble-with-too-much-t.html?_r=0.
115. Sullivan, "Gender Verification and Gender Policies in Elite Sport," 414.
116. Levy, "Either/Or."
117. More recent media attention has centered on charges that Pretorius committed premeditated murder when he shot and killed his girlfriend Reeva Steenkamp in his Pretoria home on February 14, 2013. His trial is ongoing at the time of this writing.
118. Jones and Wilson, "Defining Advantage and Athletic Performance."
119. Swartz and Watermeyer, "Cyborg Anxiety," 188.
120. Ibid.
121. Skirstad, "Gender Verification in Competitive Sport."
122. Butler, "Doing Justice to Someone," 621–636; Chase, "Hermaphrodites with Attitude," 189–211; and Fausto-Sterling, *Sexing the Body*.

Chapter 5   A Pure Playing Field Nation: The Curious Case of New Zealand

1. Danforth. "Is the 'World Game' an 'Ethnic Game' or an 'Aussie Game'?," 363–387.
2. Merry, "Transnational Human Rights and Local Activism," 39.
3. This is a colloquial reference to New Zealanders. The kiwi bird is a national icon.
4. "'Pure Playing Field Nation' to Strengthen Drug-Free Sport." Voxy.co.nz, December 5, 2008, http://www.voxy.co.nz/national/039pure-playing-field-nation039-stengthen-drug-free-sport/5/6248.
5. Anae, "From Kava to Coffee."
6. Field notes from interview by author, Auckland, August 10, 2008.
7. Grainger, "The Browning of the All Blacks."
8. Seuffert, *Jurisprudence of National Identity*, 133.
9. This term gained traction in the 1980s. It typically refers to New Zealanders of European descent, although many scholars caution that pākehā is an unstable racial

category (Liu et al. *New Zealand Identities*; Spoonley, MacPhearson, and Pearson, *Nga Patai*.

10. The word, "Māori," came to connote indigeneity after colonial contact. It had previously signified "normal," and by the mid-1970s, there was a range of Māori political activist stances, including nationalist and separatist camps. Anthony Patete provides an overview (*Māori Political Activism and the Quest for Rangatiratanga*).

11. Fairburn, "Is There a Good Case for New Zealand Exceptionalism?," 29–49; Durie, *Te Mana Te Kawanatanga*, 278.

12. Ilana Gershon, *No Family Is an Island*, 80.

13. Ibid.

14. Seuffert offers numerous examples (*Jurisprudence of National Identity*). Notable among them are the findings of Moana Jackson's report on people of Māori descent and the justice system, which stated that monoculturalism had led to disproportionately punitive levels of punishment aimed at Māori people. It also called for parallel legal systems as a mandate recognized by the signed Māori versions of the Treaty of Waitangi.

15. Jenkins, "Maori Education."

16. For more details, see Seuffert, *Jurisprudence of National Identity*.

17. Ng Shiu, "*It's like Going to the Moon*," 10. Other books explore how racialized dynamics continue to change, often with a specific on the challenges faced by Pacific peoples (Spoonley and Pearson, eds. *Tangata, Tangata*).

18. Grieg, *Immigration and National Identity in New Zealand*; Grainger, "From Immigrant to Overstayer"; Grainger, "*The Browning of the All Blacks*"; and Pearson, "Citizenship, Identity and Belonging."

19. Grainger, "From Immigrant to Overstayer," 47.

20. Ng Shiu, "*It's like Going to the Moon*," 17.

21. Ibid., 18

22. Fraser and Gordon, "A Genealogy of Dependency," 331–332.

23. Mohanram, *Black Body*, 150.

24. Ibid., 150.

25. Hall, *Feminism and Sporting Bodies*.

26. As Hokowhitu argues, racism aimed at Māori athletes still permeates these practices of inclusion ("Māori Rugby and Subversion").

27. The All Blacks most often perform "Ka Mate." Although often referred to as "the haka," this characterization incorrectly implies that it is the only one of its kind. There are various different types, and other New Zealand teams perform them (McLean, *Māori Music*).

28. Jackson and Hokowithu, "Sport, Tribes, and Technology"; Tengan, "(En)gendering Colonialism."

29. Tengan and Markham, "Performing Polynesian Masculinities in American Football," 2421.

30. Ibid., 2421–2422.

31. Ibid.

32. Hokowhitu, "Tackling Māori Masculinity."

33. While similar, each code, including rugby sevens, rugby league, touch rugby, and rugby union, has distinct rules. Of the varieties of rugby codes, rugby union is known for its amateur (and arguably elitist) roots, only professionalizing in the 1990s. In fact, during the early twentieth century in England, there was a split in rugby over the issue of professionalism. This division gave birth to a rugby league,

which is widely considered the working-class counterpart of rugby union. For more analyses of rugby union and (trans)nationalism, see Besnier, "The Athlete's Body and the Global Condition"; Grainger, "The Browning of the All Blacks"; Jackson and Hokowhitu, "Sport, Tribes, and Technology"; and Nauright and Chandler, *Making Men*. There is also a growing interest in how these dynamics affect Pacific men within the jurisdiction of the United States, especially around American football (also referred to as Gridiron) (for example, Tengan and Markham, "Performing Polynesian Masculinities in American Football"; Uperesa, "*Fabled Futures*").

34. Grainger, "From Immigrant to Overstayer," 52–53.
35. Evans and Ngarimu, *The Art of Māori Weaving*, 21–23, 86–87.
36. Mana, a pan-Oceanic concept, does not readily translate into English terms. As reflected upon by many Māori participants I spoke with, it also has spiritual roots that evidence power and integrity. Thus, the authority that accompanies this power comes with a responsibility not to abuse it. Furthermore, there are many kinds of mana, which living as well as nonliving objects have, with communal or religious significance. For earlier discussions of mana and the challenges of translation, see Keesing, "Rethinking Mana," 137–156.
37. Deeb, "Exhibiting the 'Just-Lived Past,'" 372.
38. Sport, Fitness, and Leisure Ministerial Task Force, *Getting Set: For an Active Nation*, 2001, 10, italics mine.
39. Ibid., 11.
40. Ibid., 17–23.
41. Ibid., 22.
42. Ibid., 16.
43. Ibid., 48.
44. Burrows, "Pedagogizing Families through Obesity Discourse," 131.
45. Schwartz, *Never Satisfied*.
46. After ten years as SPARC, the agency's name changed in February 2012 to Sport New Zealand, a shift that followed the launching of High Performance Sport New Zealand, an initiative focusing on elite athlete development.
47. For more information about the details of cases it hears beyond anti-doping rule violations, refer to the Sports Tribunal of New Zealand website, available at http://www.sportstribunal.org.nz/, accessed April 20, 2011.
48. SPARC, "SPARC Statement of Intent, 2007–2010," 3.
49. *Sports Anti-Doping Act* (2006), 7, accessed April 20, 2011, http://www.legislation.govt.nz/act/public/2006/0058/latest/DLM390107.html. As of 2012, the act has been revised.
50. NZOC, "NZOC Anti-Doping By-Law," 1, accessed January 10, 2012, http://www.olympic.org.nz/system/files/attachments/nzoc-anti-doping-by-law-14-december-2011-1.pdf.
51. Interview by author, Wellington, June 24, 2010.
52. Interview by author, Palmerston North, August 12, 2008.
53. Ibid.
54. Interview by author, Wellington, June 24, 2010.
55. Interview by author, Auckland, June 15, 2010.
56. Ibid.
57. Lupton, *The Imperative of Health*; Rose, *The Politics of Life Itself*.
58. Interview by author, Wellington, June 24, 2010.

59. Ibid.

60. New Zealand Law Commission, *Controlling and Regulating Drugs*, 16.

61. Data on anti-doping cases are available on the Sports Tribunal of New Zealand's website, http://www.sportstribunal.org.nz/decisions/Results-in-anti-doping-cases/. Summary information is also accessible through the Sports Tribunal's annual reports (2007–2013).

62. With regard to illicit drug use more generally, New Zealand (and other nations) have international obligations to comply with three UN drug conventions that require governments to prohibit substances listed in its schedules (unless for medical or scientific purposes). Thus, the handling of drugs is not taken lightly as this point might seem to suggest. Following the requirements of the UNESCO Convention against Doping in Sport is thus not unique as an international requirement, but it is in the sense that it focuses on sport-specific uses. Taken together, these requirements may lead to disproportionate forms of punishment, as I argue here.

63. New Zealand Law Commission, *Controlling and Regulating Drugs*, 116–117.

64. This is according to the Misuse of Drugs Acts 1975 and subsequent amendments made to it in 2000 that reflect risk as a determining factor of classification. It also takes a presumptive stance against imprisonment for the possession or use of a Class C drug, but not with regards to acts of dealing or trafficking. There are also stages within classes that specify certain subcategories of drugs.

65. Ibid. For more information, refer to Fergusson and Horwood, "Cannabis Use and Dependence" and Fergusson and Horwood, "Arrests and Convictions for Cannabis-Related Offences."

66. Interview by author, Auckland, April 1, 2010.

67. This elaborates upon a point Besnier notes in relation to Pacific people's race consciousness. Besnier writes that in comparison to residents in the Pacific Islands (specifically Tongans), it is "only among younger second- and third-generation migrants to New Zealand, Australia, and the United States that one encounters an identification with blackness" ("The Athlete's Body and the Global Condition," 507n15). That identification often surfaced when speaking with and observing young Pacific men in New Zealand. These participants often cited the appeal of black popular culture's valuing of resistance to oppressive structures that hinder such expression.

68. Interview by author, Auckland, April 10, 2010.

69. In this case, he referred to the aftermath of rape allegations aimed at Bryant and the ensuing scandal around him. Tonu did not actually mention the words, "rape" or "sex," but he did state that he found the accusations questionable because Bryant was "a married man with a beautiful wife." He also said that even if Bryant "had been" with someone else, it was likely consensual, and it was the media and his female accuser who was out to defame him. Because this was not the topic of my inquiry, I chose not proceed further in this discussion beyond how it related to his explanation of race dynamics in sport. The quote still highlights how heteronormativity is integral to his explanation.

70. Interview by author, Auckland, April 13, 2010.

71. Some of these athletes cited that they had a Māori grandparent or great-grandparent, but knew little about those ways beyond childhood stories.

72. Interview by author, Auckland, April 6, 2010.

73. Interview by author, Auckland, April 12, 2010.

74. It was common among Māori interlocutors with whom I had developed a good rapport to use "black" to reference themselves and other Māori people. They often apologized, admitting that they would not usually use language around those most pākehā.
75. Interview by author, Canberra, June 27, 2012.
76. Interview by author, Auckland, April 6, 2010.
77. New Zealand Law Commission, *Controlling and Regulating Drugs*, 222.
78. Sports Tribunal of New Zealand. "Annual Report 2007/2008," 7.
79. Interview by author, Auckland, June 16, 2010.
80. Interview by author, Auckland, June 27, 2010.
81. Interview by author, Auckland, June 29, 2010.
82. Interview by author, Auckland, June 18, 2010.
83. Sports Tribunal of New Zealand. "Annual Report 2008/2009," 8.
84. Ibid., 8.
85. New Zealand Law Commission, *Controlling and Regulating Drugs*, 25.
86. Sports Tribunal of New Zealand. "Annual Report 2007/2008," 7.
87. Ibid.
88. Ibid.
89. Wenner, *Fallen Sports Heroes, Media, and Celebrity Culture*.

Chapter 6   Conclusion

1. MacAloon, "The Ethnographic Imperative in Comparative Olympic Research," 117.
2. Field notes by author, San Diego, California, May 30, 2011.
3. Kate Schmidt, "Just Say Yes to Steroids." *Los Angeles Times*, October 18, 2007.
4. Tim Rohan, "Study Revealing Doping in Track Strikes Hurdle," *New York Times*, August 23, 2013, A1.
5. These details are deliberately obscured and vague at the athlete's request to take all measures to ensure confidentiality. There are rules regarding national representation, which can vary by sport and sometimes country, but they are often limited to athletes with dual citizenship (who can usually choose) or those with permanent residency status.
6. Field notes by author, Los Angeles, California, December 9, 2007.
7. Beamish and Ritchie, "From Fixed Capacities to Performance-Enhancement."
8. With regard to illicit drug markets, a significant body of research acknowledges that the prohibition stance is only one regulatory approach, one that emerged alongside and in reaction to the regulation of licit drugs: Braithwaite, *Markets in Vice, Markets in Virtue*; Braithwaite and Drahos, *Global Business Regulation*, Courtright, "Drug Wars"; and Seddon, *A History of Drugs*. Prohibition is not—and has never been—the only answer to tackling drug use, nor is unfettered legalization. While there is evidence that legalization often spurs a short-term increase in illicit drug use, whether or not that rate of use becomes a long-term trend depends on the extent of its commercialization and accessibility (MacCouen and Reuter, *Drug War Heresies*).
9. Braithwaite, *Markets in Vice, Markets in Virtue*.
10. Kate Schmidt. "Just Say Yes to Steroids." *Los Angeles Times*, October 18, 2007.
11. Lupton, *The Imperative of Health*.
12. Atkinson discusses how risks are inherent to any supplementation use, focusing on how they take on gendered dimensions and motivations for taking them in the

first place (even when risks are not evident or recognized by users), ("Playing With Fire").

13. The report is available at http://resources.news.com.au/files/2013/02/07/1226572/544748-acc-reoport.pdf.

14. Matthew Drummond and John Stensholt, "The Powers That Persecute." *Australian Financial Review*, February, 15, 2013, http://www.afr.com/p/national/the_powers_that_persecute_ye7fNyTiayWDQdtL3W7VgO; Paoli and Donati, *The Doping Sports Market*.

15. Jason Mazanov. "One Year On—The Real Doping Scandals of 2013," *The Conversation*, February 14, 2014, http://theconversation.com/one-year-on-the-real-doping-scandals-of-2013-22871.

16. Brad Walter. "Cronulla Sharks Players Angry and Upset over ASADA Offer That Was Too Good to Refuse." *Sydney Morning Herald,* August 22, 2014, http://www.smh.com.au/rugby-league/league-news/cronulla-sharks-players-angry-and-upset-over-asada-offer-that-was-too-good-to-refuse-20140822-107aq5.html.

17. Paul Malone, Todd Balym, and Robert Craddock. "Australian Olympic Athletes Hit Out at ASADA's 'ludicrous' Backdated Bans for NRL Players." *Australian,* August 23, 2014, http://www.dailytelegraph.com.au/sport/nrl/australian-olympic-athletes-hit-out-at-asadas-ludicrous-backdated-bans-for-nrl-players/story-fni3fbgz-1227033607968?nk=a45b4b9ab7d275a3e5bb6422ac7b7ab3.

18. The AFL Press Release is available on its website, accessed August 28, 2013, http://www.afl.com.au/news/2013-08-27/essendon-penalties.

19. Kathryn Henne and Vanessa McDermott, "Cruel Reality of Sport Business," *Canberra Times,* February 15, 2013, C19.

20. Senator the Honorable Kate Lundy, Media Release, "Important New Anti-Doping Powers for ASADA Pass through Parliament," June 27, 2013, accessed August 20, 2013, http://www.asada.gov.au/media/ministerial.html.

21. Martin Hardie and Benjamin Koh, "We Need an Advocate Against ASADA's Power in Doping in Sport," *The Conversation*, February 11, 2014, https://theconversation.com/we-need-an-advocate-against-asadas-power-in-doping-control-12119; "We're Getting Tougher on Doping Cheats—But Why?," *The Conversation*, February 20, 2013, https://theconversation.com/were-getting-tougher-on-doping-cheats-but-why-12235.

22. Paoli and Donati (*The Doping Sports Market*) discuss this in the implications of their research on Italy, a jurisdiction where doping is criminalized.

23. For these case histories, refer to *NFL Players Association v. NFL*, 582 F.3d 863, U.S. Dist. LEXIS 43576 (2009), and *Williams v. NFL,* U.S. App. LEXIS 20251 (2009).

24. Wolf offers a more detailed legal analysis ("Conflicting Anti-Doping Laws in Professional Sports"); however, she makes some judgments about the players involved and rates of doping that I am not willing to endorse here.

25. Amos and Fridman, "Drugs in Sport"; Schneider, "Privacy, Confidentiality and Human Rights in Sport."

26. Matt Slater, "Legal Threat to Anti-Doping Code." *BBC Sport*, January 22, 2009, http://news.bbc.co.uk/sport2/hi/front_page/7844918.stm.

27. David, *A Guide to the World Anti-Doping Code*, 19; Ravjani, "The Court of Arbitration for Sport," 274.

28. E-mail correspondence with author, citing press release in German, February 26, 2014.

29. Houlihan ("Civil Rights, Doping Control and the World Anti-Doping Code") provides an overview that captures many of these debates.

30. Amy Shipley, "Lance Armstrong Accuses USADA of Violating Its Own Rules in Pursuit of Doping Violations," *Washington Post*, June 29, 2012, accessed July 25, 2012, http://www.washingtonpost.com/sports/othersports/2012/06/28/gJQAEncy9V_story.html.

31. Joe Palazzolo, "Armstrong Lawsuit: Before and After," WSJ Law Blog, July 10, 2012, accessed July 25, 2012, http://blogs.wsj.com/law/2012/07/10/armstrong-lawsuit-before-and-after/.

32. Associated Press, *National Public Radio*, August 10, 2012, accessed August 13, 2012, http://www.npr.org/templates/story/story.php?storyId=158604200.

33. For more details of the events that inform the Lance Armstrong case, see Dimeo, "Why Lance Armstrong?"

34. Martin Hardie, "Is the Lance Armstrong Affair a Race to the Bottom for Cycling?," *The Conversation,* August 27, 2012, https://theconversation.edu.au/is-the-lance-armstrong-affair-a-race-to-the-bottom-for-cycling-9073.

35. There is documented disdain between Pound and former UCI president Pat McQuaid worth noting (see "Pound Says IOC May Drop Cycling from Olympics on Armstrong Confession," *Cycling News*, January 15, 2013, http://www.cyclingnews.com/news/pound-says-ioc-may-drop-cycling-from-olympics-on-armstrong-confession.

36. For a reference to these dynamics, see Gail Collins, "The Point of Lance," *New York Times*, January 16, 2013, accessed August 20, 2013, http://www.nytimes.com/2013/01/17/opinion/collins-the-point-of-lance.html.

37. Teetzel and Mazzucco, "Minor Problems."

38. Field notes from interview by author, Canberra, Australia, September 13, 2013.

39. JohnathanThurston, (jthurston06), "Thanks ASADA for the 6am visit for a urine and blood test! I nearly forgot to say thanks for bashing down the front door and waking Frankie up too! #effingtorture." July 24, 2013, Instagram.

40. Andrew Webster, "Angry Cronulla Sharks Players Reject Voluntary Six Month Ban, Claim Their Hand Is Being Forced," *Fox Sports*, March 8, 2013, accessed August 28, 2013, http://www.foxsports.com.au/league/nrl-premiership/angry-cronulla-sharks-players-reject-voluntary-six-month-ban-claim-their-hand-is-being-forced/story-fn2mcuj6–1226592916152#.UiUmnmTVczE.

41. David Ricco, "Exclusive Drugs in Sport Survey—The Results Are In," *Courier Mail*, February 16, 2013, accessed August 28, 2013, http://www.couriermail.com.au/sport/exclusive-drugs-in-sport-survey-the-results-are-in/story-fnduczvk-1226579439745.

42. Adam Lucius, "Sharks Players Plead Guilty to ASADA Charges," *ABC News Radio*, August 22, 2014, http://www.abc.net.au/newsradio/content/s4072797.htm.

43. Haraway, *Simians, Cyborgs, and Women*.

44. Haraway, "Situated Knowledges."

45. Hoag, "Assembling Partial Perspectives," 82.

46. Latour, *We Have Never Been Modern*.

47. Hobbes, *Leviathan*.

48. Duster, *Backdoor to Eugenics*. Roberts more explicitly looks at race in relation to bio-citizenship and knowledge developed and obtained from genetics (*Fatal Invention*).

49. Young, too, discusses excess in similar ways with regard to crime and punishment. The punishments of certain bodies, she writes, "exemplify that which exceeds contemporary formulations of crimo-legal tradition" (*Imagining Crime*, 77).

50. Collier, Maurer, and Suárez-Navaz, "Sanctioned Identities," 2.
51. Ibid., 2.
52. Brownell's edited collection provides an in-depth analysis of these earlier dynamics in relation to the 1904 Olympics, particularly around the display of "savages" and "natives" during the Anthropology Days (*The 1904 Anthropology Days and Olympic Games*).
53. Hajjar, "Chaos as Utopia," 3.

Appendix   Research Methods: On Secrets and Multi-Sited Storytelling

1. Ewick and Silbey, *The Common Place of Law*, 251.
2. Much of this appendix provides details not covered in the original ethics approvals for this research, although it is very much concerned with the ethics of research. To conduct this research, I received ethics clearance from the University of California, Irvine (2008-6153), and the University of New South Wales (A-13-35).
3. Because these anti-doping rules fall under licensing, the athletes observed were professional fighters. Competitive amateur boxers are typically subject to USA Boxing regulations.
4. Merry, "Transnational Human Rights and Local Activism," 39.
5. Marcus, *Ethnography through Thick and Thin*, 14.
6. Ibid.
7. Silk, Andrews, and Mason, "Encountering the Field," 11–12.
8. Silk, "Sporting Ethnography."
9. Richland (*Arguing with Tradition*, 59–64) further discusses these approaches.
10. Bauman and Briggs, "Poetics and Performance as Critical Perspectives," 69.
11. Gal, "Multiplicity and Contestation among Linguistic Ideologies," 323.
12. Briggs, *Disorderly Discourse*.
13. Terry, "Theorizing Deviant Historiography," 284.
14. Ewick and Silbey, *The Common Place of Law*, 258.
15. In doing so, I acknowledge that Clifford Geertz first called for anthropologists to think of culture as text and that others, such as Victor Turner, were influential in shifting the field to a constructivist orientation, which enabled the critical turn embraced here.
16. Richland, "Perpetuities against Rules."
17. Ibid., 434.

Bibliography

Aganthangelou, Anna M., and L. H. M. Ling. "Desire Industries: Sex Trafficking, UN Peace-keeping, and the Neo-liberal World Order." *The Brown Journal of World Affairs*, 10, no. 1 (2003): 133–148.

Al-Habet, Sayed, Kinfe Redda, and Henry J. Lee. "Uses and Abuses of Anabolic Steroids by Athletes." In *Cocaine, Marijuana, Designer Drugs: Chemistry, Pharmacology, and Behavior*, edited by Kinfe Redda, Charles A. Walker, and Gene Barnett, 211–232. Boca Raton, FL: CRC Press, 1989.

Althusser, Louis. "Ideology and Ideological State Apparatuses: Notes toward an Investigation." In *Lenin and Philosophy and Other Essays*, translated by Ben Brewster, 127–188. New York: Monthly Review Press, 1971.

Amos, Anne, and Saul Fridman. "Drugs in Sport: The Legal Issues." *Sport in Society* 12, no. 3 (2009): 356–374.

Anae, Melani. "From Kava to Coffee: The 'Browning' of Auckland." In *Almighty Auckland?*, edited by Ian Carter, David Craig, and Steve Matthewman, 89–110. Palmerston North, NZ: Dunmore Press, 2004.

Anderson, Benedict. *Imagined Communities: Reflections on the Origin and Spread of Nationalism*. New York: Verso, 1983.

Andersson, Mette. "The Relevance of the Black Atlantic in Contemporary Sport: Racial Imaginaries in Norway." *International Review for the Sociology of Sport* 42, no. 1 (2007): 65–81.

Andrews, David, and George Ritzer. "The Grobal in the Sporting Glocal." *Global Networks* 7, no. 2 (2007): 113–153.

Atkinson, Michael. "Playing with Fire: Masculinity, Health, and Sports Supplements." *Sociology of Sport Journal* 24, no. 2 (2007): 165–186.

Backhouse, Susan, Jim McKenna, Simon Robinson, and Andrew Atkin. *Attitudes, Behaviours, Knowledge and Education—Drugs in Sport: Past, Present and Future*. Montreal: World Anti-Doping Agency (2007) http://www.wada-ama.org/ rtecontent/document/ Backhouse_et_al_Full_Report.pdf.

Bale, John. "From Anthropology Days to Anthropological Olympics." In *The 1904 Anthropology Days and Olympic Games: Sport, Race, and American Imperialism*, edited by Susan Brownell, 324–342. Lincoln: University of Nebraska Press, 2008.

Balsamo, Anne. *Technologies of the Gendered Body: Reading Cyborg Women*. Durham, NC: Duke University Press, 1996.

Barclay, Kelly. "Rethinking Inclusion and Biculturalism: Towards a More Relational Practice of Democratic Justice." In *New Zealand Identities: Departures and Destinations*, edited by James H. Liu, Tim McCreanor, Tracey McIntosh, and Teresia Teaiwa, 118–139. Wellington, NZ: Victoria University Press, 2005.

Barnes, Lan. "Olympic Drug Testing: Improvements without Progress." *The Physician and Sports Medicine* 8, no. 6 (1980): 21–24.

Barney, Robert K, Stephen R. Wenn, and Scott G. Martyn. *Selling the Five Rings: The International Olympic Committee and the Rise of Olympic Commercialism*. Salt Lake City: University of Utah Press, 2002.

Bauman, Richard, and Charles L. Briggs. "Poetics and Performance as Critical Perspectives on Language and Social Life." *Annual Review of Anthropology* 19 (1990): 59–88.

Beamish, Rob, and Ian Ritchie. *Fastest, Highest, Strongest: A Critique of High-Performance Sport*. New York: Routledge, 2006.

———. "From Chivalrous 'Brothers-in-Arms' to the Eligible Athlete: Changed Principles and the IOC's Banned Substance List." *International Review for the Sociology of Sport* 39, no. 4 (2004): 355–371.

———. "From Fixed Capacities to Performance-Enhancement: The Paradigm Shift in the Science of 'Training' and the Use of Performance-Enhancing Substances." *Sport in History* 25, no. 3 (2005): 412–433.

———. "The Spectre of Steroids: Nazi Propaganda, Cold War Anxiety and Patriarchal Paternalism." *International Journal of the History of Sport* 22, no. 5 (2005): 777–795.

Beck, Ulrich. *Risk Society: Towards a New Modernity*. London: Sage, 1992.

Becker, Howard. *Outsiders: Studies in Sociology of Deviance*. New York: Free Press, 1963.

Beckett, Arnold. "The Future of the Olympic Movement." In *Drug Controversy in Sport: The Socio-ethical and Medical Issues*, edited by Ronald S. Laura and S. W. White, 25–37. Sydney: Allen and Unwin, 1991.

———. "Misuse of Drugs in Sports." *British Journal of Sports Medicine* 12 (1979): 185–194.

Besnier, Niko. "The Athlete's Body and the Global Condition: Tongan Rugby Players in Japan." *American Ethnologist* 39, no. 3 (2012): 491–510.

Bhabba, Homi K. "Narrating the Nation." In *Nation and Narrative*, edited by Homi K. Bhabba, 1–7. New York: Routledge, 1990.

Birrell, Susan. "Sport as Ritual: Interpretations from Durkheim to Goffman." *Social Forces* 60, no. 2 (1981): 354–376.

Birrell, Susan, and CL Cole. "Double Fault: Renee Richards and the Construction and Naturalization of Difference." *Sociology of Sport Journal* 7, no. 1 (1990): 1–21.

———. *Women, Sport, and Culture*. Champaign, IL: Human Kinetics, 1994.

Bourdieu, Pierre. *The Field of Cultural Production*. New York: Columbia University Press, 1993.

———. "Program for a Sociology of Sport." *Sociology of Sport Journal* 5, no. 2 (1988): 153–161.

Braithwaite, John. *Markets in Vice, Markets in Virtue*. Annandale, NSW: The Federation Press, 2005.

Braithwaite, John, and Peter Drahos. *Global Business Regulation*. Cambridge: Cambridge University Press, 2000.

Briggs, Charles. *Disorderly Discourse: Narrative, Conflict, and Inequality*. London: Oxford University Press, 1996.

Brown, Wendy. "Neo-liberalism and the End of Liberal Democracy." *Theory and Event* 7, no. 1 (2003): 1–25.

Brownell, Susan. *Training the Body for China: Sports in the Moral Order of the People's Republic*. Chicago: University of Chicago Press, 1995.

———, ed. *The 1904 Anthropology Days and Olympic Games: Sport, Race, and American Imperialism*. Lincoln: University of Nebraska Press, 2008.

Burrows, Lisette. "Pedagogizing Families through Obesity Discourse." In *The Fat Studies Reader*, edited by Esther Rothblum and Sondra Solvay, 127–140. New York: New York University Press, 2009.

Butcher, Robert, and Angela Schneider. "Fair Play as Respect for the Game." In *Ethics in Sport*, 2nd ed., edited by William J. Morgan, 119–140. Champaign, IL: Human Kinetics, 2007.

Butler, Judith. *Bodies That Matter: On the Discursive Limits of "Sex."* New York: Routledge, 1993.

———. "Doing Justice to Someone: Sex Reassignment and Allegories of Transsexuality." *GLQ: A Journal of Gay and Lesbian Studies* 7, no. 4 (2001): 621–636.

Butryn, Ted M., and Matthew A. Masucci. "It's Not about the Book: A Cyborg Counternarrative of Lance Armstrong." *Journal of Sport and Social Issues* 27, no. 2 (2003): 124–144.

Cabot, Heath. "The Governance of Things: Documenting Limbo in the Greek Asylum Procedure." *PoLAR: Political and Legal Anthropology Review* 35, no. 1 (2012): 11–29.

Calavita, Kitty. *Invitation to Law and Society: An Introduction to the Study of Real Law*. Chicago: University of Chicago Press, 2010.

Casini, Lorenzo. "Global Hybrid Public-Private Bodies: The World Anti-Doping Agency (WADA)." *International Organizations Law Review* 6, no. 2 (2009): 421–446.

Cavanagh, Sheila L., and Sykes, Heather. "Transsexual Bodies at the Olympics: The International Olympic Committee's Policy on Transsexual Athletes at the 2004 Athens Summer Games." *Body and Society* 12, no. 3 (2006): 75–102.

Chase, Cheryl. "Hermaphrodites with Attitude: Mapping the Emergence of Intersex Political Activism." *GLQ: A Journal of Gay and Lesbian Studies* 4, no. 2 (1998): 189–211.

Clarke, Adele E., Janet K. Shim, Laura Mamo, Jennifer Ruth Fosket, and Jennifer R. Fishman. "Biomedicalization: Technoscientific Transformations of Health, Illness, and U.S. Biomedicine." *American Sociological Review* 68, no 2 (2003): 161–194.

Cohen, Stan. *Folk Devils and Moral Panics: The Creation of the Mods and Rockers*. London: Routledge, 1972.

Cole, Cheryl, and Melissa Orlie. "Hybrid Athletes, Monstrous Addicts and Cyborg Natures." *Journal of Sport History* 22, no. 3 (1995): 229–239.

Cole, CL "Resisting the Canon: Feminist Cultural Studies, Sport, and Technologies of the Body." *Journal of Sport and Social Issues* 17, no. 2 (1993): 77–97.

———. "Testing for Sex or Drugs." *Journal of Sport and Social Issues* 24, no. 4 (2000): 331–333.

Cole, CL, and Harry Denny III. "Visualizing Deviance in Post-Reagan America: Magic Johnson, AIDS, and the Promiscuous World of Professional Sport." *Critical Sociology* 38, no. 4 (1994): 123–147.

Cole, CL, and Alex Molbey. "American Steroids: Using Race and Gender." *Journal of Sport and Social Issues* 29, no. 1 (2005): 3–8.

Collier, Jane F., Bill Maurer, and Liliana Suárez-Navaz. "Sanctioned Identities: Legal Constructions of Modern Personhood." *Identities* 2 no. 1–2 (1995): 1–27.

Cooky, Cheryl, Ranissa Dycus, and Shari L. Dworkin. "'What Makes a Woman a Woman?' versus 'Our First Lady of Sport': A Comparative Analysis of the United States and the South African Media Coverage of Caster Semenya." *Journal of Sport and Social Issues* 37, no. 1 (2013): 31–56.

Coubertin, Pierre de. "Chronique du Mois: Duel de Races—Le Mépris de la Mort—Défense aux Femmes—Palais des Sports—Le Prix d'un athlète." *La Revue Olympique* (July, 1910): 108–111.

———. "Olympia." In *The Olympic Idea: Discourses and Essays*, edited by Carl-Diem-Institut and Deutschen Sporthochschule Köln. Stuttgart: Hofmann, 1996 [1929].

———. "Why I Revived the Olympic Games." In *Olympism: Selected Writings*, edited by Norbert Müller. Lausanne: International Olympic Committee, 2000.

Courtwright, David. "Drug Wars: Policy Hots and Historical Cools." *Bulletin of the History of Medicine* 78, no. 2 (2004): 440–450.

Coutin, Susan. *Legalizing Moves: Salvadoran Immigrants' Struggle for U.S. Residency*. Ann Arbor: University of Michigan Press, 2003.

Coutin, Susan, and Barbara Yngvesson. "Backed by Papers: Undoing Persons, Histories, and Return." *American Ethnologist* 33, no. 2 (2006): 177–190.

Curry, Timothy. "Fraternal Bonding in the Locker Room: A Profeminist Analysis of Talk about Competition and Women." *Sociology of Sport Journal* 8, no. 2 (1991): 119–135.

Danforth, Loring M. "Is the 'World Game' an 'Ethnic Game' or an 'Aussie Game'? Narrating the Nation in Australian Soccer." *American Ethnologist* 28, no. 2 (2001): 363–387.

David, Paul. *A Guide to the World Anti-Doping Code: A Fight for the Spirit of Sport*. Cambridge: Cambridge University Press, 2008.

Davis, Laurel R., and Linda C. Delano. "Fixing the Boundaries of Physical Gender: Side Effects of Anti-drugs Campaigns in Athletics." *Sociology of Sport Journal* 9, no. 1 (1992): 1–19.

Deeb, Lara. "Exhibiting the 'Just-Lived Past': Hizbullah's Nationalist Narratives in Transnational Political Context." *Comparative Studies in Society and History* 50, no. 2 (2008): 369–399.

Dietz, Mary G. "Context Is All: Feminism and Theories of Citizenship." *Daedalus* 116, no. 4 (1987): 1–24.

Dimeo, Paul. *A History of Drug Use in Sport 1876–1976: Beyond Good and Evil*. New York: Routledge, 2007.

———. "Why Lance Armstrong? Historical Context and Key Turning Points in the 'Cleaning Up' of Professional Cycling." *International Journal of the History of Sport 31, no. 8* (2014): 951–968.

Dimeo, Paul, Thomas M. Hunt, and Matthew T. Bowers. "Saint or Sinner?: A Reconsideration of the Career of Prince Alexandre de Merode, Chair of the International Olympic Committee's Medical Commission, 1967–2002." *International Journal of the History of Sport* 28, no. 6 (2011): 925–940.

Dirix, Albert. "The Doping Problem at the Tokyo and Mexico City Olympic Games." *Journal of Sports Medicine and Fitness* 6 (1963): 183–186.

Dirix, Albert, and Xavier Sturbois. *The First Thirty Years of the International Olympic Committee Medical Commission 1967–1997*. Lausanne: International Olympic Committee (IOC Booklet Series, "History and Facts"), 1998.

Donnelly, Peter. "Prolympism: Sport Monoculture as Crisis and Opportunity." *Quest* 48, no. 1 (1996): 25–42.

Douglas, Mary. *Purity and Danger: An Analysis of the Concepts of Pollution and Taboo*. Harmondsworth, UK: Penguin, 1970 [1966].

DuBois, W. E. B. "The Prize Fighter." *Crisis* 8 (1904): 181.

Dumit, Joseph. *Drugs for Life: How Pharmaceutical Companies Define Our Health*. Durham, NC: Duke University Press, 2012.

Durie, Mason. *Te Mana Te Kawanatanga: The Politics of Māori Self-Determination*. Auckland, NZ: Oxford University Press, 1998.

Duster, Troy. *Backdoor to Eugenics*. New York: Routledge, 1990.

Dworkin, Shari L., and Cheryl Cooky. "Sport, Sex Segregation, and Sex Testing: Critical Reflections on This Unjust Marriage." *American Journal of Bioethics* 12, no. 7 (2012): 21–23.

Edwards, Harry. "Sport within the Veil: The Triumphs, Tragedies and Challenges of Afro-American Involvement." *Annals of the American Academy of Political and Social Science* 445 (1979): 116–127.

———. "Sport's Tragic Drug Connection: Where Do We Go from Here?" *Journal of Sport and Social Issues* 10, no. 1 (1986): 1–5.

Elsas, Louis, J., R. P. Hayes, and Kasinathan Muralidharan. "Gender Verification in the Centennial Olympic Games." *Journal of the Medical Association of Georgia* 86 (1997): 50–55.

Enck-Wanzer, Suzanne Marie. "All's Fair in Love and Sport: Black Masculinity and Domestic Violence in the News." *Communication and Critical/Cultural Studies* 6, no. 1 (2009): 1–18.

Epstein, Stephen. *Impure Science: AIDS, Activism, and the Politics of Knowledge*. Berkeley: University of California Press, 1996.

Ericson, Richard, Aaron Doyle, and Dean Barry. *Insurance as Governance*. Toronto: University of Toronto Press, 2003.

Ericson, Richard, and Kevin Haggerty. *Policing the Risk Society*. Toronto: University of Toronto Press, 1997.

Evans, Miriama, and Ranui Ngarimu. *The Art of Māori Weaving: The Eternal Thread/Te Aho Mutunga Kore*. Wellington, NZ: Huia, 2005.

Ewick, Patricia, and Susan Silbey. *The Common Place of Law: Stories of Law in Everyday Life*. Chicago: University of Chicago Press, 1998.

Fairburn, Miles. "Is There a Good Case for New Zealand Exceptionalism?" *ThesisEleven: Critical Theory and Historical Sociology* 92, no. 1 (2008): 29–49.

Fassin, Didier, and Richard Rechtman. *The Empire of Trauma: An Inquiry into the Condition of Victimhood*, translated by Rachel Gomme. Princeton: Princeton University Press, 2010.

Fausto-Sterling, Anne. *Sexing the Body: Gender Politics and the Construction of Sexuality*. New York: Basic, 2000.

Feldman, Allen. *Formations of Violence: The Narrative of the Body and Political Terror in Northern Ireland*. Chicago: University of Chicago Press, 1991.

Fergusson, David M., and John L. Horwood. "Cannabis Use and Dependence in a New Zealand Birth Cohort." *New Zealand Medical Journal* 113, no. 1109 (2000): 156–158.

Fergusson, David M., N. R. Swain-Campbell, and John L. Horwood. "Arrests and Convictions for Cannabis-Related Offences in a New Zealand Birth Cohort." *Drug and Alcohol Dependence* 70, no. 1 (2003): 53–63.

Fine, Gary A. *With the Boys: Little League Baseball and Preadolescent Culture*. Chicago: University of Chicago Press, 1987.

Foucault, Michel. "The Confession of the Flesh." In *Power/Knowledge: Selected Interviews and Other Writings, 1972–1977*, edited by Colin Gordon, 194–229. New York: Pantheon, 1980.

———. *The History of Sexuality, Vol. 1: An Introduction*. New York: Vintage, 1990 [1978].

———. "Nietzsche, Genealogy, History." In *The Foucault Reader*, edited by Paul Rabinow, 76–100. London: Penguin, 1991.

Fouché, Rayvon. "Cycling's 'Fix.'" *Journal of Sport and Social Issues* 33, no. 1 (2006): 97–99.

Franklin, Sarah. "Science as Culture, Cultures of Science." *Annual Review of Anthropology* 24 (1995): 163–184.

Fraser, Nancy, and Linda Gordon. "A Genealogy of Dependency: Tracing a Keyword in U.S. Discourse." *Signs: Journal of Women in Culture and Society* 19, no. 2 (1994): 309–336.

Gal, Susan. "Multiplicity and Contestation among Linguistic Ideologies." In *Language Ideologies: Practice and Theory*, edited by Bambi B. Schieffelin and Kathryn A. Woolard, 317–332. Oxford: Oxford University Press, 1997.

Gems, Gerald R. "The Politics of Boxing: Resistance, Religion, and Working Class Assimilation." *International Sports Journal* 8, no. 1 (2004): 89–103.

Gerlach, Neil, Sheryl N. Hamilton, Rebecca Sullivan, and Priscilla L. Walton. *Becoming Biosubjects: Bodies. Systems. Technology.* Toronto: Toronto University Press, 2011.

Gershon, Ilana. *No Family Is an Island: Cultural Expertise among Samoans in Diaspora.* Ithaca, NY: Cornell University Press, 2012.

Gibson-Graham, J. K. *The End of Capitalism (As We Knew It): A Feminist Critique of Political Economy.* Oxford: Blackwell, 1996.

Giddens, Anthony. *The Consequences of Modernity.* Cambridge: Polity, 1990.

———. *Modernity and Self-Identity: Self and Society in the Late Modern Age.* Palo Alto, CA; Stanford University Press.

Glassner, Barry. *The Culture of Fear: Why Americans Are Afraid of the Wrong Things.* New York: Basic, 2000.

Gleaves, John. "Doped Professionals and Clean Amateurs: Amateurism's Influence on the Modern Anti-Doping Movement." *The Journal of Sport History* 38, no. 2 (2011): 401–418.

Gleaves, John, and Matthew Llewellyn. "Sport, Drugs, and Amateurism: Tracing the Real Cultural Origins of Anti-Doping Rules in International Sport." *International Journal of the History of Sport* 31, no. 8 (2014): 839–853.

Goode, Erich. *Sport Doping as Deviance: Anti-Doping as Moral Panic.* Norderstedt, DE: Books on Demand GmbH, 2011.

Grainger, Andrew. "The Browning of the All Blacks: Pacific Peoples, Rugby, and the Cultural Politics of Identity in New Zealand." PhD diss., University of Maryland, 2008.

———. "From Immigrant to Overstayer: Samoan Identity, Rugby, and Cultural Politics of Race and Nation in Aotearoa/New Zealand." *Journal of Sport and Social Issues* 30, no. 1 (2006): 45–61.

Greig, Stuart, ed. *Immigration and National Identity in New Zealand: One People, Two Peoples, Many Peoples?* Palmerston North, NZ: Dunmore Press, 1995.

Grewal, Inderpal. *Transnational America: Feminisms, Diasporas, Neoliberalisms.* Durham, NC: Duke University Press, 2005.

Grewal, Inderpal, and Caren Kaplan, eds. *Scattered Hegemonies: Postmodernities and Transnational Feminist Practices.* Minneapolis: University of Minnesota Press, 1994.

Gusfield, Joseph. *Symbolic Crusade: Status Politics and the American Temperance Movement.* Urbana: University of Illinois Press, 1963.

Guttmann, Allen. *The Olympics: A History of the Modern Games.* Urbana: University of Illinois Press, 1992.

Haggerty, Kevin D., and Richard V. Ericson, eds. *The New Politics of Surveillance and Visibility.* Toronto: University of Toronto Press, 2006.

Hajjar, Lisa. "Chaos as Utopia: International Criminal Prosecutions as a Challenge to State Power." *Studies in Law, Politics and Society* 31 (2004): 3–23.

Hall, M. Ann. *Feminism and Sporting Bodies: Essays on Theory and Practice.* Champaign, IL: Human Kinetics, 1996.

Halliday, Terence, and Gregory Shaffer, eds. *Transnational Legal Orders.* Cambridge: Cambridge University Press, 2014.

Halse, Christine. "Bio-Citizenship: Virtue Discourse and the Birth of the Bio-Citizen." In *Biopolitics and the "Obesity Epidemic,"* edited by Jan Wright and Valerie Harwood, 45–59. New York: Routledge. 2008.

Halse, Christine, Anne Honey, and Desiree Boughtwood. "The Paradox of Virtue: (Re)thinking Deviance, Anorexia and Schooling." *Gender and Education* 19, no. 2 (2007): 219–235.

Hanson, Allan. "The Making of the Maori: Culture Invention and Its Logic." *American Anthropologist* 91, no. 4 (1989): 891–902.

Haraway, Donna. *Simians, Cyborgs, and Women: The Reinvention of Nature*. New York: Routledge, 1991.

———. "Situated Knowledges: The Science Question in Feminism and the Privilege of Partial Perspective." *Feminist Studies* 14, no. 3 (1988): 575–599.

Harding, Sandra. "Rethinking Standpoint Epistemology: What Is 'Strong' Objectivity?" In *Feminist Perspectives on Social Research*, edited by Sharlene Nagy Hesse-Biber and Michelle L. Yaisser, 39–63. New York: Oxford University Press, 2004.

Hargreaves, Jennifer. *Heroines of Sport: The Politics of Difference and Identity*. London: Routledge, 2001.

Hargreaves, John. "The Body, Sport and Power Relations." In *Sport, Leisure, and Social Relations*, edited by John Horne, David Jary, and Alan Tomlinson, 139–159. London: Routledge and Kegan Paul, 1987.

Hartmann, Douglas. *Race, Culture, and the Revolt of the Black Athlete: The 1968 Olympic Protests and Their Aftermath*. Chicago: University of Chicago Press, 2003.

Harvey, David. *A Brief History of Neoliberalism*. Oxford: Oxford University Press, 2007.

Harwood, Valerie. "Theorizing Biopedagogies." In *Biopolitics and the "Obesity Epidemic,"* edited by Jan Wright and Valerie Harwood, 15–30. New York: Routledge, 2008.

Hay, Eduardo. "Sex Determination in Putative Female Athletes." *Journal of the American Medical Association* 221, no. 9 (1972): 998–999.

Heggie, Vanessa. "Testing Sex and Gender in Sports: Reinventing, Reimagining and Reconstructing Histories." *Endeavour* 34, no. 4 (2010): 157–163.

Henne, Kathryn. "The Emergence of Moral Technopreneurialism in Sport: Techniques in Anti-Doping Regulation, 1966–1976." *International Journal of the History of Sport* 31, no. 8 (2014): 884–901.

———. *The Origins of the International Olympic Committee Medical Commission and Its Technocratic Regime: An Historiographic Investigation of Anti-Doping Regulation*. Lausanne: International Olympic Committee. (2009) http://doc.rero.ch/record/17372.

———. "The 'Science' of Fair Play: Gender and the Politics of Testing." *Signs: A Journal of Women in Culture and Society* 39, no. 3 (2014): 787–812.

———. "WADA, the Promises of Law and the Landscapes of Antidoping Regulation." *PoLAR: Political and Legal Anthropology Review* 33, no. 2 (2010): 306–325.

Hirsch, Susan F., and Mindie Lazarus-Black. "Performance and Paradox: Exploring Law's Role in Hegemony and Resistance." In *Contested States*, edited by Susan F. Hirsch and Mindie Lazarus-Black, 1–23. New York: Routledge, 1994.

Hoag, Colin. "Assembling Partial Perspectives: Thoughts on the Anthropology of Bureaucracy." *PoLAR: Political and Legal Anthropology Review* 34, no. 1 (2011): 81–94.

Hobbes, Thomas. *Leviathan Parts I and II: Revised Edition*. Edited by A. P. Martinich and Brian Battiste. Peterborough, ONT: Broadview Press, 2011.

Hoberman, John M. *Mortal Engines: The Science of Performance and the Dehumanization of Sport*. Caldwells, NJ: Blackburn Press, 2001.

———. *Testosterone Dreams: Rejuvenation, Aphrodisia, Doping*. Berkeley: University of California Press, 2006.

Hobsbawm, Eric. "Inventing Tradition." In *The Invention of Tradition*, edited by Eric Hobsbawm and Terence Ranger, 1–14. Cambridge: Cambridge University Press, 1983.

Holmes, Douglas R., and George E. Marcus. "Cultures of Expertise and the Management of Globalization: Toward the Re-functioning of Ethnography." In *Global Assemblages: Technology, Politics, and Ethics as Anthropological Problems*, edited by Aihwa Ong and Stephan J. Collier, 235–254. Malden, MA: Blackwell, 2004.

Hokowhitu, Brendan. "Māori Rugby and Subversion: Creativity, Domestication, Oppression and Decolonization." *The International Journal of the History of Sport* 26, no. 16 (2009): 2314–2334.

———. "Tackling Māori Masculinity: Genealogy of Savagery and Sport." *Contemporary Pacific* 16, no. 2 (2004): 259–284.

Hong, Fan. "Doping and Anti-Doping in Sport in China: An Analysis of Recent and Present Attitudes and Actions." *Sport in Society* 9, no. 2 (2006): 314–333.

Houlihan, Barry. "Civil Rights, Doping Control, and the World Anti-doping Code." *Sport in Society* 7, no. 3 (2004): 420–437.

———. *Dying to Win: Doping in Sport and the Development of Anti-doping Policy*. 2nd ed. Strasbourg, FR: Council of Europe, 2002.

Hunt, Thomas. *Drug Games: The International Olympic Committee and the Politics of Doping, 1960–2008*. Austin: University of Texas Press, 2011.

Hunt, Thomas, Paul Dimeo, and Scott R. Jedlicka. "The Historical Roots of Today's Problems: A Critical Appraisal of the International Anti-Doping Movement." *Performance Enhancement and Health* 1, no. 2 (2012): 55–60.

Ian, Marcia. "The Primitive Subject of Female Bodybuilding: Transgression and Other Postmodern Myths." *Differences: A Journal of Feminist Cultural Studies* 12, no. 3 (2001): 69–100.

International Olympic Committee. *The Olympic Charter*. (2004), accessed March 13, 2009, http://www.olympic.org/charter.

Jackson, Steven J. "Exorcizing the Ghost: Donovan Bailey, Ben Johnson and the Politics of Canadian Identity." *Media, Culture and Society* 26, no. 1 (2004): 121–141.

Jackson, Steven J., and Brendan Hokowhitu. "Sport, Tribes, and Technology: The New Zealand All Blacks Haka and the Politics of Identity." *Journal of Sport and Social Issues* 26, no. 2 (2002): 125–139.

Jenkins, Kuni. "Maori Education: A Cultural Experience and Dilemma for the State—A New Direction for Maori Society." In *The Politics of Learning and Teaching in Aotearoa—New Zealand*, edited by Eve Coxon, Kuni Jenkins, James Marshall, and Lauran Massey, 148–179. Palmerston North, NZ: Dunmore Press, 1994.

Jennings, Andrew. *The New Lords of the Rings: Olympic Corruption and How to Buy Gold Medals*. New York: Pocket, 1996.

Jones, Carwyn, and Cassie Wilson. "Defining Advantage and Athletic Performance: The Case of Oscar Pistorius." *European Journal of Social Science* 9, no. 2 (2009): 125–131.

Jönsson, Kutte. "Sport beyond Gender and the Emergence of Cyborg Athletes." *Sport in Society* 31, no. 2 (2010): 249–259.

Jordan-Young, Rebecca, and Katrina Karkazis. "Some of Their Parts." *Anthropology News*. (2012), accessed September 1, 2012, http://www.anthropology-news.org/index.php/2012/06/15/some-of-their-parts/.

Kanaaneh, Rhoda Ann. *Birthing the Nation: Strategies of Palestinian Women in Israel*. Berkeley: University of California Press, 2002.

Kaplan, Caren. *Questions of Travel: Postmodern Discourses of Displacement*. Durham, NC: Duke University Press, 1996.

Karkazis, Katrina. *Fixing Sex: Intersex, Medical Authority and Lived Experience*. Durham, NC: Duke University Press, 2008.

Karkazis, Katrina, Rebecca Jordan-Young, Georgiann Davis, and Silvia Camporesi. "Out of Bounds? A Critique of the New Policies on Hyperandrogenism in Elite Female Athletes." *American Journal of Bioethics* 12, no. 7 (2012): 3–16.

Keesing, Roger M. "Rethinking Mana." *Journal of Anthropological Research* 40, no. 1 (1984): 137–156.

Keys, Barbara. *Globalizing Sport: National Rivalry and International Community in the 1930s.* Cambridge, MA: Harvard University Press, 2006.

Kratz, Corinne A., and Ivan Karp. "Museum Frictions: Public Cultures/Global Transformations." In *Museum Frictions: Public Cultures/Global Transformations*, edited by Ivan Karp, Corinne A. Kratz, Lynn Szwaja, and Tomas Ybarra-Frausto, 1–33. Durham, NC: Duke University Press, 2006.

Krüger, Arnd. "The Origins of Pierre de Coubertin's *Religio Athletae*." *Olympika* 2 (1993): 91–102.

La Cava, Giuseppe. "The Use of Drugs in Competitive Sport." *Bulletin du Comité International Olympique* 78: 52–53.

Landry, Fernand, and Magdalene Yerlès, eds. *The International Olympic Committee One Hundred Years: The Idea—the Presidents—the Achievements.* Vol. 3. Lausanne: The International Olympic Committee, 1996.

Latour, Bruno. *We Have Never Been Modern.* Cambridge, MA: Harvard University Press, 1993.

Lenskyj, Helen J. *Inside the Olympic Industry: Politics, Power and Activism.* Albany: State University Press of New York, 2000.

Levi-Faur, David. "The Global Diffusion of Regulatory Capitalism." *Annals of the American Academy of Political and Social Science* 598, no. 1 (2005): 12–32.

Linnekin, Jocelyn. "Cultural Invention and the Dilemma of Authenticity." *American Anthropologist* 93, no. 2 (1991): 446–449.

Liu, James H., Tim McCreanor, Tracey McIntosh, and Teresia Teaiwa, eds. *New Zealand Identities: Departures and Destinations.* Wellington, NZ, New Zealand: Victoria University Press, 2005.

Lock, Rebecca Ann. "The Doping Ban: Compulsory Heterosexuality and Lesbophobia." *International Review for the Sociology of Sport* 38, no. 4 (2003): 397–411.

Loland, Sigmund. *Fair Play in Sport: A Modern Norm System.* London: Routledge, 2002.

Lupton, Deborah. *The Imperative of Health: Public Health and the Regulated Body.* London: Sage, 1995.

———. *Medicine as Culture: Illness, Disease, and the Body.* 3rd ed. London: Sage, 2012.

MacAloon, John. "The Ethnographic Imperative in Comparative Olympic Research." *Sociology of Sport Journal* 9, no. 2 (1992): 104–130.

———. "Olympic Games and the Theory of Spectacle of Modern Societies." In *Rite, Drama, Festival, Spectacle: Rehearsals toward a Theory of Cultural Performance*, edited by John J. MacAloon, 241–280. Philadelphia: Institute for the Study of Human Issues Press, 1984.

———. "The Olympic Idea." *The International Journal of the History of Sport* 23, no. 3 (2006): 483–527.

———. "Steroids and the State: Dubin, Melodrama, and the Accomplishment of Innocence." *Public Culture* 2, no. 2 (1990): 41–64.

MacCouen, Robert J., and Peter Reuter. *Drug War Heresies: Learning from Other Vices, Times, and Places.* Cambridge: Cambridge University Press, 2001.

Macpherson, Cluny. "From Moral Community to Moral Communities: The Foundations of Migrant Social Solidarity among Samoans in Urban Aotearoa/New Zealand." *Pacific Studies* 25, no. 1 (2002): 71–94.

———. "From Pacific Islander to Pacific People and Beyond." In *Tangata, Tangata: The Changing Ethnic Contours of New Zealand*, edited by Paul Spoonley, and David G. Pearson. Palmerston North, NZ: Thomson Dunmore Press, 2004.

Magubane, Zine. "Spectacles and Scholarship: Caster Semenya, Intersex Studies, and the Problem of Race in Feminist Theory." *Signs* 39, no. 3 (2014): 761–785.

Mangan, J. A. *Athleticism in the Victorian and Edwardian Public School: The Emergence of an Educational Ideology.* Cambridge: Cambridge University Press, 1981.

———. *The Games Ethic and Imperialism: Aspects and Diffusion of an Ideal.* London: Frank Cass.

Maraniss, David. *Rome 1960: The Olympics That Changed the World.* New York: Simon and Schuster, 2008.

Marcus, George. "Ethnography in/of the World System: The Emergence of Multi-Sited Ethnography." *Annual Review of Anthropology* 24 (1995): 95–117.

———. *Ethnography through Thick and Thin.* Princeton, NJ: Princeton University Press, 1998.

Marshall, T. H. *Class, Citizenship and Social Development.* Westport, CT: Greenwood, 1950.

Martínez-Patiño, María José. "A Woman Tried and Tested." *Lancet* 366 (2005): S38.

Martínez-Patiño, María José, Covadonga Mateos-Padorno, Aurora Martínez-Vidal, Anna María Sánchez Mozquera, José Luis García Soidán, María del Pino Díaz Pereira, and Carlos Francisco Touriño González. "An Approach to the Biological, Historical and Psychological Repercussions of Gender Verification in Top Level Competitions." *Journal of Human Sport and Exercise* 5, no. 3 (2010): 307–321.

McClintock, Anne. *Imperial Leather: Race, Gender, and Sexuality in the Colonial Contest.* London: Routledge, 1995.

McKay, James, and Helen Johnson. "Pornographic Eroticism and Sexual Grotesquerie in Representations of African American Sportswomen." *Social Identities: Journal for the Study of Race, Nation and Culture* 14, no. 4 (2008): 491–504.

McLean, Mervyn. *Māori Music.* Auckland, NZ: Auckland University Press, 1996.

McMichael, Philip. "Globalization: Myths and Realities." *Rural Sociology* 61, no. 1 (1996): 25–55.

Merry, Sally E. "Legal Pluralism." *Law and Society Review* 22, no. 5 (1988): 869–896.

———. "Transnational Human Rights and Local Activism: Mapping the Middle." *American Anthropologist* 108, no. 1 (2006): 38–51.

Messner, Michael. *Power at Play: Sports and the Problem of Masculinity.* Boston: Beacon Press, 1995.

———. "Sports and Male Domination: The Female Athlete as Contested Ideological Terrain." In *Ethics in Sport*, edited by Klaus V. Meier, Angela J. Schneider, and William J. Morgan, 267–284. Champaign, IL: Human Kinetics, 2001.

———. *Taking the Field: Women, Men, and Sports.* Minneapolis: University of Minnesota Press, 2002.

Miah, Andy. *Genetically Modified Athletes: Biomedical Ethics, Gene Doping and Sport.* London: Routledge, 2004.

Mitchell, Don. *Cultural Geography: A Critical Introduction.* Oxford: Blackwell, 2000, 269.

Mitten, Matthew J., and Hayden Opie. "'Sports Law': Implications for the Development of International, Comparative, and National Law and Global Dispute Resolution." *Tulane Law Review* 85, no. 2 (2010): 269–322.

Mohanram, Radhika. *Black Body: Women, Colonialism, and Space.* Minneapolis: University of Minnesota Press, 1999.

Møller, Verner. "Knud Enemark Jensen's Death during the 1960 Rome Olympics: A Search for Truth?" *Sport in History* 25, no. 3 (2009): 452–471.

Montoya, Michael. *Making the Mexican Diabetic: Race, Science and the Genetics of Inequality.* Berkeley: University of California Press, 2011.

Moore, Sally Falk. *Law as Process: An Anthropological Approach.* New York: Routledge and Kegan Paul, 1978.

Morgan, William. "Fair Is Fair, Or Is It?: A Moral Consideration of the Doping Wars in American Sport." *Sport in Society* 9, no. 2 (2006): 177–198.

Munday, Jennie. "Gendered Citizenship." *Sociology Compass* 3, no. 2 (2009): 249–366.

Munro, Brenna. "Caster Semenya: Gods and Monsters." *Safundi: The Journal of South African and American Studies* 11, no. 4 (2010): 383–396.

Nader, Laura. "Up the Anthropologist—Perspectives Gained from Studying Up." In *Reinventing Anthropology*, edited by Dell H. Hymes, 284–311. New York: Random House, 1972.

Nauright, John, and Timothy J. L. Chandler, eds. *Making Men: Rugby and Masculine Identity.* London: Taylor and Francis, 1996.

Nelson, Diane. *Reckoning: The Ends of War in Guatemala.* Durham, NC: Duke University Press, 2009.

New Zealand Law Commission. *Controlling and Regulating Drugs* (2010), http://www.lawcom.govt.nz/project/review-misuse-drugs-act-1975/publication/issues-paper/2010/controlling-and-regulating-drugs.

Ng Shiu, Roannie. "'It's like Going to the Moon': The Experiences of Samoan Tertiary Health Students at the University of Auckland." PhD diss., University of Auckland, 2011.

Nichter, Mark, and Jennifer Thompson. "For My Wellness, Not Just My Illness: North Americans' Use of Dietary Supplements." *Culture, Medicine and Psychiatry* 30, no. 2 (2006): 175–222.

Olsen-Acre, Haley K. "The Use of Drug Testing to Police Sex and Gender in the Olympic Games." *Michigan Journal of Gender and Law* 13, no. 2 (2007): 207–236.

Ong, Aihwa. *Flexible Citizenship: The Cultural Logics of Transnationality.* Durham, NC: Duke University Press, 1999.

———. "Mutations in Citizenship." *Theory, Culture, and Society* 23, no. 2–3 (2006): 499–505.

Park, Jin-Kyung. "Governing Doped Bodies: The World Anti-Doping Agency and the Global Culture of Surveillance." *Cultural Studies ↔ Critical Methodologies* 5, no. 2 (2005): 174–186.

Paoli, Letizia, and Alessandro Donati. *The Doping Sports Market: Understanding Supply and Demand, and the Challenges of Their Control.* New York: Springer, 2014.

Patete, Anthony. *Māori Political Activism and the Quest for Rangatiratanga in the 1970s and 1980s.* Wellington, NZ: Victoria University Stout Research Centre for New Zealand Studies, 2007.

Petryna, Adriana. "Biological Citizenship: The Science and Politics of Chernobyl-Exposed Populations." *Osiris* 19 (2004): 250–265.

———. *Life Exposed: Biological Citizens after Chernobyl.* Princeton, NJ: Princeton University Press, 2002.

Pfister, Gertrud, and Dagmar Reese. "Gender, Body Culture, and Body Politics in National Socialism." *Sport Science Review* 4, no. 4 (1995): 91–121.

Philips, Susan U. *Ideology in the Language of Judges: How Judges Practice Law, Politics, and Courtroom Control.* New York: Oxford University Press, 1998.

Phillips, Dennis. "Australian Women and the Olympics: Achievement and Alienation." *Sporting Traditions* 6, no. 2 (1990): 181–200.

Pitt, Charles D., and Cluny Macpherson. *Emerging Pluralism: The Samoan Community in New Zealand.* Auckland, NZ: Longman Paul, 1974.

Porritt, Arthur. "Doping." *The Journal of Sports Medicine and Physical Fitness* 5, no. 3 (1965): 166–168.

———. "Doping and the Use of Chemical Agents to Modify Human Performance in Sport." *Bulletin du Comité International Olympique* 90 (1965): 49–50.

Pound, Richard. *Inside Dope: How Drugs Are the Biggest Threat to Sports, Why You Should Care, and What Can Be Done About Them*. Mississauga, ONT: Wiley and Sons, 2006.

———. *Inside the Olympics: A Behind-the-Scenes Look at the Politics, Scandals and the Glory of the Games*. Mississauga, ONT: Wiley and Sons, 2004.

Povinelli, Elizabeth. *The Empire of Love: Toward a Theory of Intimacy, Genealogy, and Carnality*. Durham, NC: Duke University Press, 2006.

Pratt, Mary Louise. *Imperial Eyes: Travel Writing and Transculturation*. London: Routledge, 1992.

Prokop, Ludwig. "Drug Abuse in International Athletes." *Journal of Sport Medicine* 3, no. 2 (1975): 85–87.

Qureshi, Sadiah. "Displaying Sara Baartman, the 'Hottentot Venus.'" *History of Science* 42, no. 2 (2004): 233–257.

Rabinow, Paul, ed. *The Foucault Reader*. New York: Pantheon, 1984.

Rabinow, Paul, and Nikolas Rose. "Biopower Today." *BioSocieties* 1, no. 2 (2006): 195–217.

Rail, Geneviève, Dave Holmes, and Stuart Murray. "The Politics of Evidence on 'Domestic Terrorists': Obesity Discourses and their Effects." *Social Theory and Health* 8, no. 3 (2010): 259–279.

Ravjani, Abbas. "The Court of Arbitration for Sport: A Subtle Form of International Delegation." *Journal of International Media and Entertainment Law* 2, no. 2 (2009): 241–284.

Reinarman, Craig. "Moral Entrepreneurs and Political Economy: Historical and Ethnographic Notes on the Construction of the Cocaine Menace." *Contemporary Crises* 3, no. 3 (1979): 225–254.

Richland, Justin B. *Arguing with Tradition: The Language of Law in Hopi Tribal Court*. Chicago: University of Chicago Press.

———. "Perpetuities against Rules: Law, Ethnography, and the Measuring of Lives." *Law, Culture and the Humanities* 8, no. 3 (2010): 433–447.

Ritchie, Ian. "Pierre de Coubertin, Doped 'Amateurs' and the 'Spirit of Sport': The Role of Mythology in Olympic Anti-Doping Policies." *International Journal of the History of Sport* 31, no. 8 (2014): 820–838.

———. "Sex Tested, Gender Verified: Controlling Female Sexuality in the Age of Containment." *Sport History Review* 34, no. 1 (2003): 80–98.

Ritchie, Robert, John Reynard, and Tom Lewis. "Intersex and the Olympic Games." *Journal of the Royal Society of Medicine* 101, no. 8 (2008): 395–399.

Roberts, Dorothy. *Fatal Intervention: How Science, Politics, and Big Business Re-create Race in the Twenty-First Century*. New York: Perseus, 2011.

Roche, Maurice. "The Olympics and 'Global Citizenship.'" *Citizenship Studies* 6, no. 1 (2002): 165–181.

Rose, Nikolas. *The Politics of Life Itself: Biomedicine, Power, and Subjectivity in the Twenty-First Century*. Princeton, NJ: Princeton University Press, 2006.

———. *Powers of Freedom: Reframing Political Thought*. Cambridge: Cambridge University Press, 1999.

Rose, Nikolas, and Carlos Novas. "Biological Citizenship." In *Global Assemblages: Technology, Politics, and Ethics as Anthropological Problems*, edited by Aihwa Ong and Stephan J. Collier, 439–463. Malden, MA: Blackwell, 2005.

Rowe, David, and Geoffrey Lawrence. "Beyond National Sport: Sociology, History and Post-modernity." *Sporting Traditions* 12, no. 2 (1996): 3–16.

Rubin, Gayle S. "Thinking Sex: Notes for a Radical Theory of the Politics of Sexuality." In *Deviations: A Gayle Rubin Reader*, 137–181. Durham, NC: Duke University Press, 2011.

Sánchez, Francisco J., María Martínez-Patiño, and Eric Vilain. "The New Policy on Hyperan-drogenism in Elite Female Athletes Is Not about 'Sex Testing.'" *Journal of Sex Research* 50, no. 2 (2013). doi: 10.1080/00224499.2012.752429.

Sarat, Austin, and Thomas R. Kearns, eds. *Law in Everyday Life*. Ann Arbor: University of Michigan Press, 1993.

Schantz, Otto J. "Pierre de Coubertin's Concepts of Race, Nation, and Civilization." In *The 1904 Anthropology Days and Olympic Games: Sport, Race, and American Imperialism*, edited by Susan Brownell, 156–188. Lincoln: University of Nebraska Press, 2008.

Schneider, Angela J. "Privacy, Confidentiality and Human Rights in Sport." *Sport in Society* 7, no. 3 (2004): 438–456.

Schwartz, Hillel. *Never Satisfied: A Cultural History of Diets, Fantasies and Fat*. New York: Free Press, 1986.

Scott, Colin. "Regulating in Global Regimes." University College Dublin Working Papers in Law, Criminology and Socio-Legal Studies, Research Paper No. 25 (2010), 1–17.

Seddon, Toby. *A History of Drugs: Drugs and Freedom in the Liberal Age*. Abingdon, UK: Routledge-Cavendish, 2010.

Sekula, Allen. "Body and the Archive." *October* 39 (1986): 3–64.

Seuffert, Nan. *Jurisprudence of National Identity: Kaleidoscopes of Imperialism and Globalisation from Aotearoa New Zealand*. Oxford: Ashgate, 2006.

Sheridan, Heather. "Conceptualizing 'Fair Play': A Review of the Literature." *European Physical Education Review* 9, no. 2 (2003): 163–184.

Silk, Michael L. "Sporting Ethnography: Philosophy, Methodology, and Reflection." In *Qualitative Methods in Sports Studies*, edited by David. L. Andrews, Daniel S. Mason, and Michael. L. Silk, 65–103. Oxford: Berg, 2005.

Silk, Michael L., David L. Andrews, and Daniel Mason. "Encountering the Field: Sports Studies and Qualitative Research." In *Qualitative Methods in Sports Studies*, edited by David. L. Andrews, Daniel S. Mason, and Michael L. Silk, 1–20. Oxford: Berg, 2005.

Silliman, Jael, and Anannya Bhattacharjee, eds. *Policing the National Body: Race, Gender and Criminalization*. Cambridge, MA: South End Press, 2000.

Simon, Jonathan. *Governing through Crime: How the War on Crime Transformed American Democracy and Created a Culture of Fear*. Oxford: Oxford University Press, 2007.

Skirstad, Berit. "Gender Verification in Competitive Sport: Turning Research into Action." In *Values in Sport: Elitism, Nationalism, Gender Equality and the Scientific Manufacture of Winners*, edited by Torbjörn Tännsjö and Claudio Tamburrini, 116–122. London: E&FN Spon, 2000.

Smart, Barry. "Not Playing Around: Global Capitalism, Modern Sport and Consumer Cul-ture. *Global Networks* 7, no. 2 (2007): 113–134.

Smith, Dorothy. *Institutional Ethnography: A Sociology for People*. New York: AltaMira, 2005.

Smith, Earl, and Angela J. Hattery. "Hey Stud: Race, Sex and Sports." *Sexuality and Culture* 10, no. 2 (2006): 3–32.

Soule, Bastien, and Ludovic Lestrelin. "The Puerto Affair: Revealing the Difficulties of the Fight against Doping." *Journal of Sport and Social Issues* 35, no. 2 (2011): 186–208.

Spoonley, Paul, Cluny MacPhearson, and David Pearson, eds. *Nga Patai: Racism and Ethnic Relations in Aotearoa/New Zealand*. Palmerston North, NZ: Dunmore, 1996.

Spoonley, Paul, and David G. Pearson, eds. *Tangata, Tangata: The Changing Ethnic Contours of New Zealand.* Palmerston North, NZ: Thomson Dunmore Press, 2004.

Sport and Recreation New Zealand. "SPARC Statement of Intent, 2007–2010" (2007), accessed April 20, 2011, http://www.sparc.org.nz/Documents/Publications/Statement %20of%20Intent/SPARC-Statement-of-Intent-2010–2013.pdf.

Sports Tribunal of New Zealand. "Annual Report 2007/2008" (2008), http://www .sportstribunal.org.nz/Global/Annual%20Reports/annual-report-2007–08.pdf.

———. "Annual Report 2008/2009" (2009), http://www.sportstribunal.org.nz/Global/ Annual%20Reports/Sports-Tribunal-Annual-Report-09-WEB.pdf.

———. "Annual Report 2009/2010" (2010), http://www.sportstribunal.org.nz/Global/ Annual%20Reports/Sports_Tribunal_Annual%20Report_10.pdf.

———. "Annual Report 2010/2011" (2011), http://www.sportstribunal.org.nz/Global/ Annual%20Reports/Sports_Tribunal_Annual_Report_11.pdf.

———. "Annual Report 2011/2012" (2012), http://www.sportstribunal.org.nz/Global/ Annual%20Reports/Sports_Tribunal_Annual_Report%2012.pdf.

———. "Annual Report 2012/2013" (2013), http://www.sportstribunal.org.nz/Global/ Annual%20Reports/Sports_Tribunal_%20Annual_Report_13.pdf.

Steel, Graeme. "Anti-Doping in Sport—What Is WADA's Mandate?" *Performance Enhancement and Health* 2, no. 2 (2013): 78–79.

Stokvis, Ruud. "Moral Entrepreneurship and Doping Cultures in Sport." ASSR Working Paper Series, Amsterdam School for Social Science Research (2003): 1–25.

Strathern, Marilyn. "Cutting the Network." *The Journal of the Royal Anthropological Institute* 2, no. 3 (1996): 517–535.

———. *Partial Connections.* Savage, MD: Rowman and Littlefield, 1991.

Sullivan, Claire F. "Gender Verification and Gender Policies in Elite Sport: Eligibility and 'Fair Play.'" *Journal of Sport and Social Issues* 35, no. 4 (2011): 400–419.

Swartz, Leslie, and Brian Watermeyer. "Cyborg Anxiety: Oscar Pistorius and the Boundaries of What It Means to Be Human." *Disability in Society* 23, no. 2 (2008): 187–190.

Sykes, Heather. "Transsexual and Transgender Policies in Sport." *Women in Sport and Physical Activity Journal* 15, no. 1 (2006): 3–13.

Tamburrini, Claudio. "Are Doping Sanctions Justified? A Moral Relativistic View." *Sport in Society* 9, no. 2 (2006): 199–211.

Taussig, Karen Sue. *Ordinary Genomes: Science, Citizenship, and Genetic Identities.* Durham, NC: Duke University Press, 2009.

Teetzel, Sarah. "On Transgendered Athletes, Fairness and Doping: An International Challenge." *Sport in Society* 9, no. 2 (2006): 227–251.

Teetzel, Sarah, and Marcus Mazzucco. "Minor Problems: The Recognition of Young Athletes in the Development of International Anti-Doping Policies." *International Journal of the History of Sport* 31, no. 8 (2014): 914–933.

Tengan, Ty P. Kāwika. "(En)gendering Colonialism: Masculinities in Hawai'i and Aotearoa." *Cultural Values* 6, no. 3 (2002): 239–256.

Tengan, Ty P. Kāwika, and Jesse Makani Markham. "Performing Polynesian Masculinities in American Football: From 'Rainbows to Warriors.'" *International Journal of the History of Sport* 26, no. 16 (2009): 2412–2431.

Terry, Jennifer. "Theorizing Deviant Historiography." In *Feminists Revision History*, edited by Anne-Louise Shapiro, 276–303. New Brunswick, NJ: Rutgers University Press, 1994.

Therberge, Nancy. "A Critique of Critiques: Radical and Feminist Writings on Sport." *Social Forces* 60, no. 2 (1981): 341–353.

Todd, Jan, and Terry Todd. "Significant Events in the History of Drug Testing and the Olympic Movement." In *Doping in Elite Sport: The Politics of Drugs in the Olympic Movement*, edited by Wayne Wilson and Edward Derse, 65–128. Champaign, IL: Human Kinetics, 2001.

Trubek, David M., and Louise G. Trubek. "Hard and Soft Law in the Construction of Social Europe: The Roles of the Open Method of Co-ordination." *European Law Journal* 11, no. 3 (2005): 343–364.

Turner, Bryan S. *Citizenship and Social Theory*. Thousand Oaks, CA: Sage, 1993.

Ungerleider, Steven. *Faust's Gold: Inside the East German Doping Machine*. New York: St. Martin's Press, 2001.

Uperesa, Fa'anofo L. "Fabled Futures: Development, Gridiron Football, and Transnational Movement in American Samoa." PhD diss., Columbia University, 2010.

Vannini, April, and Barbara Fornssler. "Girl, Interrupted: Semenya's Body, Gender Verification Testing, and Public Discourse." *Cultural Studies ↔ Critical Methodologies* 11, no. 3 (2011): 243–257.

Vaughan, Diane. *Uncoupling: Turning Points in Intimate Relationships*. New York: Oxford University Press, 1986.

Vertinsky, Patricia. "Weighs and Means: Examining the Surveillance of Fat Bodies through Physical Education Practices in the late 19th and Early 20th Centuries." *Journal of Sport History* 35, no. 3 (2008): 401–420.

Viloria, Hida. "Gender Rules in Sport—Leveling the Playing Field, Or Reversed Doping?" *The Global Herald*, April 11, 2011. http://theglobalherald.com/?p=14837.

Wackwitz, Laura A. "Verifying the Myth: Olympic Sex Testing and the Category Woman." *Women's Studies International Forum* 26, no. 6 (2003): 553–560.

Wahlert, Lance, and Autumn Fiester. "Gender Transports: Privileging the 'Natural' in Gender Testing Debates for Intersex and Transgender Athletes." *American Journal of Bioethics* 12, no. 7 (2012): 19–21.

Walby, Silvia. "Is Citizenship Gendered?" *Sociology* 28, no. 2 (1994): 379–395.

Wenner, Lawrence A., ed. *Fallen Sports Heroes, Media, and Celebrity Culture*. New York, Peter Lang, 2013.

———, ed. *Sports, Media, and Society*. Thousand Oaks, CA: Sage, 1989.

West, Candace, and Don H. Zimmerman. "Doing Gender." *Gender and Society* 1, no. 2 (1989): 125–151.

Wiederkehr, Stefan. "We Shall Never Know the Exact Number of Men Who Have Competed in the Olympics Posing as Women: Sport, Gender Verification and the Cold War." *International Journal of the History of Sport* 26, no. 4 (2009): 556–572.

Williams, Yohuru R. "American Exported Black Nationalism: The Student Nonviolent Coordinating Committee, the Black Panther Party, and the Worldwide Freedom Struggle, 1967–1972." *Negro History Bulletin* 60, no. 3 (1997): 13–20.

Witherspoon, Kevin B. *Before the Eyes of the World: Mexico and the 1968 Olympics*. DeKalb: Northern Illinois University Press, 2008.

Wolf, Roberta F. "Conflicting Anti-Doping Laws in Professional Sports: Collective Bargaining Agreements v. State Law." *Seattle University Law Review* 34, no. 4 (2011): 1605–1636.

Woodland, Les. *Dope: The Use of Drugs in Sport*. London: David and Charles, 1980.

World Anti-Doping Agency. *World Anti-Doping Code* (2009), accessed April 11, 2011, http://www.wada-ama.org/rtecontent/document/code_v2009_En.pdf.

Wrynn, Alison. "The Human Factor: Science, Medicine and the International Olympic Committee, 1900–70." *Sport in Society* 7, no. 2 (2004): 211–231.

Wrynn, Alison, and Maureen Smith. "Women in the 2012 Olympic and Paralympic Winter Games: An Analysis of Participation and Leadership Opportunities." East Meadow, NY: Women's Sports Foundation, 2013.

Young, Alison. *Imagining Crime: Textual Outlaws and Criminal Conversations.* Thousand Oaks, CA: Sage, 1996.

Index